GCSE

SPANISH

John Bates

Longman

LONGMAN REVISE GUIDES

SERIES EDITORS:
Geoff Black and Stuart Wall

TITLES AVAILABLE:
Art and Design
Biology*
Business Studies
Chemistry*
Computer Studies
Economics
English*
English Literature*
French
Geography
German
Home Economics
Information Systems*
Mathematics*
Mathematics: Higher Level*
Music
Physics*
Religious Studies
Science*
Sociology
Spanish
Technology*
World History

* new editions for Key Stage 4

Longman Group Ltd,
*Longman House, Burnt Mill, Harlow,
Essex CM20 2JE, England
and Associated Companies throughout the world.*

© Longman Group Limited 1994

All rights reserved; no part of this publication may be reproduced, stored in a retrieval system, or transmitted in any form or by any means, electronic, mechanical, photocopying, recording, or otherwise without either the prior written permission of the Publishers or a licence permitting restricted copying in the United Kingdom issued by the Copyright Licensing Agency Ltd, 90 Tottenham Court Road, London W1P 9HE.

First Published 1994
Third Impression 1995

ISBN 0 582 22652 X   PPR

British Library Cataloguing-in-Publication Data

A catalogue record for this book is
available from the British Library

Set by 19QQ in 10/12pt Century Old Style

Produced by Longman Singapore Publishers Pte Ltd
Printed in Singapore

Contents

	Editors' Preface	iv
	Acknowledgements	iv
CHAPTER 1	The Examinations	1
2	Preparing for the Examination	7
3	Subject Content: Topics, Settings and Vocabulary	13
4	Listening: Basic Level	55
5	Listening: Higher Level	76
6	Speaking: Basic Level	101
7	Speaking: Higher Level	116
8	Reading: Basic Level	135
9	Reading: Higher Level	165
10	Writing: Basic Level	193
11	Writing: Higher Level	215
12	Grammar	235
	Index	247

EDITORS' PREFACE

Longman Revise Guides are written by experienced examiners and teachers, and aim to give you the best possible foundation for success in examinations and other modes of assessment. Examiners are well aware that the performance of many candidates falls well short of their true potential, and this series of books aims to remedy this, by encouraging thorough study and a full understanding of the concepts involved. The Revise Guides should be seen as course companions and study aids to be used throughout the year, not just for last minute revision.

Examiners are in no doubt that a structured approach in preparing for examinations and in presenting coursework can, together with hard work and diligent application, substantially improve performance.

The largely self-contained nature of each chapter gives the book a useful degree of flexibility. After starting with the opening general chapters on the background to the GCSE, and the syllabus coverage, all other chapters can be read selectively, in any order appropriate to the stage you have reached in your course.

We believe that this book, and the series as a whole, will help you establish a solid platform of basic knowledge and examination technique on which to build.

Geoff Black and Stuart Wall

ACKNOWLEDGEMENTS

I am grateful to the following Examination Groups for permission to reproduce questions which have appeared in their examination papers. The answers, or hints on any answers, are solely the responsibility of the author.

Commonwealth of the Bahamas Ministry of Education (BGCSE); Midland Examining Group (MEG); Northern Examinations and Assessment Board (NEAB); Northern Ireland Council for Curriculum, Examinations and Assessment (NICCEA); Southern Examining Group (SEG); University of London Examinations and Assessment Council (ULEAC); Welsh Joint Education Committee (WJEC).

We are also grateful to T Murray, for various illustrations.

John Bates

GETTING STARTED

This book sets out to help you to develop the skills you need as a candidate for GCSE Spanish. It will set out for you the exact requirements of your examination and will cover in detail the four key language skills of listening, speaking, reading and writing. It will provide examples of questions set at both Basic and Higher Levels. No matter which Examining Group's GCSE you are taking, you will find every chapter relevant. You can use the chapters in any order to suit your revision plan.

As well as covering the four key language skills, this book will provide you with the vocabulary and phrases that you will be expected to know (Chapter 3). The *topic areas* used to group this vocabulary and the *settings* (places) in which you will be expected to use it are also identified. The rules of grammar, so important in learning any language, are covered in Chapter 12.

Try the questions and exercises provided in each chapter yourself before checking the answers provided. In some chapters you will also find *student's answers* to questions with the examiner's comments on the strengths and weaknesses of those answers. You will be given *review sheets* for each skills-based chapter to help you check your understanding of the content of that chapter. Active learning on your part involving *doing* questions, exercises and examples is one of the best ways of preparing for your examinations.

CHAPTER 1

THE EXAMINATIONS

AIMS OF GCSE SPANISH

THE NATURE OF THE EXAMINATION

THE DEFINED CONTENT

ASSESSMENT

GRADES – MINIMUM ENTRY REQUIREMENTS

WRITING

IGCSE

BGCSE

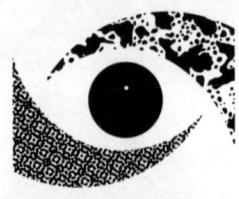

ESSENTIAL PRINCIPLES

1 > AIMS OF GCSE SPANISH

The general aims of your GCSE in Spanish, or in any language

The GCSE National Criteria are a set of rules laid down by the Secretary of State that are followed by all GCSE Examining Groups in England, Wales and Northern Ireland. The *aims* listed for Modern Languages are:

1. to develop the ability to use the foreign language effectively for purposes of practical communication;

2. to form a sound base of the skills, language and attitudes required for further study, work and leisure;

3. to offer insights into the culture and civilization of countries where the language is spoken;

4. to develop an awareness of the nature of language and language learning;

5. to provide enjoyment and intellectual stimulation;

6. to encourage positive attitudes to foreign language learning and to speakers of foreign languages and a sympathetic approach to other cultures and civilizations;

7. to promote learning skills of a more general application (e.g. analysis, memorizing, drawing inferences).

Obviously not all of these can be directly tested in the GCSE examinations, where the emphasis is very firmly on understanding and effective practical communication in Spanish.

2 > THE NATURE OF THE EXAMINATION

Tasks set will be realistic ones

Examiners are looking for what you achieve to award marks

All parts of the examination are based on situations that you might find yourself in when dealing with Spanish speakers. The tasks set are ones that you might realistically have to carry out in real life. All reading and listening material is authentic Spanish material (possibly edited), not artificial texts invented purely to test English-speaking (or Welsh-speaking) candidates.

A key aspect of the GCSE is that it should test what candidates **know, understand and can do**. The emphasis is on success and the tasks set are therefore realistic in the demands they make on candidates. Marks are awarded for what is actually achieved, rather than being deducted for every mistake (which was often the rule in earlier examinations). There are sections which everyone, no matter what their level of ability, can do successfully and even the most able candidates are required to demonstrate their competence in performing quite simple tasks, before moving on to harder parts of the examination.

3 > THE DEFINED CONTENT

The Examining Groups define what you must know

Each of the Examining Groups has been required to publish a Defined Content, which includes:

- a list of the *topic areas* to be covered
- a list of the *tasks* students should be able to perform
- a list of all the *vocabulary* they will need at the different levels of the examination
- a list of the *grammar* they are expected to know

Candidates (and their teachers) can be absolutely sure that they will not be tested on any unforeseen vocabulary or grammar. (Up to 15% of the words in any Listening or Reading test may be from outside the published list but understanding of such words will not be required of candidates in order to answer the questions set.) The Defined Content of each of the different Examining Groups has been used in preparing the Vocabulary and Grammar chapters of this Longman GCSE Revise Guide.

4 > ASSESSMENT

Because of the National Criteria, the requirements for GCSE Spanish are very similar for the examinations set by the different Examining Groups. In almost all Spanish syllabuses the final examination counts for 100% of the marks and there is no coursework component.

The four language skills of listening, speaking, reading and writing are examined separately. The tests in the different skills are divided into two levels, so that there are normally eight tests:

> *Tests are at two levels for each skill*

- Basic Listening
- Basic Speaking
- Basic Reading
- Basic Writing
- Higher Listening
- Higher Speaking
- Higher Reading
- Higher Writing

The Speaking Tests will be conducted by your own teacher between March and May and will almost certainly be tape-recorded. The Listening, Reading and Writing Tests take place between late May and the first week in July. Some Examining Groups set all the Basic level papers on one day and all the Higher on another, while other Groups prefer to examine the same skill at both levels on the same day.

Grid showing GCSE Examining Group components:

EXAMINING GROUP	MEG			NEAB		NISEAC		SEG		ULEAC		WJEC	
LEVEL	B	H1	H2	B	H	B	H	GL	EL	B	H	B	H
Listening													
Time allowed (minutes)	20	20	20	30	30	30	30	30	35	30	30	30	40
Recorded on Cassette	Yes	Yes	Yes	Yes	Yes	Yes	Yes	Yes	Yes	Yes	Yes	Yes	Yes
Questions and answers in E/W	E	E	E	E	E	E	E	E	E	E	E	E/W	E/W
Speaking													
Time allowed (minutes)	10	12	15	5-10	10-15	10	15	10	17	10	20	10	15
Role-plays	2	+1		2	+2V	2	+2	2	+2V	2	+1	2	+2
Conversation	C	C	C	C	C	C	C	C	C	C	C	C	C
Notes or picture stimulus			C										
Reading													
Time allowed (minutes)	25	25	25	25	40	45	40	30	40	30	30	30	40
Questions and answers in E/W	E	E	E	E	E	E	E	E	E	E	E	E/W	E/W
Writing													
Time allowed (minutes)	25	30	35	25	50	45	50	30	60	45	60	30	70
Number of words		100	150		NS +NS		200		100 +100		100 +100		110 +110
Lists/Forms	C					*			*		*		*
Messages	C			*C		*		C	*		*		*
Postcards	C			*C		*			*		*		*
Letters		CO		C	C		*	C	C	CO	O	C	CO
Visual/pictures					*		*		*		O		*
Narrative/ Topic/Report			CO		*		*		*		O		CO

KEY:

B	=	Basic	EL	=	Extended Level	C	=	Compulsory
H	=	Higher	E	=	English	CO	=	Compulsory element but with choice of question
H1	=	Higher Part 1	W	=	Welsh			
H2	=	Higher Part 2	V	=	Visual stimulus	*	=	Could appear
GL	=	General level	O	=	Option	NS	=	Not specified
						CL	=	Core level

❝ Basic must come before Higher in any skill ❞

ALL candidates are entered for, and must attempt, the three 'Common core' elements – Basic Listening, Basic Speaking and Basic Reading.

In addition candidates may CHOOSE to enter for the other elements of the examination, but they cannot enter for the Higher level in any skill without entering the Basic level in that same skill.

The system is designed to allow candidates to enter for what they *can do*, and to allow for maximum flexibility. In this way a candidate should be able to avoid being faced with an impossible task on the day of the examination.

There are three Examining Groups that have slight variations in the pattern outlined above:

The Southern Examining Group (SEG) calls its levels 'General Level' (= Basic) and 'Extended Level' (= Higher).

The Bahamas Ministry of Education calls its levels, 'Core Level' (= Basic) and 'Extended Level' (= Higher).

The Midland Examining Group (MEG) has divided its Higher Level into two parts (Higher Part 1 and Higher Part 2) in order to give greater flexibility. Higher Part 1 takes candidates up to about a good Grade C standard, while Higher Part 2 then takes them further to allow them to show performance at Grade A or B level.

Time allowances for Higher Level Speaking include the time for the Basic Level test but it is assumed that Higher Level candidates will complete the Basic test in slightly less time than other candidates.

Note that the time allowances for MEG Higher Level Reading and Writing are based on the assumption that candidates who are correctly entered for Higher Level will complete the Basic papers well within the time allowed and move straight on to the Higher papers.

5 > GRADES – MINIMUM ENTRY REQUIREMENTS

❝ Remember, Basic Listening, Basic Speaking and Basic Reading are the core ❞

The following table sets out the *minimum* entry requirements for the different grades. Everyone has to do the 'Core', namely Basic Listening, Basic Speaking and Basic Reading. After that you are free to choose which additional tests you take.

Highest grade possible	Minimum entry required
Grade E	Core (Basic Listening + Basic Reading + Basic Speaking)
Grade D	Core + any one other test
Grade C	Core + Basic Writing + any one other test
Grade B	Core + Basic Writing + Higher Writing + any one other test
Grade A	Core + Basic Writing + Higher Writing + any two other tests
Grade A*	All tests

Notes:
MEG Higher Level tests are divided into Part 1 and Part 2. Two Part 1 tests in different skills count the same as one complete Higher test.

SEG calls its levels 'General' (= Basic) and 'Extended' (= Higher).

Remember that if you take only the minimum you will have to perform very well in all those tests to achieve the grades shown. You are strongly advised to attempt at least one additional element beyond the minimum requirement for the grade you are hoping to get.

6 > WRITING

> *Basic and Higher Writing are needed for the higher grades*

You will have noticed that Writing is mentioned specifically in the table of Minimum Entry Requirements. The National Criteria require a Basic Level Writing test to have been taken by anyone awarded Grades C, B or A. In addition, the Criteria require a Higher Level Writing test to have been taken if Grade B or A is to be awarded. (For MEG this means both Higher Part 1 and Higher Part 2 Writing.)

It is worth pointing out that the requirement is to *enter for* (and actually attempt) Writing. Provided that you do so, you can make up for poor performance in Writing by doing well in other elements (but you will then certainly need to take more than the minimum number of elements for the grade you are hoping to achieve).

7 > IGCSE

The International GCSE (IGCSE) is not normally available to students in the United Kingdom unless they are studying at an International School. The aims are the same as those of the other GCSE Examining Groups and the major differences in the examinations are that all the questions are in Spanish and in the Listening and Reading papers the answers also have to be written in Spanish.

8 > BGCSE

The Bahamas GCSE (BGCSE) has the same aims as the UK Examining Groups. The examination components, the language tested and the grades awarded are very much in line with those of the other Groups. The three additional elements (reading aloud, dictation and translation into English) are not included in examinations after 1995.

EXAMINING GROUPS

Examining Group addresses:

MEG

Midland Examining Group
1 Hills Road, Cambridge CB1 2EU
Telephone: 01223 553311
    Fax: 01223 460278

NEAB

Northern Examinations and Assessment Board
Devas Street, Manchester M15 6EX
Telephone: 0161 953 1180
    Fax: 0161 273 7572

NICCEA

Northern Ireland Council for Curriculum, Examinations and Assessment
Beechill House, 42 Beechill Road, Belfast BT8 4RS
Telephone: 01232 704666
    Fax: 01232 799913

SEG

Southern Examining Group
Stag Hill House, Guildford GU2 5XJ
Telephone: 01483 506506
    Fax: 01483 300152

ULEAC

University of London Examinations and Assessment Council
Stewart House, 32 Russell Square, London WC1B 5DN
Telephone: 0171 331 4000
    Fax: 0171 631 3369

WJEC

Welsh Joint Education Committee
245 Western Road, Cardiff CF5 2YX
Telephone: 01222 561231
    Fax: 01222 571234

IGCSE

International General Certificate of Secondary Education
University of Cambridge Local Examinations Syndicate
1 Hills Road, Cambridge CB1 2EU
Telephone: 01223 61111
Fax: 01223 460278

BGCSE

Bahamas GCSE
Ministry of Education
P.O. Box N-3913
Nassau-N.P.
Bahamas

When contacting the Examining Groups you will need to ask for the Publications Department and request an order form to be sent to you. Be prepared to send a cheque or postal order with your actual order.

GETTING STARTED

In this chapter we shall look at ways of preparing for the Spanish GCSE examinations. We shall first consider **study skills** of a general nature, which should help you to make best use of your time in the period leading up to the GCSE, and which can generally be applied to other subjects as well. Then we shall consider briefly the four **language skills** of listening, speaking, reading and writing. Finally we shall consider a few general techniques that are important in the examination room itself.

As you prepare for the examination, remember that most examiners are also teachers who are fully aware of the hopes and fears of students as they prepare for examinations. The questions are set in such a way as to give you the opportunity to demonstrate what you know, understand and can do. The examiners are looking for opportunities to award you marks, not to take them away!

PREPARING FOR THE EXAMINATION

ATTITUDE TO THE COURSE

ORGANIZATION

PLANNING YOUR REVISION

HOW TO REVISE

LEARNING SPANISH

IN THE EXAMINATION

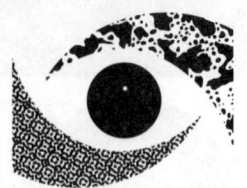

ESSENTIAL PRINCIPLES

1 > ATTITUDE TO THE COURSE

❝ You must be motivated to do well ❞

❝ There is no substitute for practice ❞

Success in GCSE is based firmly on what *you* have done during the course. In particular, a positive attitude and a desire to learn are essential. It is no good taking things easy on the assumption that you will be able to do some work at the end and then do well in the examination. Remember that at Basic Level you are expected to know about 1500 specified Spanish words and at Higher Level a further 700 or so. You cannot learn all of those in the last two weeks before the examination. Remember also that, since performance in Spanish is a skill, it needs to be practised regularly – and in all practice you must aim for success. Never be satisfied with work of a lower standard than you know you are capable of producing.

2 > ORGANIZATION

❝ Being well organized ❞

- **Have a routine.** Having set times when you do your work takes away much of the strain of actually making up your mind to get started.
- **Have a suitable place to study.** Keep it tidy so that you are not put off by the clutter.
- **Do work as it is set.** Don't let a backlog build up – and don't allow your regular work in Spanish to be squeezed out by the demands of coursework in other subjects.
- **Make sure you learn some new words each week.** Set yourself a target – e.g. 20 new words on a particular topic (eating in a restaurant, etc) each week.
- **Revise work regularly.** Check that you can remember the vocabulary or grammar points you learned last month, last year, etc.
- **Learn from what you have done.** Check every piece of work that has been marked for you and make sure you have learnt any lessons from the marking. Work out where your weaknesses are and then plan what to do to eliminate them.
- **Plan times for relaxation and leisure interests.** These are important. If there is something you particularly want to do that requires a change in your study routine, plan it in advance so that your work gets done and, equally importantly, you enjoy the activity without having to worry about work.

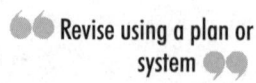

❝ Revise using a plan or system ❞

- **Plan well ahead.** Set specific times of the week where you will concentrate on Spanish GCSE.
- **Make sure you know what each examination involves.** Check the language skills chapters in this book. Your teachers and the Examining Groups themselves can provide further information, if needed.
- **Use questions from examinations of previous years for practice.** You will find many such questions in this book.
- **Use the Review Sheets from this book.** You will find these for each language skills chapter.
- **Make the most of your strengths.** Be sure to revise thoroughly the things you are good at so that you get high marks for them.
- **Work at your weaknesses.** However, don't let them depress you. Remember that you can make up for any weakness in one skill by doing particularly well in another.
- **Identify the sort of questions that are likely to be set.** Many of the tasks are very similar from one year to another – because there is a limit to the number of different things you are likely to have to do in any situation. (How many different tasks can you think of that you might reasonably have to perform in a shop?)

4 HOW TO REVISE

Make your revision active

Concentration is often the main problem with revision. If you are not careful, you can sit in front of a book, with your eyes moving steadily over the pages, only to realize after half an hour that you have not been thinking about what you are studying at all. Your mind has been on the television programme you watched last night, or on your plans for the coming weekend or an argument you have had. Mechanically passing your eyes over the page in that way is not revision and is of no use at all.

So how can you maintain concentration? You need to be *actively* involved in what you are doing.

- **Write notes**. One way is by writing notes, but that means notes that actively engage your mind. Again it is all too easy to copy notes mechanically, without thinking about them at all, with your mind somewhere completely different. So make sure that you set yourself tasks that make you think before you write.

- **Self-check**. Test yourself on the material you are revising. Then make sure you go back and learn thoroughly what you didn't know.

- **Keep a checklist of things revised**. Keep a checklist of what you have revised and are sure you now know. It will be helpful in planning your future revision and it should also give you a sense of achievement. In learning vocabulary in Chapter 3 there are boxes to tick as you complete certain tasks. You can use this idea in other ways as well.

- **Set targets**. Set yourself sensible targets and give yourself small rewards when you achieve them. If you can successfully complete a particular item of revision in forty minutes, give yourself a break. (And if you complete it with thorough knowledge in thirty minutes – give yourself an extra ten minutes' break! Remember, what is important is what you learn, not how many hours you have spent at your desk!)

- **Practise vocabulary by using it in likely tasks**. Think how you might have to *use* the words, rather than simply what they mean. You can imagine you are the customer in a shop, or trying to change money, etc.

- **Vary your activities and what you revise**. This will allow you to maintain concentration for longer.

- **Work with a friend**. Practise speaking together. Test each other, both orally and in writing.

Don't work late the night before an examination and don't indulge in panic revision just before the examination – that can often prevent you recalling effectively what you revised earlier. What you don't know by the day before is almost always best left.

5 LEARNING SPANISH

GENERAL

1. Although the four skills are tested separately, they are very closely linked in real life. This means, for example, that any work you do to improve your listening techniques will also have a positive 'spin-off' effect on the other three skills.

2. Vocabulary-learning is a chore, but it is a necessary part of your preparation. Make sure you begin early and learn steadily, over the weeks, remembering to test yourself as you learn. Chapter 3 will help you to work your way through the topic areas you have to study in depth.

3. Grammar is an important part of any language. Although the emphasis in the GCSE is less 'academic' than in earlier examinations, the more accurate you are the higher the marks you will gain – and this is particularly true at Higher Level. Grammar is important in helping us to understand what we hear and read, as well as in helping us to express ourselves clearly. Again, be methodical:

   – go over exercises you have done in class Do them again and see if you can improve on your earlier performances;

Some hints on learning grammar

   – use the Grammar section at the end of this book;

   – draw up a practical checklist for use before and during the examination.

4. Working with a friend can often be a helpful change from working on your own. This is especially important for speaking and vocabulary work.

CHAPTER 2 PREPARING FOR THE EXAMINATION

LISTENING

This is at first sight the most difficult skill to practise on your own, but there are still plenty of things you can do. In the chapters on Listening we go into detail about some of these, but the following will serve as an introduction.

There is an increasing number of language programmes on radio and television. Watch them whenever you can. Make recordings where that is possible, so that you can listen to them again. You will need to check details yourself, because broadcast series are constantly changing.

❝ Make use of radio and television ❞

Most courses now have cassettes to accompany them, so make sure you hear them at school. You may be able to borrow listening material (both course material and past examination recordings) from your teacher or from your local library. An audio cassette is available to accompany this book. It will help you to develop your listening (and speaking) skills.

Depending on where you live, you may be able to pick up Spanish radio stations. Or you could try Radio Spectrum International's Spanish Service, broadcasting on weekdays from 2 pm to 3 pm and on Saturdays from 10 am to 11 am, on 558 khz medium wave. (You will hear an interesting mixture of Spanish and South American accents.) It's a good idea to tune in occasionally to some Spanish language stations – and don't worry if you can't understand very much at first. Just see, first of all, if you can recognize the occasional word. If you can do that, fairly quickly you will find that you recognize more and more and you will develop a sense of positive achievement. (If, instead, you concentrate on the fact that there is much you do not understand, you will make much less progress.)

❝ Listen to real Spanish ❞

If you have any Spanish-speaking contacts, use them. Speak to people, ask penfriends to record some Spanish for you – you can help them with their English. Blank cassettes are very cheap!

SPEAKING

We deal with preparations for Speaking in depth in later chapters, but you should bear the following considerations in mind:

- The topic lists and language tasks in Chapter 3 will provide you with a lot of essential material for the Speaking tests. Make sure you know what tests you have to do and which topic areas they cover. Try to anticipate likely activities for role-plays and areas for conversation.

- Learn thoroughly the key expressions, especially for the role-plays. Several of them occur remarkably often in the examinations – because they are used so often in real life.

❝ Learn key expressions ❞

- Get used to the sound of your own voice because the Speaking tests will almost certainly be recorded.

- Get as much practice as you can with your teacher, friends – anyone who speaks Spanish.

- Use this book and your textbook fully and cover all the examples they provide.

READING

Reading is in some ways the easiest skill to revise, because material is more readily available. At GCSE you are required to read a wide range of texts in different styles, so the more you read the better.

Make full use of your course textbook. It will no doubt contain much reading material, and the more modern courses provide an excellent range of texts suitable for GCSE. Re-read articles you have read before, note down vocabulary that you did not know without looking it up. This is an invaluable step on the way to learning vocabulary.

❝ Take every reading opportunity in Spanish ❞

There are some interesting readers in schools or libraries. Find out what there is and take advantage of what is 'on the doorstep'.

There are also short magazines especially designed for foreign-language learners. Mary Glasgow Publications Ltd, Brookhampton Lane, Kineton CV35 0JB, telephone (0926) 640606 is an invaluable source for magazines, readers, puzzle-books.

WRITING

Grammar and spelling will be important but the main thing is to get the message across. The more accurate you are, though, the more marks you will gain, especially at Higher Level.

Repetition can help

- Go over exercises done in class. Try them again.
- Work your way through the writing tasks in this book and in your course textbook, then go over them again.
- Use the grammar section in this book to help you.

6 > IN THE EXAMINATION

MEMORY AIDS

Don't forget your 'supports' such as mnemonics, tables, key aids and checklists which you have developed during your preparation for the written examinations. Once you have been told you can start, make a quick note of your 'supports' *before* you start answering the questions.

Hints when you are in the exam itself

READ THE QUESTIONS CAREFULLY

Read the questions carefully and make sure you answer **ALL** parts of the question, that you cover **ALL** tasks. This applies to **ALL FOUR SKILLS**!

PRESENTATION

Whatever people may say to the contrary, a tidy, well-presented script which is easy on the eye and easy to read **DOES** create a favourable impression on examiners. It does not mean that they will award you more marks, but it will certainly do you no harm, and if an examiner cannot read clearly what you have written, then he or she cannot award marks!

TIMING

Timing is critical. First check that you know exactly how long you have for each test.

Use your time wisely

You will have been working to timed exercises in your preparation for the examination so you should have a clear idea of how long you will need for a particular exercise. Make sure you distribute your time in the examination wisely so that you don't spend too long on one question and then have to rush things at the end. You should also include in your schedule enough time to **RE-READ** and to **CHECK** your answers. This is especially important for the Writing tests, but is also important for the other skills. In the chapters on writing there are suggestions for drawing up your own grammar checklist and using it in the examination.

PLANNING ANSWERS

In the Writing papers, especially at Higher Level, you will need to plan carefully what to write, by making notes of key vocabulary, structures and idioms, *before* you write your answer.

You will have to keep to fairly strict word limits, and in some cases the space provided for your answer will not allow you to write much, e.g. for postcards.

You must also remember that you have to cover *all* the tasks, so you have to leave yourself enough words and room to do this.

In both Basic and Higher Level Writing you will be attempting to 'show off' what you know, so it's a great help to jot down a few interesting items of vocabulary and some idioms before you start writing your actual answer – but do make sure they are not completely irrelevant to the task you have been set!

ANSWER ALL THE QUESTIONS

There may be occasions when you are genuinely stuck on a particular question. Do not waste time over it. Write yourself a note of the question number and go on to the next question. Don't forget to come back to the unanswered question later though!

If all else fails, don't just leave a blank space – make a sensible guess based on what seems possible. Remember, you never lose out by 'having a go'.

RE-READ AND CHECK

Use your checklist wisely, make sure you have in fact covered all you were required to.

Now you are ready to move to Chapter 3 and to start getting down to the real work. Work your way thoroughly through the book and persevere. It will be worth it. **GOOD LUCK!**

CHAPTER 3

SUBJECT CONTENT: TOPICS, SETTINGS AND VOCABULARY

TOPICS

SETTINGS

COMBINATION OF TOPICS AND SETTINGS

ACTIVE AND RECEPTIVE USE

LANGUAGE TASKS

LEARNING VOCABULARY

VOCABULARY LISTS

GETTING STARTED

The National Criteria have required the Examining Groups to publish in their DEFINED CONTENT lists of vocabulary and phrases that candidates are expected to know. Although, in Listening and Reading papers, up to 15% of words may come from *outside* the lists, no questions may be set that depend on knowledge of words that are not listed. The vocabulary lists contain about 1400–1500 words for Basic Level and a further 700 or so for Higher Level. There are many words that occur in the lists of all the Examining Groups but there is also considerable variety. It is not practical to reproduce all the lists in this book but this chapter is based on the vocabulary lists of all the major Examining Groups and if you know the words in this chapter you will do well.

The chapter includes some advice on how to learn vocabulary effectively. The main message is to learn a little but often.

ESSENTIAL PRINCIPLES

1 > TOPICS

All of the Examining groups provide a list of the **Topic Areas** to be covered at Basic and Higher Level. The names chosen by the groups vary a little and there is also some variation in the way certain areas are classified. For example, banking is included under shopping by some groups, and under travel or services by others. There is, however, a large measure of agreement on what is included in the Topic Areas. The vocabulary given by the Examining Groups is listed here under the following headings:

The main Topic Areas

- Key Words and Expressions
- House and Home – Life at Home
- School and College
- Free Time and Entertainment
- Holidays
- Social Relationships
- Shopping
- Services
- Personal Identification
- Geographical surroundings
- Work and Careers
- Travel
- Accommodation
- Health and Welfare
- Food and Drink
- Weather

Some Examining Groups list Language Problems as a topic. Vocabulary needed for dealing with that topic is included in the section on 'Key Words and Expressions', under the sub-heading 'Knowledge, Meaning and Understanding'.

2 > SETTINGS

The Examining Groups also list the *Settings* – the places where you will be expected to use the vocabulary. The settings are:

'Settings' or places in which you must use your vocabulary

- Home
- School/college
- Places of Entertainment
- Private Transport
- Tourist Information Office
- Cafés and Restaurants
- Country, Seaside
- Garage, Petrol Station
- Lost Property Office, Police Station
- Town
- Place of Work
- Places of Interest
- Public Transport
- Shops and Markets
- Hotels, Campsites etc.
- Dentist's, Doctor's, Chemist's
- Bank, Exchange Office

3 > COMBINATION OF TOPICS AND SETTINGS

Each topic can appear in different settings

Each topic may occur in a number of different settings. So, for example, you may be required to give your name (Topic Area : Personal Identification) in almost any setting, e.g. when meeting people on holiday at the seaside, when booking a room at a Hotel or Youth Hostel, at the Doctor's, or when reporting lost property at the Police Station.

The combinations of settings and topic areas is perhaps shown more clearly by the following table:

CHAPTER 3 **ESSENTIAL PRINCIPLES** 15

TOPICS	SETTINGS	Home	Town	School/college	Place of work	Places of entertainment	Private transport	Public transport	Tourist Information Office	Shops, markets	Café, restaurant	Hotels campsites etc.	Dentist, doctor, chemist	Garage, petrol station	Bank, exchange office	Lost property, police station
Personal identification				■	■							■	■			■
House and home – Life at home																
Geographical surroundings																
School and college																
Work and careers																
Free time and entertainment																
Travel																
Holidays																
Accommodation																
Social relationships																
Health and welfare																
Shopping																
Food and drink																
Services																
Weather																
Language problems																

You could shade or colour the squares where the topics and settings are most likely to coincide. Personal identification, for instance, is most likely to be required at school, your place of work, at a hotel, at the dentist's, and at the lost property office or police station. So these squares have been shaded in for you. Spend a few moments considering where the other vocabulary topics are most likely to be useful.

4 > ACTIVE AND RECEPTIVE USE

Most words and expressions are for active use

In the same way that the examination is divided into Basic and Higher Levels, what you are required to do is also divided into two sections: Active and Receptive. *Active* use means what you will be expected to say or write, and *Receptive* use refers to what you are expected to understand (listening or reading). There are some differences in the requirements of the individual Examining Groups on this issue, so in the Topic Areas I have listed the most common words and expressions without indicating whether they are for active or receptive use. The vast majority are for active use, so you must try to learn to use as many as possible and to ensure that you understand the rest. Do remember that you are free to use words which do not appear as long as they are relevant – indeed their use is encouraged. This is of course even more important at Higher Level.

5 > LANGUAGE TASKS

A comprehensive list of the things you will be expected to do is given below. It may appear somewhat off-putting at first, but you will soon see that there are many things, such as giving your name and age, that you can already do well. It also gives you a clear point of reference as to what else you need to learn!

You need to work your way through the list systematically and to check that you can perform all the tasks. To help you to check your progress through the tasks, two boxes are provided next to each task. You can tick off (or even date) items as you learn them and again when you have been tested at a later date (either by yourself or by a friend or by a member of your family).

PERSONAL IDENTIFICATION

You should be able to give information about yourself and others (e.g. members of your family or host family) and to seek information from others on the following points:

Learnt   Tested

- Names (including spelling out your own name) ☐ ☐
- Home Address (including spelling out the name of your home town ☐ ☐
- Telephone Numbers ☐ ☐
- Ages and Birthdays ☐ ☐
- Nationality ☐ ☐
- General Descriptions including sex, marital status, physical appearance, character or disposition of yourself and others ☐ ☐
- Description of clothing ☐ ☐
- Religion ☐ ☐
- Likes and Dislikes (with regard to people and other topics in the syllabus ☐ ☐

HOUSE AND HOME – LIFE AT HOME

House and Home

You should be able to discuss where and under what conditions you and others live, and be able to:

- Say whether you live in a house, flat etc., and ask others the same ☐ ☐
- Describe your house, flat, etc. and its location ☐ ☐
- Find out about and give details of rooms, garage, garden, etc., as appropriate ☐ ☐
- Mention or enquire about availability of the most essential pieces of furniture, amenities, services ☐ ☐
- Say whether you have a room of your own and describe your room or the room where you sleep ☐ ☐
- Say what jobs you do around the home ☐ ☐
- Ask where places and things are in a house ☐ ☐
- Say you need soap, toothpaste, or a towel ☐ ☐
- Invite someone to come in, sit down ☐ ☐

Learnt   Tested

- Thank somebody for hospitality ☐ ☐
- Offer and ask for help to do something about the house ☐ ☐
- Ask permission to use or do things when a guest of a Spanish-speaking family ☐ ☐

Life at Home

You should be able to give and seek information about:

- Members of the Family ☐ ☐
- Description of Members of the Family and their Occupations ☐ ☐
- Description of Family Pets ☐ ☐
- Daily Routine ☐ ☐
- What time you usually get up and go to bed, have meals, how you spend your evenings and weekends. Ask others about the same ☐ ☐
- What you do to help at home ☐ ☐
- How much pocket money you get and what you do with it ☐ ☐

GEOGRAPHICAL SURROUNDINGS

You should be able to give information about your home town or village and surrounding areas, and seek information from others, with respect to:

- Location ☐ ☐
- Character ☐ ☐
- Amenities, attractions, features of interest, entertainment ☐ ☐

You should also be able to:

- Express a simple opinion about your own town or someone else's town ☐ ☐
- Give full descriptions of your home town/village or that of others, and of the surrounding area and region ☐ ☐
- Outline possibilities for sight-seeing ☐ ☐
- Give your opinion of your home town/village: what is good about it; what is not so good about it; how

CHAPTER 3 **ESSENTIAL PRINCIPLES**

Learnt Tested

- long you have been living there; how you would improve it ☐ ☐
- Name and talk about places you have visited ☐ ☐

SCHOOL AND COLLEGE

You should be able to exchange information and opinions about:

- Your school/college and its facilities; state the type, size and location of your school and describe the buildings ☐ ☐
- Daily routines: when school/college begins and ends; how many lessons there are and how long they last; break times and lunch times; homework; how you travel to and from school ☐ ☐
- Your school/college year and holidays; subjects studied and preferences; clubs, sports, trips and other activities ☐ ☐

You should be able to:

- Discuss what sort of education you have had, propose to continue with, at what types of educational institution ☐ ☐
- Talk about examinations ☐ ☐
- Talk about special events in the school year, e.g. plays, sports day, visits ☐ ☐

WORK AND CAREERS

You should be able to:

- Discuss any spare-time job you have, including working hours, earnings and nature of work ☐ ☐
- Discuss your plans and hopes for the future, including: plans for work after the completion of full-time education ☐ ☐
- Give reasons for your choice of career ☐ ☐
- Say what jobs members of your family have ☐ ☐

FREE TIME AND ENTERTAINMENT

General

Learnt Tested

- State your hobbies and interests ☐ ☐
- Ask about the hobbies and interests of other people ☐ ☐
- Discuss your evening, weekend and holiday activities and those of other people ☐ ☐
- Discuss your interest and involvement in: sport and sporting events; intellectual and artistic pursuits; youth clubs, societies ☐ ☐
- Give and seek information about leisure facilities ☐ ☐
- Express simple opinions about: radio and TV, films, performances ☐ ☐
- Agree or disagree with other people's opinions ☐ ☐
- Ask if someone agrees with you ☐ ☐
- Describe and comment on the leisure and entertainment facilities of the area you live in ☐ ☐
- Discuss in more detail your interests/activities ☐ ☐
- Discuss films/plays/concerts, etc. in greater detail ☐ ☐
- Describe how you usually spend a period of free time, e.g. an evening or weekend ☐ ☐
- Describe how you spent a recent period of free time ☐ ☐
- Describe what you would like to do ☐ ☐

Places of entertainment

- Buy entry tickets for cinema or theatre, concert, swimming pool, football match, sports centre ☐ ☐
- Find out the cost of seats or entry ☐ ☐
- Find out or state the starting/finishing times ☐ ☐
- State or ask what sort of film or play it is ☐ ☐
- Ask if the film or event is/was good ☐ ☐

CHAPTER 3 SUBJECT CONTENT: TOPICS, SETTINGS AND VOCABULARY

Learnt Tested

- Express an opinion (about the film or event) ☐ ☐
- Agree or disagree with other people's opinions ☐ ☐
- Ask if someone agrees with your opinion ☐ ☐

TRAVEL

General

- Say how you get to your school/college/place of work (means of transport, if any; duration of journey) ☐ ☐
- Understand and give information about other journeys ☐ ☐

Public Transport

- Ask if there is a bus, train, tube, coach, plane or boat to a particular place ☐ ☐
- Buy tickets, stating:
  destination
  single or return
  class of travel
  day of travel ☐ ☐
- Ask about the cost of tickets ☐ ☐
- Ask about times of departure and arrival ☐ ☐
- Inform someone about proposed times of departure and arrival ☐ ☐
- Ask and check whether it is:
  the right platform
  the right station
  the right line or bus, coach or stop ☐ ☐
- Check that it is the right flight or sailing ☐ ☐
- Ask about the location of facilities, e.g. bus stop, waiting room, information office, toilets ☐ ☐
- Ask if and/or where it is necessary to change buses, trains, or coaches ☐ ☐
- Ask or state whether a seat is free ☐ ☐
- Understand information given in brochures and tables ☐ ☐
- Write a letter about requirements for travel arrangements ☐ ☐

Learnt Tested

- Give above information to others ☐ ☐
- Say what you have lost at the lost property office ☐ ☐
- Ask how to get to a place by bus, train, tube, coach, plane or boat ☐ ☐
- Give above information to others ☐ ☐
- Reserve a seat ☐ ☐
- Say where you would like to sit ☐ ☐
- Ask for information, timetables, or a plan ☐ ☐
- Ask about price reductions and supplements ☐ ☐
- Make arrangements for taking, leaving or sending luggage ☐ ☐
- Deal with an element of the unexpected in travel arrangements, e.g. delayed or cancelled departures, mislaid tickets, documents, lost luggage ☐ ☐
- State whether you have anything to declare at the Customs ☐ ☐

Private Transport

- Buy petrol by grade, volume or price ☐ ☐
- Ask for the tank to be filled up ☐ ☐
- Ask the cost ☐ ☐
- Ask someone to check oil, water and tyres ☐ ☐
- Ask where facilities are ☐ ☐
- Ask about the availability of facilities nearby ☐ ☐
- Check on your route ☐ ☐
- Obtain and give information about routes, types of roads, traffic rules, parking facilities ☐ ☐
- Report a breakdown, giving location and other relevant information ☐ ☐
- Ask for technical help ☐ ☐
- Pay and ask for a receipt ☐ ☐

Finding the way

- Attract the attention of a passer-by ☐ ☐
- Ask where a place is ☐ ☐

CHAPTER 3 **ESSENTIAL PRINCIPLES**

Learnt Tested

- Ask the way (to a place) ☐ ☐
- Ask if it is a long way (to a place) ☐ ☐
- Ask if a place is nearby ☐ ☐
- Ask if there is a place or an amenity nearby ☐ ☐
- Understand directions ☐ ☐
- Ask if there is a bus, train or coach ☐ ☐
- Ask someone to repeat what they have said ☐ ☐
- Say you do not understand ☐ ☐
- Thank people ☐ ☐
- Give directions to strangers ☐ ☐
- State and enquire about distances ☐ ☐

HOLIDAYS

General

- Say where you normally spend your holidays; how long they last; who you go on holiday with; what you normally do; understand others giving the above information ☐ ☐
- Describe a previous holiday: where you went; how you went; who you went with and for how long; where you stayed; what the weather was like; what you saw and did; what your general impressions were; understand others giving the above information ☐ ☐
- Describe your holiday plans ☐ ☐
- Say whether you have been abroad and give details if applicable ☐ ☐
- Understand others giving above information ☐ ☐
- Supply information about travel documents ☐ ☐

Tourist Information

- Ask for and understand information about a town or region (maps, brochures of hotels and camp-sites) ☐ ☐
- Ask for and understand details of excursions, shows, places of interest (location, costs, times) ☐ ☐

Learnt Tested

- Give above information about your own area or one you have visited to others, e.g. prospective tourists ☐ ☐
- React to (i.e. welcome or reject) suggestions about activities and places of interest ☐ ☐
- Write a short letter asking for information and brochures about a town or region and its tourist facilities or attractions ☐ ☐

ACCOMMODATION

General

- Describe accommodation you use or have used ☐ ☐
- Write a short letter asking about the availability and price of accommodation at an hotel, campsite or youth hostel and about amenities available ☐ ☐
- Write a short letter booking such accommodation ☐ ☐
- Read and understand relevant information about accommodation, e.g. brochures ☐ ☐
- Make complaints ☐ ☐

Hotel and Boarding House

- Ask if there are rooms available ☐ ☐
- State when you require a room/rooms and for how long ☐ ☐
- Say what sort of room is required ☐ ☐
- Ask the cost (per night, per person, per room) ☐ ☐
- Say it is too expensive ☐ ☐
- Ask to see the room(s) ☐ ☐
- Accept or reject a room ☐ ☐
- Check in ☐ ☐
- Say that you have (not) reserved accommodation ☐ ☐
- Identify yourself ☐ ☐
- Ask if there is a particular facility (e.g. restaurant) in or near the hotel, campsite etc. ☐ ☐

CHAPTER 3 SUBJECT CONTENT: TOPICS, SETTINGS AND VOCABULARY

Learnt Tested

- Ask where facilities are, e.g. telephone, car park, lift, lounge ☐ ☐
- Ask if meals are included ☐ ☐
- Ask what meals are available ☐ ☐
- Ask the times of meals ☐ ☐
- Ask for your key ☐ ☐
- Say you would like to pay ☐ ☐

Youth Hostel

- Ask if there is any room ☐ ☐
- State when and for how long ☐ ☐
- State how many males and females require accommodation ☐ ☐
- Say you have (not) reserved ☐ ☐
- Identify yourself ☐ ☐
- Ask the cost (per night, per person or facility) ☐ ☐
- Ask if there is a particular facility in or near the hostel ☐ ☐
- Ask where facilities are ☐ ☐
- Say you would like to pay ☐ ☐
- Ask about meal times ☐ ☐
- Ask about opening and closing times ☐ ☐
- Ask about rules and regulations ☐ ☐
- Say you have a sleeping bag ☐ ☐
- Say you wish to hire a sleeping bag ☐ ☐

Camp-site

- Ask if there is any room ☐ ☐
- State when and for how long ☐ ☐
- Say you have (not) reserved ☐ ☐
- Identify yourself ☐ ☐
- Say how many tents, caravans, people or vehicles it is for ☐ ☐
- Say how many children and adults are in the group ☐ ☐
- Ask the cost (per night, per person, per tent, caravan, vehicle or facility) ☐ ☐
- Say it is too expensive ☐ ☐
- Ask if there is a particular facility on or near the site ☐ ☐
- Ask where the facilities are ☐ ☐
- Buy essential supplies ☐ ☐
- Ask about rules and regulations ☐ ☐

SOCIAL RELATIONSHIPS

Relations with Others (General)

Learnt Tested

You should be able to:

- Say whether you are a member of any clubs/groups; if so, which clubs and what activities are involved ☐ ☐
- Give information about your friends ☐ ☐
- Say if you have any friends in foreign countries ☐ ☐

Making Acquaintances

- Greet someone and respond to greetings ☐ ☐
- Ask how someone is and reply to similar enquiries ☐ ☐
- Say that you are pleased to meet someone ☐ ☐
- Introduce yourself (see also Personal Identification) ☐ ☐
- Introduce an acquaintance to someone else ☐ ☐
- Give, receive and exchange gifts ☐ ☐
- Make a telephone call ☐ ☐

Arranging a meeting or an activity

You should be able to:

- Find out what a friend wants to do ☐ ☐
- Ask what is on TV or at the cinema ☐ ☐
- Express preferences for an activity (e.g. watching TV, going out, visiting a friend) ☐ ☐
- Invite someone to go out (stating when and where) ☐ ☐
- Invite someone or suggest going to a particular place, event or on a visit ☐ ☐
- Accept or decline invitations ☐ ☐
- State that something is possible, impossible, probable or certain ☐ ☐
- Thank and apologize ☐ ☐
- Express pleasure ☐ ☐
- Ask about, suggest or confirm a time and place to meet ☐ ☐
- Ask about and state the cost (of entry, etc.) ☐ ☐

Learnt Tested   *Learnt Tested*

- Express surprise, pleasure, regret, doubt, certainty ☐ ☐
- Apologise for late arrival ☐ ☐
- State likes and dislikes ☐ ☐

Current Affairs

You should be able to follow the recounting or discussion of current issues and events of general news value, and of interest to 16-year old students, and to express your reaction to such items.

HEALTH AND WELFARE

General

- State how you feel (well, ill, better, hot, cold, hungry, thirsty, tired) ☐ ☐
- Ask others how they feel ☐ ☐
- Ask about taking a bath or shower ☐ ☐
- Ask for soap, toothpaste, towel ☐ ☐
- Refer to parts of the body where you are in pain or discomfort ☐ ☐
- Call for help ☐ ☐
- Warn about danger ☐ ☐
- Say you would like to rest or go to bed ☐ ☐

Illness and injury

You should be able to:

- Report minor ailments (e.g. temperature, cold, sunburn) ☐ ☐
- Ask for items in a chemist's and ask if they have anything for particular ailments ☐ ☐
- Say you would like to lie down ☐ ☐
- Respond to an enquiry about how long an ailment or symptom has persisted ☐ ☐
- Say you would like to see a doctor or dentist ☐ ☐
- Report injuries ☐ ☐
- Deal with contact with the medical services ☐ ☐
- Say whether you take medicine regularly, and, if so, what ☐ ☐
- Say whether or not you are insured ☐ ☐

- Tell others about medical facilities, surgery hours ☐ ☐

Accident

You should be able to:

- Ask or advise someone to 'phone (doctor, police, fire brigade, ambulance, consulate, acquaintance) ☐ ☐
- Ask for someone's name and address ☐ ☐
- Suggest filling in a road accident form ☐ ☐
- Describe an accident ☐ ☐
- Report that there has been an accident ☐ ☐
- Ask or say whether it is serious ☐ ☐
- Deny responsibility and say whose fault it was ☐ ☐

SHOPPING

General

You should be able to:

- Ask for information about supermarkets, shopping centres, markets, shops ☐ ☐
- Ask where specific shops and departments are ☐ ☐
- Discuss shopping habits ☐ ☐

Shops and Markets

You should be able to:

- Ask whether particular goods are available ☐ ☐
- Ask for particular items (mentioning e.g. colour, size, who it is for, etc.) ☐ ☐
- Find out how much things cost ☐ ☐
- Say an item is (not) satisfactory ☐ ☐
- Say an item is too expensive, small, big, etc. ☐ ☐
- Say you will (not) take something ☐ ☐
- Express a preference ☐ ☐
- State quantity required (including weights, volumes, containers) ☐ ☐
- Find out opening and closing times ☐ ☐
- Say that is all you require ☐ ☐
- Enquire about costs and prices ☐ ☐

Learnt Tested

- Pay for items ☐ ☐
- Say whether things are (too) expensive ☐ ☐
- State whether you have enough money ☐ ☐
- Understand currencies used in major Spanish-speaking countries, including written and printed prices ☐ ☐
- Ask for small change ☐ ☐
- Return unsatisfactory goods and ask for a refund or replacement ☐ ☐

FOOD AND DRINK

General

You should be able to:

- Discuss your likes, dislikes and preferences and those of others ☐ ☐
- Discuss your typical meals, meal times, and eating habits ☐ ☐
- Buy food and drink (see Shops and Markets) ☐ ☐
- Explain to a visitor what a dish is, or what it contains ☐ ☐

Café, Restaurant and Other Public Places

- Attract the attention of the waiter/waitress ☐ ☐
- Order a drink or snack ☐ ☐
- Order a meal ☐ ☐
- Ask for a particular fixed-price menu ☐ ☐
- Say how many there are in your group ☐ ☐
- Ask for a table (for a certain number) ☐ ☐
- Ask about availability of certain dishes and drinks ☐ ☐
- Ask the cost of dishes and drinks ☐ ☐
- Ask for an explanation or description of something on the menu ☐ ☐
- Expess opinions about a meal or dish ☐ ☐
- Accept or reject suggestions ☐ ☐
- Ask if the service charge is included ☐ ☐

Learnt Tested

- Ask about the location of facilities (e.g. toilets, telephone) ☐ ☐

At Home

- Express hunger and thirst ☐ ☐
- Ask about time and place of meals ☐ ☐
- Ask for food and table articles (including asking for more, a little, a lot) ☐ ☐
- React to offers of food (accept, decline, apologise, express pleasure) ☐ ☐
- Express likes, dislikes and preferences ☐ ☐
- Express appreciation and pay compliments ☐ ☐
- Respond to a toast, e.g. 'Salud' ☐ ☐

SERVICES

Post Office

- Ask where a post-office or letter box is ☐ ☐
- Ask how much it costs to send letters, postcards or parcels to a particular country or within the country ☐ ☐
- Say whether you would like to send letters, postcards or parcels ☐ ☐
- Buy stamps of a particular value ☐ ☐
- Find out opening and closing times ☐ ☐
- Say that is all you require ☐ ☐
- Send a telegram ☐ ☐

Bank or Exchange Office

- Say you would like to change travellers' cheques or money ☐ ☐
- Ask for coins or notes of a particular denomination ☐ ☐
- Give proof of identity (e.g. show passport) ☐ ☐
- Cope with any likely eventuality that may arise while using a bank or foreign exchange office to change currency or cheques ☐ ☐

CHAPTER 3 **ESSENTIAL PRINCIPLES** 23

Learnt Tested   *Learnt Tested*

Telephone

- Give and seek information about where 'phone calls can be made ☐ ☐
- Ask if you can make a 'phone call ☐ ☐
- Ask for a telephone number and give your own telephone number ☐ ☐
- Answer a 'phone call, stating who you are ☐ ☐
- Make a 'phone call and ask to speak to someone ☐ ☐
- Ask someone to ring you up ☐ ☐
- Find out if others can be contacted by 'phone ☐ ☐
- Tell others you will ring up ☐ ☐
- Ask for coins ☐ ☐
- Ask for a reversed charge call ☐ ☐

Lost Property

- Report a loss or theft, stating what you have lost, when and where it was lost or left and describing the item (size, shape, colour, make, contents) ☐ ☐
- Express surprise, pleasure, disappointment, anger ☐ ☐

Having things repaired and cleaned

- Report an accident, damage done or breakdown ☐ ☐
- Ask if shoes, clothes, camera, etc. can be repaired ☐ ☐
- Explain what is wrong and ask if shoes, etc. can be repaired ☐ ☐
- Ask for, and offer, advice about getting something cleaned or repaired ☐ ☐
- Ask for an item of clothing to be cleaned ☐ ☐
- Arrange for clothing to be washed ☐ ☐
- Find out how long it will take, what it will cost, when an item will be ready ☐ ☐
- Thank, complain, express disappointment, pleasure ☐ ☐
- Suggest the need for repair or cleaning and report or comment on any action taken ☐ ☐

WEATHER

- Describe or comment on current weather conditions ☐ ☐
- Ask about weather conditions in the country you are visiting ☐ ☐
- Describe the climate of your own country and ask about the climate in another country ☐ ☐
- Understand simple predictions about weather conditions ☐ ☐
- Understand spoken and written weather forecasts ☐ ☐

LANGUAGE PROBLEMS

(Dealt with in the vocabulary list of 'Key Words and Expressions' under the sub-heading 'Knowledge, Meaning and Understanding')

- State whether or not you understand ☐ ☐
- Ask someone to repeat what they have said ☐ ☐
- Ask for and understand the spelling out of names, etc. ☐ ☐
- Ask if someone speaks English or Spanish ☐ ☐
- State how well or how little you speak and understand Spanish ☐ ☐
- Ask what things are called in Spanish or English ☐ ☐
- Ask what words or phrases mean ☐ ☐
- Say you do not know (something) ☐ ☐
- Say that you have forgotten (something) ☐ ☐
- Ask whether, or state that, something is correct ☐ ☐
- Say for how long you have been learning Spanish and any other languages you know ☐ ☐
- Ask someone to explain something, to correct mistakes ☐ ☐
- Ask how something is pronounced ☐ ☐

6 > LEARNING VOCABULARY

This is, for most people, one of the tedious tasks of language learning but it has to be done, and it has to be done over the weeks and months if you are to acquire a working knowledge of 1500–2200 words by the time you take your examination. So how can you make sure that the hard work you do is effective?

- **Learn vocabulary regularly**; ideally every day (and certainly at least twice a week).

- **Work in short sessions**. For most people, about 10 minutes at one go is enough. After that, words don't seem to lodge in the memory so well. Three 10-minute spells of vocabulary learning are far more effective than one 30-minute session. So do ten minutes now, then do something else and come back to the vocabulary, maybe half an hour or an hour later.

- **Be systematic**; keep a record of what you have learnt, so that you can plan your future learning successfully.

> *Hints for learning vocabulary*

- **Work by topic and by specific areas within each topic**. It is much easier to remember words learnt in a group which is linked with one type of situation (e.g. ordering food in the restaurant) than to recall a list of words whose only link is that they begin with the letter 'a'.

- **Test yourself regularly as you learn** (or ask someone else to test you), so that you can concentrate on the words you still don't know well enough. Some words can be learnt almost on sight; others prove far more difficult. So don't spend the same amount of time on each word!

- **Start by making sure you know the English for the Spanish words**, then reverse the process and make sure you can give the Spanish when you see or hear the English.

- **Say each word aloud at some point** (or at least think how you would pronounce it). Remember you have to speak the words as well as write them – so make sure you can say them correctly.

- **Think how you might use the word in a real situation**. Putting it into a sentence is one of the most effective ways of 'fixing' a word in the memory.

- If you record the words on a cassette, leaving a gap between the English word and its Spanish equivalent, you can use your cassette recorder or personal stereo as a means of testing yourself at odd times, such as when you are getting dressed, doing your hair or even travelling. Your aim is to say (or think) the correct Spanish word during the gap before you hear it on the cassette.

- Many people who enjoy using computers find the computer can be a great help in learning words and their spellings, using the word processor and, if they have one, the spelling checker. (You have to take care to enter Spanish words correctly in the spelling checker!)

And when you are learning vocabulary, don't forget that, if you are to use a word correctly, you will need to know:

- the **correct spelling**, including accents;

- if it is **masculine or feminine** – so learn the gender with the word;

> *Important for using a word correctly*

- if it is a **radical-changing verb** – so learn the letters (*ue*), (*ie*) or (*i*) that are printed after the radical-changing verbs in the vocabulary lists (and check the Grammar section if you are unsure how radical-changing verbs work!).

If you say or write words incorrectly though in a way that a Spanish-speaker with no knowledge of English would understand, you will be given credit for effective communication but you will not gain good marks for quality of language – and that can be quite important at Higher Level if you are aiming for a high grade.

KEY WORDS AND EXPRESSIONS

VOCABULARY LISTS

Underlying all the topic areas areas are certain key words and expressions that are not necessarily related to any specific topic but are likely to be essential in dealing with almost any. They are usually listed in the Examining Groups' syllabuses within sections headed 'Functions' and 'Notions'. In this section I have not attempted to give an exhaustive list of the Functions and Notions in the GCSE syllabuses but merely to set out the most common expressions that you will need and that have not been included in the topic sections that follow.

Expressions marked with an asterisk * are normally required at *Higher Level* only.

> 🙶 Useful words and expressions which do not fit the topic areas below 🙷

> 🙶 Remember – an asterisk means needed for Higher Level only 🙷

ser *to be*
estar *to be*
tener *to have*
hay *there is/ there are*

ir (a) *to go (to)*
venir (de) *to come (from)*
entrar (en) *to enter, go in (to)*
salir *to go out, to depart*
llegar *to arrive*
subir *to go up*
bajar *to go down*
quedar (se) *to stay*
estar en casa *to be at home*
ir a casa *to go home*
volver (ue) a casa *to return home*

pasar *to happen*
suceder * *to happen*
tener lugar * *to take place*
bueno *good*
malo *bad*
mejor *better*
peor *worse*
grande *big*
pequeño *small*
mayor *greater, older*
menor *lesser, younger*
más grande *bigger*
más pequeño *smaller*

aquí *here*
allí *there*
ahí *there (near the person being addressed)*
en alguna parte *somewhere*
en ninguna parte * *nowhere*
en todas partes *everywhere*
(For other expressions of place – see 'Geographical Surroundings')

aunque *although*
como *as*
pero *but*
porque *because*
y *and*

con *with*
sin *without*
para *for*
por *by, through, because of*

alguien *someone*
algo *something*
alguno / algún / alguna... *some...*
cada (uno/una) *each (one)*
nada *nothing*
nadie *nobody*
todos *all, everyone*
todo el mundo *everybody*

EMOTIONS

(no) estar contento *to be (un)happy*
gozar de *to enjoy*
inquietarse por * *to worry about*
llorar *to cry, weep*
odiar *to hate*
preocuparse (por) * *to worry (about)*
pasarlo bien *to enjoy oneself*
querer (ie) *to wish, to love*
reírse (de)* *to laugh (at)*
tener miedo (de) *to be afraid (of)*
alegre *happy*
triste *sad*
preocupado (por) * *worried (about)*
de buen humor *in a good mood*
de mal humor *in a bad mood*

TIME

el año *year*
el día *day*
la estación *season (of the year)*
la fecha *date*
la hora *hour*
el mes *month*
el minuto *minute*
la semana *week*
el rato * *short while*
el segundo *second*
el siglo * *century*
el tiempo *time*

este año *this year*
el año pasado *last year*
el año que viene *next year*
el año siguiente * *the following year*
al día siguiente * *the following day*
esta semana *this week*
el fin de semana *(at) the weekend*
quince días *a fortnight*
¿Cuánto tiempo...? *For how long...?*
durante mucho tiempo *for a long time*

la mañana *morning*
la tarde *afternoon, early evening*
la noche *late evening, night*
la madrugada * *early morning*
durar * *to last*
por la mañana *in the morning*
a las diez de la mañana *at 10 o'clock in the morning*

la primavera *Spring*
el verano *Summer*
el otoño *Autumn*
el invierno *Winter*

enero *January*
febrero *February*
marzo *March*
abril *April*
mayo *May*
junio *June*
julio *July*
agosto *August*
se(p)tiembre *September*
octubre *October*
noviembre *November*
diciembre *December*

¿Qué fecha es? *What is the date?*
Es el 5 de marzo *It is the 5 March*
¿A cuántos estamos? *What is the date?*
Estamos a 5 de marzo *It is the 5 March*
a principios de enero *at the beginning of January*
a mediados de octubre *in mid-October*
a fines de diciembre *at the end of December*

lunes *Monday*
martes *Tuesday*
miércoles *Wednesday*
jueves *Thursday*
viernes *Friday*
sábado *Saturday*
domingo *Sunday*

el domingo *on Sunday*
los viernes *on Fridays*
el jueves que viene *next Thursday*
el lunes por la mañana *on Monday morning*
el sábado que viene por la tarde *next Saturday afternoon*

el día de Año Nuevo *New Year's Day*
el día de Reyes *Epiphany, Twelfth Night*
la Semana Santa *Holy Week, Easter*
las vacaciones de Semana Santa *the Easter holidays*

el Viernes Santo *Good Friday*
la Nochebuena *Christmas Eve*
el día de Navidad *Christmas Day*
la Nochevieja *New Year's Eve*

hoy *today*
mañana *tomorrow*
pasado mañana *the day after tomorrow*
ayer *yesterday*
anteayer *the day before yesterday*
anoche *last night*
mañana por la mañana *tomorrow morning*
hoy día *these days*

actualmente *at the present time*
ahora *now*
ahora mismo *right now, straightaway*
al mismo tiempo *at the same time*
antes *before, earlier*
de nuevo *again*
de repente *suddenly*
después *afterwards, later*
en seguida *at once, immediately*
entonces *then, at that time*
finalmente *finally*
luego *then, next*
más tarde *later*
por fin *finally, at last*
pronto *soon*
tarde *late*
temprano *early*
todavía *still*
todavía no *not yet, still not*
ya *already, by now*
ya no *no longer*
al final *at the end, in the end*
al principio *at the beginning*
hace tres horas *three hours ago*
a menudo *often*
a veces *sometimes*
de vez en cuando * *from time to time*
generalmente *generally*
nunca *never*
casi nunca *hardly ever*
pocas veces *rarely*
raramente *rarely*
siempre *always*
todos los días *every day*
una vez al año *once a year*

a partir de *(starting) from*
antes de *before*
desde *since, from*
después de *after*
durante *during, for*
hasta *until*
como *as*
cuando *when*
en cuanto * *as soon as*
mientras * *while*

TIME OF DAY

¿A qué hora...? *At what time...?*
a la una *at one o'clock*
a las dos *at two o'clock*
a las tres y media *at half past three*
a las cinco y cuarto *at quarter past five*
a las doce menos cuarto *at quarter to twelve*
a las diez y veinte *at twenty past ten*
a las ocho menos diez *at ten to eight*
a las siete y pico *just after seven*
¿Qué hora es? *What time is it?*
Es la una *It is one o'clock*
Son las dos *It is two o'clock*
¿Qué hora era? *What time was it?*
Eran las seis y veinte *It was twenty past six*
aproximadamente *about, approximately*
a eso de... *at about...*
en punto *exactly*
dar * *to strike*
daban las cinco * *It was striking five*
las siete de la tarde *seven o'clock in the evening*
la una de la madrugada * *one o'clock in the morning*

SPEED

a gran velocidad *at great speed*
a toda velocidad *at full speed*
de prisa *quickly*
despacio *slowly*
lentamente *slowly*
rápidamente *rapidly*
lento *slow*
rápido *quick*
tener prisa *to be in a hurry*
darse prisa * *to hurry*
a noventa kilómetros por hora *at 90 kilometres per hour*

NUMBERS

1	uno, un, una
2	dos
3	tres
4	cuatro
5	cinco
6	seis
7	siete
8	ocho
9	nueve
10	diez
11	once
12	doce
13	trece
14	catorce
15	quince
16	dieciséis
17	diecisiete
18	dieciocho
19	diecinueve
20	veinte
21	veintiuno/a
22	veintidós
23	veintitrés
24	veinticuatro
25	veinticinco
26	veintiséis
27	veintisiete
28	veintiocho
29	veintinueve
30	treinta
31	treinta y uno/a
32	treinta y dos
40	cuarenta
41	cuarenta y uno/a
50	cincuenta
60	sesenta
70	setenta
80	ochenta
90	noventa
100	ciento, cien
101	ciento uno
200	doscientos/as
300	trescientos/as
400	cuatrocientos/as
500	quinientos/as
600	seiscientos/as
700	setecientos/as
800	ochocientos/as
900	novecientos/as
1000	mil
2000	dos mil
100 000	cien mil
1 000 000	un millón
2 000 000	dos millones

NOTES: a) dos, tres, *and* seis *take an accent when added to the end of another word (e.g.* dieciséis*).*
b) *The word* y *occurs only between the tens and units from 31 to 99.*
c) cien *is used before a noun (e.g.* cien personas*) but not before an additional part of the number (e.g.* ciento cincuenta y seis*).*
d) millón *and* millones *take* de *before a noun, but not before a continuation of the number (e.g.* tres millones de personas *but* cuatro millones trescientos mil*).*

Ordinal numbers:
1° primero/a *first*
2° segundo/a *second*
3° tercero/a *third*

4° cuarto/a *fourth*
5° quinto/a *fifth*
6° sexto/a *sixth*
7° séptimo/a *seventh*
8° octavo/a *eighth*
9° noveno/a *ninth*
10° décimo/a *tenth*

QUESTION WORDS

¿Adónde...? *Where...to?*
¿Cómo...? *How...?*
  ¿Cómo? *I beg your pardon? What? (asking someone to repeat)*
  ¿Cómo te llamas? *What is your name?*
  ¿Cómo se llama? *What is his/her name?*
  ¿Cómo es (son)...? *What is (are)... like?*
¿Cuál? *Which one?*
  ¿Cuál de...? *Which one of...?*
¿Cuándo...? *When...?*
¿Cuánto/a...? *How much...?*
  ¿Cuántos/as...? *How many...?*
¿Dónde...? *Where...?*
¿Por qué...? *Why...?*
¿Qué...? *What...?*
  ¿Qué libro...? *Which book...? What book...?*
¿Quién...? *Who...? (singular)*
  ¿Quiénes...? *Who...? (plural)*
  ¿A quién...? *To whom....? Who...to? Whom...?*
  ¿De quién es (son)...? *Whose is (are)...?*

KNOWLEDGE, MEANING AND UNDERSTANDING

el error *error, mistake*
la palabra *word*
la mentira * *lie*
la verdad *truth*
comprender *to understand*
conocer *to be acquainted with*
corregir (i) *to correct*
decir *to say, tell*
entender (ie) *to understand*
escribir *to write*
equivocarse * *to be wrong, to make a mistake*
explicar * *to explain*
hablar *to speak*
llamarse *to be called*
mentir (ie) * *to lie*
negar (ie) * *to deny*
pronunciar * *to pronounce*
querer decir *to mean*
repetir (i) *to repeat*
saber *to know, to know how to*
(no) tener razón *to be right (wrong)*
correcto *correct*
verdadero *real*

¿Cómo se escribe? *How is it spelt?*
¿Cómo se llama esto? *What is this called*
¿Cómo se pronuncia esta palabra? * *How do you pronounce this word?*
¿Conoce usted Londres? *Do you know London?*
¿Está bien esto? *Is this right?*
Es verdad *It is true*
¿Habla usted inglés? *Do you speak English?*
Hable más despacio por favor *Speak more slowly, please*
Llevo tres años estudiando el español * *I have been studying Spanish for three years*
¿Me puede explicar...? * *Can you explain to me...?*
¿Me puede corregir esto, por favor? * *Could you correct this for me, please?*
No entiendo *I don't understand*
No es verdad *It is untrue*
No sé *I don't know*
¿Qué quiere decir...? *What does ... mean?*
Repita usted, por favor *Please would you repeat that*
¿Sabes dónde está mi reloj? *Do you know where my watch is?*
Se me ha olvidado *I have forgotten*

PERSONAL IDENTIFICATION

NAME

Basic
el apellido *surname*
el nombre (de pila) *first name*
  llamarse *to be called*
  escribir *to write*
  firmar *to sign*
  señor *Mr, Sir*
  señora *Mrs, madam*
  señorita *Miss*
  don *title used with first name (masc.)*
  doña *title used with first name (fem.)*
  Sr. /Sra. /Srta. *Mr, Mrs, Miss*
D. /Da. *title used with first name*
Letters of the alphabet

Basic phrases
¿Cómo se escribe....? *How do you spell....?*
Me llamo.... *My name is....*
Se llama.... *His/her name is....*

ADDRESS

Basic
la avenida *avenue*
la calle *street*

la casa *house, home*
la ciudad *town, city*
la dirección *address*
el domicilio *home*
el número *number*
el país *country*
el piso *flat, storey*
la plaza *square*
el pueblo *village*
la provincia *province, (= county)*
las señas *address*
el sobre *envelope*
vivir *to live*

Basic phrase
Vivo en.... *I live in/at....*

TELEPHONE
Basic
¿Dígame? *Hello (when answering)*
Oiga *Hello (when ringing)*
la guía (telefónica) *telephone directory*
llamar (por teléfono) *to call, to telephone*
marcar (un número) *to dial (a number)*
el número de teléfono *telephone number*
telefonear *to telephone*
tener teléfono *to have a telephone*

Basic phrases
¿Cuál es tu número de teléfono? *What is your telephone number?*
¿Está Pepe? *Is Pepe there?*

AGE
Basic
el año *year*
el cumpleaños *birthday*
la edad *age*
la fecha de nacimiento *date of birth*
el lugar de nacimiento *place of birth*
el mes *month*
el santo *Saint's day*
nacer *to be born*
morir *(ue) to die*

Basic phrases
Nací en.... *I was born in....*
Tengo.... años *I am .... years old*

Higher
cumplir 16 años *to have one's 16th birthday*

NATIONALITY AND COUNTRIES
Basic
alemán *German*
americano *American*
escocés *Scottish*
español *Spanish*
francés *French*
galés *Welsh*
inglés *English*
irlandés *Irish*

Alemania *Germany*
Escocia *Scotland*
España *Spain*
los Estados Unidos *the United States*
Francia *France*
Inglaterra *England*
Irlanda *Ireland*
el País de Gales *Wales*

el carné de identidad *identity card*
la documentación *identity document*
extranjero *foreign*
la nacionalidad *nationality*
el pasaporte *passport*

Basic phrases
¿De dónde es usted? *Where are you from?*
¿Dónde naciste? *Where were you born*
Nací en.... *I was born in....*
Soy inglés (inglesa) *I am English*

Higher
Gran Bretaña *Great Britain*
el Reino Unido *the United Kingdom*
natural de... *born in...*
el país de origen *country of origin*

FOR A FULLER LIST OF COUNTRIES AND NATIONALITIES SEE 'HOLIDAYS'.

PEOPLE
Basic
el adulto *adult*
el/la amigo/a *friend*
el/la bebé *baby*
Caballeros *Gentlemen*
la chica *girl*
el chico *boy, youth*
la gente *people*
el hombre *man*
el/la joven *young person*
la muchacha *girl*
el muchacho *boy*
la mujer *woman, wife*
la niña *young girl*
el niño *young boy*
la novia *girlfriend, fiancée, bride*
el novio *boyfriend, fiancé, bridegroom*
la religión *religion*
la señora *lady*
Señoras *Ladies*
el señor *gentleman*
la viuda *widow*

el   viudo *widower*
casado *married*
católico *Catholic*
divorciado *divorced*
mayor *older*
protestante *Protestant*
soltero *single, unmarried*

THE FAMILY AND RELATIVES
Basic
el/la   abuelo/a *grandfather/grandmother*
los   abuelos *grandparents*
el/la   esposo/a *husband/wife*
la   familia *family*
el/la   hermano/a *brother/sister*
el/la   hijo/a *son/daughter*
la   madre *mother*
       mamá *mum*
el   marido *husband*
el   matrimonio *married couple*
la   mujer *wife*
el   padre *father*
       papá *dad*
el/la   pariente *relative*
el/la   primo/a *cousin*
el/la   sobrino/a *nephew/niece*
el/la   tío/a *uncle/aunt*
       casarse con *to marry*
       mayor *elder*
       menor *younger*
       primero *first*
       último *last*

Basic phrases
Mi hermana está casada (con...) *My sister is married (to...)*
Se va a casar (con...) *S/he is going to get married (to...)*
Mis padres están separados *My parents are separated*
Sus padres están divorciados *His/her/their parents are divorced*

Higher
el/la   cuñado/a *brother/sister-in-law*
el/la   nieto/a *grandson/granddaughter*
el/la   suegro/a *father/mother-in-law*

DESCRIBING PEOPLE
(a) Physical appearance
Basic
la   barba *beard*
el   bigote *moustache*
la   cara *face*
las   gafas *glasses*
los   ojos *eyes*
el   pelo *hair*
      alto *tall*
      azul *blue*
      bajo *short*
      blanco *white*
      bonito *pretty*
      calvo *bald*
      castaño *brown*
      corto *short*
      débil *weak*
      delgado *slim, thin*
      feo *ugly*
      fuerte *strong*
      gordo *fat*
      grande *big, large*
      gris *grey*
      guapo *good-looking*
      hermoso *beautiful, handsome*
      joven *young*
      marrón *brown*
      pequeño *small*
      moreno *dark (of skin or hair)*
      negro *black, dark brown (of eyes)*
      largo *long*
      redondo *round*
      rubio *fair, blonde*
      verde *green, hazel (of eyes)*
      viejo *old*
      llevar *to wear*

Basic phrases
¿Cómo es? *What is s/he like?*
Tiene barba *He has a beard*
Tiene la cara redonda *S/he has a round face*
Tiene el pelo largo *S/he has long hair*
Tiene el pelo corto *S/he has short hair*
Tiene los ojos azules *S/he has blue eyes*
Lleva gafas *S/he wears glasses*

Higher
pálido *pale*
parecerse a *to resemble*
pelirrojo *red-haired*
raro *strange*
tostado *sunburnt*
vestir (i) *to wear*

(b) Character
Basic
activo *active*
alegre *cheerful*
amable *kind, nice, likeable*
antipático *nasty, unfriendly*
divertido *amusing*
estúpido *stupid*
extraño *strange*
imbécil *stupid*
inteligente *intelligent*
listo *clever*
loco *mad*
malhumorado *ill-tempered, grumpy*
malo *wicked, naughty*

trabajador/a hard-working. (handwritten)

perezoso *lazy*
pobre *poor*
rico *rich*
serio *serious*
simpático *friendly, likeable, nice*
tímido *shy*
tonto *stupid, silly*
tranquilo *calm*
triste *sad*

Higher
parecer *to seem*
vivo *lively*

Higher Phrase
Parece muy simpático *He seems very nice*

LIKES AND DISLIKES

Basic
detestar *to detest*
gustar *to like (see phrases)*
odiar *to hate*
preferir (ie) *to prefer*

Basic phrases
Me gusta la música *I like music*
Me gustan las uvas *I like grapes*
A mi hermana le gustan los calamares *My sister likes squid*

FOR CLOTHING – SEE 'CLOTHES' IN THE 'SHOPPING' SECTION.

FOR PEOPLE'S JOBS – SEE 'WORK AND CAREERS'.

FOR INTERESTS AND HOBBIES – SEE 'FREE TIME AND ENTERTAINMENT'

HOUSE AND HOME – LIFE AT HOME

HOUSE
Basic
el ascensor *lift*
el balcón *balcony*
la calefacción (central) *(central) heating*
la casa *house, home*
el chalet (chalé) *detached house*
la chimenea *fireplace, chimney*
el edificio *building*
la electricidad *electricity*
la entrada *entrance*
la escalera *stairs*
el garaje *garage*
el gas *gas*
la granja *farm*
la habitación *room*
el jardín *garden*
la lámpara *lamp*
el lujo *luxury*
la luz *light*
la llave *key, switch*
la pared *wall*
el patio *courtyard*
el piso *flat, floor, storey*
la planta baja *ground floor*
el primer piso *first floor*
la puerta *door*
la puerta principal *front door*
la puerta de la calle *front door*
el suelo *floor*
el techo *ceiling*
el tejado *roof*
la terraza *large balcony*
la ventana *window*

abajo *downstairs*
alquilar *to rent*
abrir *to open*
arreglar *to tidy, to mend*
cerrar (ie) *to close*
cerrar (ie) con llave *to lock*
arriba *upstairs*
cerca de *near*
cómodo *comfortable*
funcionar *to work properly*
lejos de *far from*
limpiar *to clean*
llamar a la puerta *to knock at the door, ring the doorbell*
lujoso *luxurious*
moderno *modern*
nuevo *new*
pasar la aspiradora *to hoover*
salir de casa *to go out*
viejo *old*
vivir *to live*
volver (ue) a casa *to return home*

Higher
amueblado *furnished*
el apartamento *appartment, flat*
mudarse *to move house*
la persiana *blind*
pintado (de blanco) *painted (white)*
la reja *window grill*
tocar el timbre *to ring the bell*

ROOMS
Basic
la cocina *kitchen*
el comedor *dining room*
el (cuarto de) baño *bathroom*
el dormitorio *bedroom*
los muebles *furniture*
el salón *lounge, sitting room*
el vestíbulo *entrance hall*
el wc (wáter) *toilet*
el rincón *corner*

Higher
el cuarto de estar *living room*

el desván *loft, attic*
el pasillo *corridor, passage*
el sótano *cellar*

BEDROOM
Basic

la almohada *pillow*
el armario *cupboard, wardrobe*
la cama *bed*
la cama individual *single bed*
la cama de matrimonio *double bed*
la cómoda *chest of drawers*
la manta *blanket*
la mesilla *bedside table*
la sábana *sheet*
la silla *chair*
el tocador *dressing table*
    despertarse (ie) *to wake up*
    dormir (ue) *to sleep*
    levantarse *to get up*

Higher

la colcha *bedspread*
el despertador *alarm clock*
    dormirse (ue) *to go to sleep*
    hacer la cama *to make the bed*
    vestirse (i) *to dress*

BATHROOM
Basic

el agua (fem.) *water*
el baño *bath*
el cepillo (de dientes) *(tooth) brush*
el champú *shampoo*
la ducha *shower*
el espejo *mirror*
el jabón *soap*
el lavabo *washbasin*
la pasta de dientes *toothpaste*
el wáter (wc) *toilet*
la toalla *towel*
    afeitarse *to shave*
    bañarse *to have a bath*
    ducharse *to have a shower*
    lavarse *to have a wash*
    lavarse las manos *to wash one's hands*
    caliente *hot*
    frío *cold*

Higher

el grifo *tap*
    abrir el grifo *to turn the tap on*
    arreglarse *to get ready (e.g. in order to go out)*
    cerrar (ie) el grifo *to turn the tap off*
    peinarse *to do one's hair*

KITCHEN
Basic

la aspiradora *vacuum cleaner*
la cacerola *saucepan*
la cafetera *coffee pot*
la cocina de gas *gas cooker*
la cocina eléctrica *electric cooker*
el congelador *freezer*
el fregadero *kitchen sink*
el fregaplatos *dishwasher*
el frigorífico *refrigerator*
la lavadora *washing machine*
la nevera *refrigerator*
la plancha *iron*
el plato *plate*
la sartén *frying pan*
la taza *cup*
    cocinar *to cook*
    cortar *to cut*
    fregar (ie) los platos *to wash up*
    lavar la ropa *to do the washing*
    limpiar *to clean*
    limpio *clean*
    planchar la ropa *to do the ironing*
    preparar la comida *to cook the meal*

Higher

la basura *rubbish*
el cubo de la basura *waste bin, dustbin*
el estante *shelf*
el jarro *jug*
    barrer *to sweep*
    calentar (ie) *to heat, to warm*
    congelar *to freeze*
    hervir (ie) *to boil*

DINING ROOM
Basic

el aparador *sideboard*
la mesa *table*
la silla *chair*
la cuchara *spoon*
el cuchillo *knife*
el mantel *table cloth*
el tenedor *fork*
el vaso *glass, tumbler*
    beber *to drink*
    cenar *to have the evening meal*
    comer *to eat, have lunch*
    desayunar *to have breakfast*
    merendar (ie) *to have an afternoon snack*
    poner la mesa *to lay the table*
    quitar la mesa *to clear the table*
    sentarse (ie) *to sit down*
    tomar café *to have coffee*
    tomar el desayuno *to have breakfast*

Higher

la cucharita *teaspoon*
la servilleta *napkin, serviette*

LIVING ROOM

Basic

- la alfombra *carpet*
- la butaca *armchair*
- la cortina *curtain*
- la chimenea *fireplace*
- el cuadro *picture*
- el estéreo *stereo*
- el florero *vase*
- la foto *photo*
- la radio *radio*
- el sillón *armchair*
- el sofá *sofa, settee*
- la televisión *television*
- el tocadiscos *record player*
- el vídeo *video*
- descansar *to rest*
- oír música *to listen to music*
- ver la televisión *to watch television*

Higher

- encender (ie) *to switch on*

GARDEN

Basic

- el árbol *tree*
- el banco *bench*
- la flor *flower*
- la fuente *fountain*
- la hierba *grass*
- las legumbres *vegetables*
- el patio *(court)yard*
- la planta *plant*
- cultivar *to cultivate, grow*

Basic phrase

- trabajar en el jardín *to work in the garden*

Higher

- el césped *lawn, turf*
- el estanque *pond*
- el árbol frutal *fruit tree*
- el manzano *apple tree*
- el peral *pear tree*

Higher phrases

- cortar la hierba *to cut the grass*
- regar (ie) las plantas *to water the plants*

ANIMALS AND PETS

Basic

- el animal *animal, pet*
- el burro *donkey*
- el caballo *horse*
- la cabra *goat*
- el cerdo *pig*
- el conejo *rabbit*
- la gallina *hen*
- el/la gato/a *cat*
- la oveja *sheep*
- el pájaro *bird*
- el pez (rojo) *(gold)fish*
- el/la perro/a *dog*
- el ratón *mouse*
- la tortuga *tortoise*
- la vaca *cow*

DAILY ROUTINE

Basic

- el día *day*
- la mañana *morning*
- la tarde *afternoon, early evening*
- la noche *night, late evening*
- el desayuno *breakfast*
- la comida *meal, lunch*
- la merienda *afternoon snack*
- la cena *evening meal, evening dinner*

- el sueldo *pocket money*

- acostarse (ue) *to go to bed*
- ayudar *to help*
- bajar *to go downstairs*
- bañarse *to have a bath*
- cenar *to have the evening meal*
- comer *to eat, have lunch*
- charlar *to chat*
- desayunar *to have breakfast*
- despertarse (ie) *to wake up*
- dormir (ue) *to sleep*
- ducharse *to have a shower*
- hablar *to speak*

- ir al colegio *to go to school*
- ir al trabajo *to go to work*
- lavarse *to have a wash*
- levantarse *to get up*
- limpiar *to clean*
- salir *to go out*
- subir *to go upstairs*
- tener sueño *to be tired*

Higher

- la madrugada *the early morning*
- almorzar (ue) *to have lunch*
- barrer *to sweep*
- dormir (ue) la siesta *to have a siesta*
- dormirse (ue) *to go to sleep*
- madrugar *to get up early*
- merendar (ie) *to have an afternoon snack*
- peinarse *to do one's hair*
- quitar el polvo *to do the dusting*
- vestirse (i) *to get dressed*

FOR PART-TIME JOBS – SEE 'WORK AND CAREERS'

GEOGRAPHICAL SURROUNDINGS

TOWN OR VILLAGE
Basic
- la capital *capital, large town*
- la ciudad *town, city*
- el pueblo *village, small town*

- los almacenes *department store*
- el ayuntamiento *town hall*
- el bar *bar, pub*
- la biblioteca *library*
- el café *café*
- el castillo *castle*
- la catedral *cathedral*
- el cine *cinema*
- el club *club*
- el colegio *school*
- correos *post office*
- la discoteca *disco*
- el edificio *building*
- la escuela *school*
- la estación *station*
- la estación de metro *underground station*
- el estadio *stadium*
- el estanco *shop for stamps and tobacco*
- la iglesia *church*
- el instituto *(state secondary) school*
- el mercado *market*
- el museo *museum, art gallery*

- la oficina *office*
- la piscina *office*
- la plaza de toros *bull ring*
- el quiosco *kiosk*
- el restaurante *restaurant*
- la tienda *shop*
- la torre *tower*

Higher
- la comisaría *police station*
- la muralla *wall, fortification*

Basic
- la acera *pavement*
- el aparcamiento *car park*
- la avenida *avenue*
- la calle *street*
- la calle mayor *main street, high street*
- el cruce *crossroads*
- la esquina *corner (of street)*
- el paseo *walk, avenue*
- el paso de peatones *pedestrian crossing*
- la plaza *square*
- la plaza mayor *main square*
- el puente *bridge*

- las afueras *outskirts, suburbs*
- el autobús *bus*
- el autocar *long distance bus, coach*
- el barrio *district of town*

- el buzón *letter box*
- la cabina telefónica *telephone kiosk*
- el centro *centre*
- la distancia *distance*
- la estatua *statue*
- el/la habitante *inhabitant*
- la industria *industry*
- el jardín zoológico (el zoo) *zoo*
- el lago *lake*
- el metro *the underground*
- el monumento *monument*
- la orilla *bank (of river or lake)*
- el parque *park*
- la playa *beach*
- el puerto *harbour, port*
- el río *river*
- el sitio *place*
- el tráfico *traffic*
- el transporte público *public transport*
- el/la vecino/a *neighbour*
- andar *to walk*
- aparcar *to park*
- cruzar *to cross*
- dar un paseo *to go for a walk*
- dar una vuelta *to go for a stroll*
- encontrar (ue) *to meet*
- pasear *to walk, stroll*
- quedar(se) *to stay*
- torcer (ue) *to turn*
- vivir *to live*

Higher
- el embotellamiento *traffic jam*
- el escaparate *shop window*
- el farol *street lamp*
- el semáforo *traffic lights*
- acercarse (a) *to approach*
- alejarse (de) *to go away (from)*
- atravesar (ie) *to cross*
- dirigirse a *to go towards*
- perderse *to get lost*

IN THE COUNTRY
Basic
- la agricultura *agriculture*
- el bosque *wood, forest*
- el campo *country, field*
- el campesino *country-dweller*
- la colina *hill*
- la costa *coast*
- la finca *farm, country estate*
- la granja *farm*
- el mar *sea*
- la montaña *mountain*
- el paisaje *landscape, countryside*
- la playa *beach, seaside*
- la provincia *province*
- la región *region*
- la sierra *mountain range, mountains*

Higher
- los alrededores *area around*
- la autopista *motorway*
- la carretera *main road*
- el monte *mountain, hill*
- el prado *meadow*
- el valle *valley*

POSITIONS/DIRECTIONS
Basic
- alrededor de *around*
- allí *there*
- antes de *before*
- aquí *here*
- cerca de *near*
- debajo de *below, underneath*
- delante de *in front of*
- dentro de *inside*
- a la derecha (de) *on the right (of)*
- después de *after*
- detrás de *behind*
- encima de *above, on top of*
- enfrente de *opposite*
- entre *between*
- al este (de) *to the east (of)*
- al final de *at the end of*
- frente a *opposite, facing*
- fuera de *outside*
- hasta *as far as*
- a la izquierda (de) *on the left (of)*
- al lado de *beside, next to*
- a lo largo de *along*
- lejos de *far from*
- al norte (de) *to the north (of)*
- al oeste (de) *to the west (of)*
- todo derecho *straight on*
- todo recto *straight on*
- todo seguido *straight on*
- al sur (de) *to the south (of)*

DESCRIPTIONS
Basic
- ancho *wide*
- antiguo *ancient, former*
- estrecho *narrow*
- feo *ugly*
- histórico *historic*
- importante *important*
- industrial *industrial*
- interesante *interesting*
- largo *long*
- limpio *clean*
- moderno *modern*
- municipal *municipal*
- pintoresco *picturesque*
- sucio *dirty*
- tranquilo *quiet*

Higher
- cercano *nearby*
- ruidoso *noisy*
- sano *healthy*

SCHOOL AND COLLEGE

BUILDINGS AND TYPES
Basic
- el colegio *school, college*
- la escuela *school*
- el instituto *state secondary school*
- la universidad *university*
- mixto *mixed, co-educational*

- el aula (fem.) *classroom*
- la biblioteca *library*
- el campo de deportes *sports field*
- el despacho *office, study*
- el gimnasio *gymnasium*
- el laboratorio *laboratory*
- la oficina *large office*
- el patio *yard, playground*
- la piscina *swimming pool*
- la sala de profesores *staff room*
- el salón de actos *school hall*
- el taller *workshop*

SCHOOL AND COLLEGE ROUTINE
Basic
- la asignatura *subject*
- el/la alumno/a *pupil*
- el bolígrafo *ball-point pen*
- la cartera *brief-case*
- el castigo *punishment*
- la clase *lesson, class*
- el club *club*
- el concierto *concert*
- el cuaderno *exercise book*
- el curso *school year*
- el deber *homework*
- el/la director(a) *head teacher, principal*
- el ejemplo *example*
- el/la estudiante *student*
- los estudios *studies*
- el examen *examination*
- la falta *mistake*
- la goma *rubber*
- la hora de comer *lunchtime*
- el horario (de clases) *timetable*
- el intercambio *exchange*
- el/la interno/a *boarder*
- el libro *book*
- el ordenador *computer*
- la pizarra *blackboard*
- el/la profesor(a) *teacher*
- el lápiz *pencil*
- el papel *paper*
- la pluma *pen*
- el recreo *recreation, break*
- la regla *ruler, rule*
- el resultado *result*

el/la	subdirector(a)	*deputy head, vice-principal*
el	trimestre	*term*
el	uniforme	*uniform*

aburrirse *to be bored*
aprender *to learn*
aprobar (ue) *to pass (an examination)*
castigar *to punish*
contestar *to answer*
copiar *to copy*
corregir (i) *to correct, to mark*
escoger *to choose*
escribir *to write*
escuchar *to listen*
estudiar *to study*
ir al colegio *to go to school*
leer *to read*
obedecer *to obey*
pasar la lista *to call the register*
practicar *to practise, to play (a sport)*
preguntar *to ask*
prohibir *to forbid*
repetir (i) *to repeat*
sacar buenas (malas) notas *to get good (bad) marks*
suspender *to fail (see Phrases below)*
tener lugar *to take place*
tomar parte en *to take part in*
trabajar *to work*
venir al colegio *to come to school or college*
volver (ue) (a casa) *to return (home)*

Basic phrases

Saco buenas notas en español *I get good marks in Spanish*
Soy miembro del club de dibujo *I am a member of the art club*
Si apruebo en matemáticas... *If I pass in Mathematics...*
Si me suspenden en geografía... *If I fail Geography...*
Si le(la) suspenden en geografía... *If he (she) fails in Geography...*

Higher

el bachillerato *advanced level qualification*
EGB (Educación General Básica) *general education*
el ejercicio *exercise*
asistir (a) *to attend, be present (at)*
enseñar *to teach*
portarse bien (mal) *to behave well (badly)*
presentarse a un examen *to take an examination*
tener éxito *to be successful*

SUBJECTS

Basic

el alemán *German*
el arte *Art Appreciation, History of Art*
la asignatura *subject*
la biología *Biology*
las ciencias *Science*
la cocina *Cookery*
el comercio *Commerce, Business Studies*
los deportes *Sport, Games*
el dibujo *Art, Drawing*
la educación física *Physical Education*
el español *Spanish*
la física *Physics*
el francés *French*
la geografía *Geography*
la gimnasia *Gymnastics, Physical Education*
la historia *History*
la informática *Information Technology*
el inglés *English*
el latín *Latin*
las lenguas *Languages*
las matemáticas *Mathematics*
la mecanografía *Typewriting*
la música *Music*
la química *Chemistry*
la religión *Religious Studies*
la taquigrafía *Shorthand*
la tecnología *Technology*
los trabajos manuales *Craft*
aburrido *boring*
difícil *difficult*
fácil *easy*
favorito *favourite*
interesante *interesting*
pesado *boring*
preferido *favourite*
práctico *practical*
útil *useful*

Basic phrase

Mi asignatura preferida es la música *My favourite subject is Music*

Higher

los idiomas *Languages*
ser fuerte en... *to be good at...*

FOR ITEMS OF SCHOOL UNIFORM – SEE 'SHOPPING: CLOTHES'.

FOR DESCRIPTIONS OF PEOPLE – SEE 'PERSONAL IDENTIFICATION'.

FOR LOCATION OF BUILDINGS – SEE 'GEOGRAPHICAL SURROUNDINGS'.

FOR SPORTS AND EXTRA-CURRICULAR ACTIVITIES – SEE 'FREE TIME AND ENTERTAINMENT'.

WORK AND CAREERS

OCCUPATIONS

Basic

el	actor	*actor*
la	actriz	*actress*
el	ama de casa (fem.)	*housewife*
el/la	artista	*artist(e)*
la	azafata	*air hostess*
el	bombero	*fireman, firefighter*
el/la	cantante	*singer*
el/la	camarero/a	*waiter/waitress*
el/la	carnicero/a	*butcher*
el/la	cartero/a	*postman/postwoman*
el/la	científico/a	*scientist*
el/la	cobrador/cobradora	*bus conductor/conductress*
el/la	cocinero/a	*cook*
el/la	comerciante	*trader, dealer, merchant*
el/la	compañero/a de trabajo	*colleague*
el/la	conductor/conductora	*driver*
el	constructor	*builder*
el	cura	*priest*
el/la	dentista	*dentist*
el/la	dependiente/dependienta	*shop assistant*
el/la	director/directora	*director, manager, headteacher*
el/la	dueño/a	*owner, proprietor*
el/la	electricista	*electrician*
el/la	empleado/a	*clerk, office worker*
el/la	empleado/a de banco	*bank clerk*
el	empleo	*job*
el/la	enfermero/a	*nurse*
el/la	estudiante	*student*
el	fontanero	*plumber*
el/la	fotógrafo/a	*photographer*
el/la	funcionario/a	*Civil Servant*
el/la	granjero/a	*farmer*
el/la	ingeniero/a	*engineer*
el/la	jardinero/a	*gardener*
el/la	jefe	*boss, leader*
el/la	maestro/a	*(primary school) teacher*
el/la	maquinista	*machinist, engine driver*
el	marinero	*sailor*
el/la	mecanógrafo/a	*typist*
el/la	médico/a	*doctor*
el	minero	*miner*
el/la	músico/a	*musician*
el	paro	*unemployment*
el/la	peluquero/a	*hairdresser*
el/la	periodista	*journalist, reporter*
el	pescador	*fisherman*
el/la	policía	*policeman/policewoman*
el	portero	*porter, doorman*
el/la	profesor/profesora	*teacher*
el/la	propietario/a	*owner*
el	puesto	*post, job, position*
el/la	recepcionista	*receptionist*
el	repartidor de periódicos	*paperboy*
el/la	representante	*representative*
el/la	secretario/a	*secretary*
el	soldado	*soldier*
el/la	taquimecanógrafo/a	*shorthand typist*
el/la	técnico/a	*technician*
el/la	telefonista	*telephonist*
el/la	tendero/a	*shopkeeper*
el	trabajo	*work*
el/la	vendedor/vendedora	*salesperson*

Basic phrases

Mi hermana es peluquera *My sister is a hairdresser*
Mi madre trabaja como secretaria *My mother works as a secretary*
Quiero ser dentista *I want to be a dentist*
Trabajo los sábados en una tienda *I work on Saturdays in a shop*
Voy a trabajar en un banco *I am going to work in a bank*

Higher

el/la	abogado	*lawyer*
el/la	agente	*agent*
el	albañil	*bricklayer*
el/la	arquitecto/a	*architect*
el/la	cajero/a	*cashier*
el	carpintero	*carpenter*
el	chófer	*driver*
el/la	deportista	*sportsman/sportswoman*
el	desempleo	*unemployment*
el/la	encargado/a	*person in charge, foreman*
el/la	escritor/escritora	*writer*
el/la	fabricante	*manufacturer*
el/la	gerente	*manager*
el	hombre de negocios	*business man*
el/la	juez	*judge*
el	lechero	*milkman*
el	obrero	*workman*
el/la	piloto	*pilot, racing driver*
el/la	verdulero/a	*greengrocer*

SOME PLACES AND ORGANIZATIONS FOR WORK AND STUDY

Basic

la	agencia de viajes	*travel agency*
el	ayuntamiento	*town hall, town council*
el	banco	*bank*
la	biblioteca	*library*
el	café	*café*
el	colegio	*school, college*
la	compañía	*company*

CHAPTER 3 SUBJECT CONTENT: TOPICS, SETTINGS AND VOCABULARY

la enseñanza *education*
la escuela *(primary) school)*
la fábrica *factory*
los grandes almacenes *department store*
el hotel *hotel*
el instituto *(state secondary) school*
la oficina *office*
el restaurante *restaurant*
la tienda *shop*

Higher
la compañía de seguros *insurance company*
la empresa *firm*
el taller *workshop*
la universidad *university*

cobrar *to earn, be paid*
conseguir (i) *to achieve, succeed in*
continuar *to continue*
estudiar *to study*
ganar *to earn*
gastar *to spend*
interesar *to interest*
seguir (i) *to continue*
suspender *to fail (a candidate) in an examination*
trabajar *to work*
aburrido *boring*
cansado *tiring*
difícil *difficult*
entretenido *entertaining*
fácil *easy*
interesante *interesting*

ASPECTS OF WORK

Basic
la ambición *ambition*
los estudios *studies*
los gastos *expenses, costs*
la propina *tip*
el proyecto *project, plan*
el salario *wages*
el sueldo *salary*
ahorrar *to save*
aprender *to learn*
aprobar (ue) *to pass (examinations)*
ayudar *to help*

Higher
los ahorros *savings*
el anuncio *advertisement*
la formación *vocational training*
la huelga *strike*
el oficio *the trade, job*
el porvenir *future*
el seguro *insurance*
la tarea *task*
cansarse *to become tired*
solicitar (un puesto) *to apply for (a post)*
agotador *exhausting*

FREE TIME AND ENTERTAINMENT

HOBBIES AND INTERESTS

Basic
la actividad *activity*
el ajedrez *chess*
el álbum *album*
la caña de pescar *fishing rod*
la colección *collection*
el dibujo *drawing, art*
el disco *record*
el drama *drama*
la exposición *exhibition*
la excursión *excursion*
el fin de semana *weekend*
la fotografía *photography, photograph*
el grupo *group*
la guitarra *guitar*
el instrumento *instrument*
el interés *interest*
el juego *game*
la lectura *reading*
el libro *book*
el magnetofón *cassette-recorder, tape-recorder*
la música *music*
la novela *novel*
el ordenador *computer*
la orquesta *orchestra*
el parque *park*
el pasatiempo *pastime, hobby*

el paseo *walk*
el periódico *newspaper*
la pesca *fishing*
la revista *magazine*
la pintura *painting*
el sello *stamp*
el tocadiscos *record-player*

bañarse *to bathe*
coleccionar *to collect*
coser *to sew*
dar una vuelta *to go for a stroll*
dar un paseo *to go for a walk*
dibujar *to draw*
fumar *to smoke*
gustar *to like (see phrases below)*
interesar *to interest (see phrases below)*
invitar *to invite*
ir de compras *to go shopping*
jugar a las cartas *to play cards*
leer *to read*
pasarlo bien *to enjoy oneself*
pasear *to walk*
pescar *to fish*
pintar *to paint*
preferir (ie) *to prefer*
saber *to know how to*
sacar fotos *to take photographs*

salir *to go out*
soler (ue) *to be in the habit of*
tocar *to play (an instrument)*
al aire libre *in the open air*

Basic phrases

Me gusta mucho la música pop *I very much like pop music*
Me interesan los sellos españoles *I am interested in Spanish stamps*
Lo paso muy bien con mis amigos/as *I enjoy myself with my friends*
¿Sabes tocar la guitarra? *Can you play the guitar?*

Higher

las	aficiones	*interests*
la	novela policíaca	*detective novel*
la	novela ciencia-ficción	*science-fiction novel*
el	parque de atracciones	*amusement park*
el	parque zoológico	*zoo*
	divertirse (ie)	*to enjoy oneself*
	ser aficionado/a (a)	*to be keen (on)*

SPORTING ACTIVITIES

Basic

el	atletismo	*athletics*
el	baloncesto	*basketball, netball*
la	bicicleta	*bicycle*
el	campo	*field*
la	carrera	*race*
el	ciclismo	*cycling*
el	club (de deportes)	*(sports) club*
el	concurso	*competition*
el	deporte	*sport*
los	deportes de invierno	*winter sports*
el/la	deportista	*sports player*
la	entrada	*(entrance) ticket*
el	equipo	*team*
la	equitación	*horse-riding*
el	esquí	*ski-ing*
el	estadio	*stadium*
el	footing	*jogging*
el	fútbol	*football*
la	gimnasia	*gymnastics*
la	natación	*swimming*
el	partido	*match*
el	patinaje	*skating*
la	piscina	*swimming pool*
la	plancha de vela	*windsurfing*
el	polideportivo	*sports centre*
el	tenis (de mesa)	*(table) tennis*
el	tiempo libre	*free time*
la	vela	*sailing*
el	voleibol	*volleyball*
	correr	*to run*

deportivo *sporting, sporty*
esquiar *to ski*
ganar *to win*
jugar (ue) *to play*
montar a caballo *to go horse-riding*
montar en bicicleta *to ride a bicycle*
nadar *to swim*
patinar *to skate*
perder *to lose*
practicar *to play (regularly)*
saltar *to jump*

Basic phrases

¿Qué deportes practicas? *What sports do you play?*
Juego al tenis *I play tennis*
¿A qué hora empieza el partido? *At what time does the match begin?*
¿Cuánto vale la entrada? *How much does a ticket cost?*

Higher

el/la	campeón/campeona	*champion*
el	campeonato	*championship*
la	pista	*track, court*
	empatar	*to draw (a match)*
	entrenarse	*to train*

ENTERTAINMENT

Basic

el	actor	*actor*
la	actriz	*actress*
el	aire acondicionado	*air conditioning*
el	baile	*dance, ball*
la	butaca	*seat (at cinema/theatre)*
el/la	cantante	*singer*
el	cine	*cinema*
el	club (de jóvenes)	*(youth) club*
el	concierto	*concert*
la	corrida	*bullfight*
los	dibujos animados	*cartoon films*
la	discoteca	*disco*
la	entrada	*(entry) ticket*
el	espectáculo	*show, spectacle*
la	fila	*row*
la	música clásica	*classical music*
la	música pop	*pop music*
la	música rock	*rock music*
la	película	*film*
la	plaza de toros	*bull-ring*
el	programa	*programme*
la	radio	*radio*
la	sala de fiestas	*dance hall*
la	taquilla	*ticket office*
la	televisión	*television*
el	teatro	*theatre*
los	toros	*bullfight, bullfighting*
el	vídeo	*video*
	bailar	*to dance*

empezar (ie) *to begin*
oír *to listen to (music, radio)*
sacar una entrada *to buy a ticket*
terminar *to finish*
ver *to watch (television, film, match)*

la sesión de la tarde *matinée*
la sesión de la noche *evening performance/showing*
hacer cola *to queue*
tener lugar *to take place*

Basic Phrases
¿A qué hora empieza? *At what time does it begin?*
Dos entradas para esta noche *Two tickets for tonight*

Higher
la sala de fiestas *dance hall*

Higher phrase
¿Qué tal la película? *What was the film like?*

SEE ALSO 'TRAVEL' AND 'HOLIDAYS'.

TRAVEL

GENERAL
Basic
la aduana *Customs*
el cinturón *(seat) belt*
el/la conductor/a *driver*
el destino *destination*
el equipaje *luggage*
la frontera *frontier*
la llegada *arrival*
la maleta *suitcase*
la oficina de turismo *tourist office*
la parada *stop*
el pasaporte *passport*
el retraso *delay*
la ventanilla *window (of vehicle)*
el viaje *journey*
el/la viajero/a *traveller*
bajar (de) *to get off/out of (a vehicle)*
durar *to last*
llegar a *to arrive (in)*
salir de *to depart, leave (from)*
subir a *to get in/on (a vehicle)*
viajar *to travel*

Higher
el chófer *driver*
las obras *roadworks*
hacer la maleta *to pack*

PUBLIC TRANSPORT
Basic
el autocar *coach, long-distance bus*
el autobús *bus (local)*
el avión *plane*
el barco *ship*
el ferrocarril *railway*
el helicóptero *helicopter*
el metro *the underground*
el taxi *taxi*
el tren *train*

la agencia de viajes *travel agency*
el aeropuerto *airport*
el andén *platform*
la azafata *air hostess*
el billete *ticket*
el billete de ida *single ticket*
el billete sencillo *single ticket*
el billete de ida y vuelta *return ticket*
la cantina *refreshment room*
el cinturón (de seguridad) *seat belt*
el coche *carriage*
el coche-cama *sleeping car*
el coche-comedor *dining car*
el coche-restorán *restaurant car*
la consigna *left luggage office*
el departamento *compartment*
el despacho de billetes *ticket office*
la estación *station*
la estación de autobuses *bus station*
la estación de metro *tube station*
el expreso *express train (normally at night)*
el horario *timetable*
el jefe de estación *station master*
la línea *line, bus route*
la máquina *engine*
el mozo *porter*
la parada del autobús *bus stop*
el pasajero *passenger*
el precio del billete *fare*
el puerto *port, harbour*
el rápido *express (normally daytime)*
la RENFE *Spanish National Railways*
el revisor *ticket inspector*
la reserva *advance booking, reservation*
la sala de espera *waiting room*
la salida *departure, exit*
la taquilla *ticket office*
el/la taquillero/a *ticket office clerk*
la tarifa *fare*
la vía *track*
aterrizar *to land*
cambiar *to change*
coger *to catch*
despegar *to take off*
directo *direct*
hacer transbordo *to change*
perder (ie) *to miss*
próximo *next*
sacar un billete *to buy a ticket*
volar (ue) *to fly*

Basic phrases

¿A qué hora sale el próximo tren para...? *At what time does the next train for... depart?*
¿De qué andén sale? *What platform does it leave from?*
¿Es directo? *Is it a through train?*
¿Hay que hacer transbordo? *Do I/we have to change?*
¿Qué puerta es? *What gate is it?*

Higher

el	aterrizaje	*landing (of plane)*
el	despegue	*take-off*
el	paso subterráneo	*underpass, subway*
la	pista	*runway*
la	señal de alarma	*alarm bell (communication cord)*
la	terminal (aérea)	*(airport) terminal*

abrochar *to fasten (seat belt)*
anunciar *to announce*
asomarse *to look/lean out of a window or door*
desembarcar *to disembark*
embarcar(se) *to embark*
marearse *to be seasick/travel sick*

PRIVATE TRANSPORT

Basic

la	bicicleta	*bicycle*
el	coche	*car*
el	peatón	*pedestrian*

hacer autostop *to hitch hike*
ir a pie *to walk*

el	aceite	*oil*
el	agua (fem.)	*water*
el	aire	*air*
el	aparcamiento	*car park*
el/la	autostopista	*hitch hiker*
el	carnet de conducir	*driving licence*
el/la	ciclista	*cyclist*
la	estación de servicio	*service station*
el	faro	*headlamp*
el	freno	*brake*
la	gasolina	*petrol*
el	mapa	*map*
el	motor	*engine*
el	plano (de la ciudad)	*(town) plan*
	normal	*2-star petrol*
el	neumático	*tyre*
el	radiador	*radiator*
la	rueda	*wheel*
los	servicios	*toilets*
	súper	*4-star petrol*
la	velocidad	*speed*
el	volante	*steering wheel*

aparcar *to park*
arreglar *to put right*
comprobar (ue) *to check*
conducir *to drive*
faltar *to be missing*
frenar *to brake*
funcionar *to work properly*
hacer falta *to be needed*
limpiar *to clean*
llenar *to fill*
necesitar *to need*
quedarse sin *to run out of*
reparar *to repair*
lleno *full*

Basic phrases

Lleno, por favor *Fill it up, please*
Nos hemos quedado sin gasolina *We've run out of petrol*
No funcionan los faros *the headlights aren't working*
Por favor, compruebe los neumáticos *Would you please check the tyres*
Veinte litros de súper, por favor *20 litres of 4-star, please*

Higher

la	avería	*breakdown*
la	batería	*(car) battery*
la	bombilla	*(light) bulb*
el	depósito	*petrol tank*
el	desvío	*detour, diversion*
la	gasolinera	*petrol station*
el	maletero	*boot*
la	matrícula	*registration number*
el	parabrisas	*windscreen*
el	peaje	*toll*
el	pinchazo	*puncture*
la	rueda de repuesto	*spare wheel*
el	seguro	*insurance*
el	tubo de escape	*exhaust pipe*

adelantar *to overtake*
arrancar *to start up, to move off*
averiarse *to break down*
cargar *to load*
reventarse (ie) *to burst*

FINDING THE WAY

Basic

la	autopista	*motorway*
la	calle	*street*
la	carretera	*main road*
el	cruce	*crossroads*
la	dirección	*direction*
la	distancia	*distance*
la	esquina	*corner*
el	paso de peatones	*pedestrian crossing*
la	plaza	*square*
el	puente	*bridge*
el	río	*river*
el	semáforo	*traffic lights*

a la derecha *to/on the right*
a la izquierda *to/on the left*
al final de *at/to the end of*
al lado de *beside, next to*
al norte de *to the north of*
al sur de *to the south of*
al este de *to the east of*
al oeste de *to the west of*
cerca de *near*
debajo de *below*
delante de *in front of*
detrás de *behind*
en *in, at*
enfrente de *opposite*
frente a *opposite*
lejos de *far from*
por *along, via*
por aquí *near here, this way*
todo derecho *straight on*
todo recto *straight on*
todo seguido *straight on*

bajar *to go down*
cruzar *to cross*
doblar la esquina *to turn the corner*
pasar delante de *to go past*
seguir (i) *to continue, follow*
subir *to go up*
tomar *to take*
torcer (ue) *to turn*

Basic phrases

¿Está lejos? *Is it far?*
¿Hay un banco por aquí? *Is there a bank near here?*
¿Por dónde se va a la catedral? *Which way is the Cathedral?*
Antes de llegar al cruce *Before you reach the crossroads*
Baje la calle, cruce la plaza *Go down the street, cross the square*
Está a unos tres kilómetros *It's about three kilometres away*
Está a unos diez minutos andando *It's about ten minutes on foot*
Está a unos dos minutos en coche *It's about two minutes by car*
Está al final de la Calle Mayor *It's at the end of the High Street*
No entiendo *I don't understand*
Siga todo recto *Go straight on*
¿Tienen un mapa de carreteras? *Have you a road map?*
Tome la primera calle a la derecha *Take the first street on the right*
Tuerza a la izquierda *Turn left*

Higher

la   autopista de peaje *toll motorway*
     atravesar (ie) *to cross*

HOLIDAYS

Basic

   Alemania *Germany*
   Escocia *Scotland*
   España *Spain*
los Estados Unidos *the United States*
   Francia *France*
   Grecia *Greece*
   Inglaterra *England*
   Irlanda *Ireland*
   Italia *Italy*
el País de Gales *Wales*

   alemán *German*
   americano *American*
   escocés *Scottish*
   español *Spanish*
   francés *French*
   galés *Welsh*
   inglés *English*
   irlandés *Irish*
   italiano *Italian*

Higher

   Austria *Austria*
   Bélgica *Belgium*
   Dinamarca *Denmark*
   Europa *Europe*
   Gran Bretaña *Great Britain*
   Méjico *Mexico*
   Portugal *Portugal*

el Reino Unido *the United Kingdom*
   Rusia *Russia*
   Suiza *Switzerland*

   austríaco *Austrian*
   belga *Belgian*
   danés *Danish*
   europeo *European*
   británico *British*
   griego *Greek*
   mejicano *Mexican*
   portugués *Portuguese*
   ruso *Russian*
   suizo *Swiss*

Basic

la aduana *Customs*
el bañador *swimming costume, swimming trunks*
el carné de identidad *identity card*
la costa *coast*
la documentación *identity document*
el folleto *brochure*
la foto *photograph*
la frontera *frontier*
las gafas de sol *sunglasses*
la lista de hoteles *list of hotels*
la loción bronceadora *sun lotion*
el mar *sea*

la	montaña *mountain*			turístico *for tourists*
el	monumento (histórico) *(historic) monument*		el	año pasado *last year*
			el	año que viene *next year*
la	nacionalidad *nationality*		el	verano pasado *last summer*
la	oficina de turismo *tourist office*		el	verano que viene *next summer*
el	pasaporte *passport*			este año *this year*
la	playa *beach, seaside*			este verano *this summer*
la	sierra *the mountains*			
el	sol *sun*			

Basic phrases

¿A qué hora se abre el castillo? *At what time does the castle open?*
¿Tiene un horario de autobuses? *Have you a bus timetable?*
Un folleto sobre la región, por favor *May I have a leaflet about the region, please*
Un plano de la ciudad, por favor *A map of the town, please*

la	sombra *shade*
la	toalla *towel*
el	traje de baño *swimming costume*
el/la	turista *tourist*
el	turismo *tourism*
las	vacaciones *holidays*
las	vacaciones de Navidad *Christmas holidays*
las	vacaciones de Semana Santa *Easter holidays*
las	vacaciones de verano *Summer holidays*
la	visita *visit*

alojarse *to stay (lodge)*
bañarse *to bathe*
descansar *to rest*
(estar) de vacaciones *(to be) on holiday*
hacer turismo *to tour*
ir al extranjero *to go abroad*
ir de vacaciones *to go on holiday*
pasar las vacaciones en casa *to spend the holidays at home*
quedarse en casa *to stay at home*
sacar una foto *to take a photograph*
tenderse (ie) al sol *to lie in the sun*
tomar el sol *to sunbathe*
visitar *to visit*
extranjero *foreign*

Higher

la	bahía *bay*
la	insolación *sunstroke, heatstroke*

broncearse *to sunbathe, get a tan*
hace un año *a year ago*
hace dos años *two years ago*
hospedarse *to stay (lodge)*

SEE ALSO 'GEOGRAPHICAL SURROUNDINGS' FOR PLACES TO BE VISITED.

SEE ALSO 'ACCOMMODATION'.

SEE ALSO 'FREE TIME AND ENTERTAINMENT' FOR OTHER HOLIDAY ACTIVITIES.

SEE ALSO 'TRAVEL'.

ACCOMMODATION

Basic

el	albergue juvenil *youth hostel*
el	camping *campsite*
el	hostal *boarding house, cheap hotel*
el	hotel *hotel*
el	parador *inn, parador, state hotel*
la	pensión *boarding house, guest house*

HOTEL AND BOARDING HOUSE

Basic

el	agua caliente (fem.) *hot water*
el	agua corriente (fem.) *running water*
el	agua fría (fem.) *cold water*
el	ascensor *lift*
le	balcón *balcony*
el	baño *bath (bathroom)*
la	cama *bed*
la	cama individual *single bed*
la	cama de matrimonio *double bed*
el/la	camarero/a *waiter/waitress*
la	ducha *shower*
la	ficha *registration card*
la	habitación *(bed)room*
la	habitación doble *double room*
la	habitación individual *single room*
	media pensión *half board*
	pensión completa *full board*
la	piscina *swimming pool*
el	portero *porter, doorkeeper*
la	recepción *reception desk*
el/la	recepcionista *receptionist*
el	restaurante *restaurant*

incluido *included*
sólo dormir *room only (no meals)*
llenar una ficha *to fill in a registration card*
quejarse (de) *to complain (about)*
reservar *to book in advance*

Basic phrases

¿Hay una habitación libre? *Have you a free room?*
¿Está incluido el desayuno? *Is breakfast included?*
¿Dónde se puede aparcar? *Where can we park?*
¿Hay teléfono/televisión en la habitación? *Is there a telephone/tv in the room?*
¿Se sirven comidas? *Do you serve meals?*
¿Para cuántas noches? *For how many nights?*
¿Para cuántas personas? *For how many people?*
¿Tiene reserva? *Do you have a reservation?*
Está completo *It's fully booked*
Quiero reservar... *I'd like to reserve...*
Para 5 noches a partir del 8 de julio *For 5 nights from the 8 July*
No funciona el/la.... *The... does not work*

Higher

el	albergue *inn*
la	casa de huéspedes *guest house*
el	gerente *manager*
el/la	hotelero/a *hotelier*

THE YOUTH HOSTEL

Basic

la	cocina *kitchen*
el	comedor *dining room*
el	dormitorio *bedroom*
el	saco de dormir *sleeping bag*

alquilar *to hire*
prestar *to lend*

Basic phrase

¿A qué hora se cierra? *At what time does it close?*
¿Me puede prestar...? *Can you lend me...? May I borrow...?*
¿Se puede alquilar...? *Is it possible to hire...?*
No se permite *It is not allowed*

THE CAMPSITE

Basic

la	cafetería *café, cafeteria*
la	caravana *caravan*
el	colchón (de aire) *(inflatable) mattress*
las	duchas *showers*
el	encargado *manager*
la	fuente *fountain*
la	mochila *rucksack*
el	saco de dormir *sleeping bag*
los	servicios *toilets, washing facilities*
la	sombra *shade*
la	tienda (de campaña) *tent*

potable *drinkable*
hacer camping *to camp*
montar la tienda *to put up the tent*

Basic phrases

¿Hay sitio (para esta noche)? *Is there any room (for tonight)*
¿Hay sitio a la sombra? *Is there any room in the shade?*

Higher

| el | cubo de la basura *dustbin, waste bin* |

SOCIAL RELATIONSHIPS

GREETINGS, GOOD WISHES AND FAREWELLS

Basic

Adiós *Goodbye*
Bienvenido/a *Welcome*
Buen viaje *Have a good journey*
Buena suerte *Good luck*
Buenas noches *Good night, Good evening*
Buenas tardes *Good afternoon*
Buenos días *Good morning*
Felices Pascuas *Happy Christmas*
(Muchas) Felicidades *Best wishes, Happy birthday*
Felicitaciones *Congratulations*
Gracias *Thank you*
De nada *Don't mention it, It's a pleasure*
Hasta luego *See you soon*
Hasta mañana *See you tomorrow*
Hasta el sábado *See you on Saturday*
Hola *Hello*
¿Qué tal? *How are you?*
Muy bien, gracias *Very well thank you*
Salud *Good health*

Higher

Enhorabuena *Congratulations*
No hay de qué *Don't mention it, It's a pleasure*
Que te vaya bien *Good luck*
Que tengas suerte *Good luck*

MEETING PEOPLE

Basic

el/la	amigo/a *friend*
la	gente *people*
la	persona *person*
la	sorpresa *surprise*

felicitar *to greet, congratulate*
presentar *to introduce*
amable *kind, friendly*
encantado/a *delighted*

Basic phrases

Te presento a mi amigo Juan *May I introduce my friend Juan?*
Mucho gusto *How do you do? Pleased to meet you*
Encantado/a *How do you do? Pleased to meet you*
¡Qué sorpresa verte aquí! *What a surprise to meet you here!*

Higher

agradecer *to thank*

ARRANGING TO MEET

Basic

la cita *appointment, date*
el guateque *party*
la invitación *invitation*
la lástima *pity*
la pena *pity*

acompañar *to accompany*
buscar *to go and pick up*
invitar *to invite*
olvidar *to forget*
poder (ue) *to be able (to)*
preferir (ie) *to prefer*
sentir (ie) *to be sorry*
venir *to come*
verse *to see one another, to meet*
Claro *Of course*
Con mucho gusto *With great pleasure*
De acuerdo *Agreed*
de veras *really*
desde luego *of course*
estupendo *great, marvellous*
imposible *impossible*
Lo siento *I'm sorry (expressing regret)*
No comprendo *I don't understand*
Perdona (perdone) *I'm sorry (apologizing)*
¡Qué bien! *How nice!*
¡Qué lástima! *What a pity*
¡Qué pena! *What a pity*
Vale *That's all right. Agreed*

Basic phrases

Te invito a un guateque *I'd like to invite you to a party*
Lo siento. No puedo ir. *I'm sorry. I can't go.*
¿Por qué no? *Why not?*
¿Quieres un café? *Would you like a coffee?*
No tengo tiempo *I haven't time*
No me gustan las películas de ciencia-ficción *I don't like sci-fi films*
Te invito a tomar una cerveza *I'd like to invite you to have a beer*
Depende *It depends*
¿A qué hora? *At what time?*
¿Dónde nos vemos? *Where shall we meet?*
Delante del cine *Outside the cinema*
Me gustó mucho *I really liked it*

Higher

citarse *to arrange to meet*
impedir (i) *to prevent*
ofrecer *to offer*
prometer *to promise*
tener ganas de *to feel like*

Higher phrases

No importa *it doesn't matter*
Me es igual *I don't mind. It's all the same to me*
No vale la pena *It's not worth it*
Te veré a las ocho *I'll see you at eight o'clock*

FOR POSSIBLE SOCIAL ACTIVITIES SEE 'FREE TIME AND ENTERTAINMENT'.

ON THE TELEPHONE

Basic

el teléfono *telephone*
el número (de teléfono) *(telephone) number*
hablar *to speak*
llamar (por teléfono) *to telephone, to call*
marcar *to dial*

Basic phrases

Diga *Hello (when answering the telephone)*
Oiga *Hello (when the other person answers the telephone)*
Oiga, ¿está María? *Hello. Is María in?*
¿Quién habla? *Who's speaking?*
Soy Pedro *It's Pedro speaking*
Está comunicando *It's engaged*

POSTCARDS AND LETTERS

Basic

la carta *letter*
la postal *post card*
el/la corresponsal *penfriend*
el sobre *envelope*
escribir *to write*
recibir *to receive*

echar *to post*
mandar *to send*

Basic phrases

Querido Pablo: *Dear Pablo,*
Querida Luisa: *Dear Luisa,*
Saludos a tus padres *Greetings to your parents*

Muy señor mío: *Dear Sir,*
Estimado Señor González:
Dear Mr Gonzalez,
Muchos recuerdos a tu familia *Remember me to your family*
Recibe un fuerte abrazo de *(ending for letter to a friend)*
Un cordial saludo de *(ending for letter to friend's parent)*
Le saluda atentamente *Yours faithfully,*

FOR FULLER ADVICE ON LETTER WRITING SEE CHAPTER 11.

HEALTH AND WELFARE

THE HUMAN BODY

Basic

la	boca	*mouth*
el	brazo	*arm*
la	cabeza	*head*
la	cara	*face*
el	corazón	*heart*
el	cuello	*neck*
el	cuerpo	*body*
el	dedo	*finger, toe*
el	diente	*(front) tooth*
el	estómago	*stomach*
la	espalda	*back*
la	garganta	*throat*
el	hombro	*shoulder*
la	lengua	*tongue*
la	muela	*(back) tooth*
la	nariz	*nose*
el	oído	*ear*
el	ojo	*eye*
el	pie	*foot*
la	pierna	*leg*

Higher

el	codo	*elbow*
la	frente	*forehead*
el	hueso	*bone*
el	labio	*lip*
la	mejilla	*cheek*
la	muñeca	*wrist*
el	pecho	*breast, chest*
la	piel	*skin*
la	rodilla	*knee*
el	rostro	*face*
el	tobillo	*ankle*
la	uña	*nail*
el	vientre	*belly*

ILLNESSES, INJURIES, PAINS AND SYMPTOMS

Basic

el	apetito	*appetite*
el	catarro	*cold*
el	dolor	*pain, ache*
la	fiebre	*temperature, fever*
la	herida	*injury*
la	insolación	*sunstroke, heatstroke*
el	resfriado	*cold*
la	salud	*health*
la	sed	*thirst*
el	síntoma	*symptom*

caerse *to fall*
cortar(se) *to cut (oneself)*
doler (ue) *to hurt*
herirse (ie) *to get injured*
romperse *to break*
vomitar *to vomit*

bien *well*
enfermo *ill, unwell*
herido *injured*
malo *ill*
mejor *better*
roto *broken*
¡Socorro! *Help!*

Basic phrases

¿Qué le duele? *Where does it hurt?*
¿Qué le pasa? ¿Qué te pasa? *What's the matter with you?*
¿Qué tal? *How are you?*
Estoy enfermo/a *I am ill*
Está mucho mejor *S/he is much better*
Me duele la cabeza *I have a headache*
Me duele una muela *I have toothache*
Le duele la espalda *S/he has backache*
No puedo dormir *I cannot sleep*
No puede andar *S/he cannot walk*
No puedo mover el pie *I cannot move my foot*
No tengo apetito *I have no appetite*
Me he roto el brazo *I have broken my arm*
Se ha roto la pierna *S/he has broken his/her leg*
Tengo fiebre *I have a temperature*

Higher

la	enfermedad	*illness*
la	gripe	*influenza*
la	picadura	*sting, insect bite*
la	quemadura	*burn*
la	tos	*cough*

desmayarse *to faint*
estar en peligro *to be on the danger list, be in danger*
hacerse daño *to hurt oneself*
hincharse *to swell*
mejorar *to improve*
morir (ue) *to die*
picar *to sting, bite*
quemarse *to get burnt*
sentirse (ie) *to feel*
temblar (ie) *to shiver, tremble*
torcer(se) *to twist*
toser *to cough*
constipado *having a cold*
mareado *feeling sick*
muerto *dead*
peor *worse*
sano *healthy*
sin sentido *unconscious*

Higher phrases

Estoy constipado *I have a cold*
Me he hecho daño en el pie *I've hurt my foot*
Me he quemado el dedo *I have burnt my finger*
Me he torcido el tobillo *I have twisted my ankle*
Me ha picado una avispa *I have been stung by a wasp*
Me siento enfermo/a *I feel ill*
Se me ha hinchado el pie *My foot has swollen up*
Se ha quedado sin sentido *S/he has become unconscious*
Tiene un ojo hinchado *S/he has a black eye*

TREATMENT

Basic

la	ambulancia	*ambulance*
la	aspirina	*aspirin*
la	cama	*bed*
el	centro de urgencia	*first aid post*
la	crema	*cream*
el/la	enfermero/a	*nurse*
la	farmacia	*chemist's shop*
el	hospital	*hospital*
la	loción	*lotion*
el	medicamento	*medicine, drug*
la	medicina	*medicine*
el/la	médico/a	*doctor*
el	puesto de socorro	*First Aid post*
la	receta	*prescription*
la	venda	*bandage*

descansar *to rest*
guardar cama *to stay in bed*
quedarse en la cama *to stay in bed*
sacar *to take out, extract*
tratar *to treat*

Basic phrases

¿Tiene algo para el dolor de cabeza? *Have you anything for a headache?*
Me ha sacado una muela *He's taken a tooth out for me*
Lleve esta receta a la farmacia *Take this prescription to the chemist's*
No salga usted al sol *Don't go out in the sun*
Tome usted aspirina *Take aspirin*

Higher

el	empaste	*filling (in tooth)*
la	pastilla	*pill, tablet*
el	socorro	*help*
la	tirita	*(sticking) plaster*

cuidar *to look after*

SHOPPING

SHOPS

Basic

el	ascensor	*lift*
la	caja	*cash desk, check-out*
la	carnicería	*butcher's*
la	confitería	*sweet shop*
el	departamento	*department, section*
la	droguería	*hardware store*
la	escalera	*stairs*
el	estanco	*tobacco and stamp shop*
la	farmacia	*chemist's*
la	frutería	*fruit shop*
los	grandes almacenes	*department store*
la	lechería	*dairy*
la	librería	*bookshop*
el	mercado	*market*
la	panadería	*baker's (for bread only)*
la	papelería	*stationer's*
la	pastelería	*cake shop*
la	perfumería	*perfume shop*
la	pescadería	*fishmonger's*
la	planta	*floor, storey*
la	planta baja	*the ground floor*
la	planta segunda	*the second floor*
la	sección	*department, section*
el	supermercado	*supermarket*
la	tienda de comestibles	*grocer's*
la	tienda de recuerdos	*souvenir shop*
la	tienda de ultramarinos	*grocer's*
la	verdulería	*greengrocer's*
la	zapatería	*shoe shop*

Basic phrases

¿Dónde está la sección de caballeros? *Where is the menswear section?*

¿Dónde está la sección de señoras? *Where is the ladieswear section?*
¿Dónde se puede comprar....? *Where can one buy...?*
¿Hay una farmacia por aquí? *Is there a chemist's near here?*

Higher

el	escaparate	*shop window*
la	ferretería	*ironmonger's, hardware shop*
el	mostrador	*counter*
el	sótano	*basement*
la	tabacalera	*tobacco shop*

CLOTHES
Basic

el	abrigo	*overcoat*
el	algodón	*cotton*
la	blusa	*blouse*
las	botas	*boots*
los	calcetines	*socks*
la	camisa	*shirt*
la	camiseta	*vest*
el	cinturón	*belt*
la	corbata	*tie*
el	cuero	*leather*
la	chaqueta	*jacket*
la	falda	*skirt*
los	guantes	*gloves*
el	impermeable	*raincoat*
el	jersey	*pullover, sweater*
la	lana	*wool*
las	medias	*stockings*
la	moda	*fashion*
el	número	*size*
el	pantalón	*pair of trousers*
el	pantalón corto	*shorts*
el	par de	*pair of*
la	ropa	*clothes*
la	ropa interior	*underwear*
el	sombrero	*hat*
el	traje	*suit*
el	traje de baño	*swimming costume, swimming trunks*
los	(pantalones) vaqueros	*jeans*
el	vestido	*dress*
los	vestidos	*clothes*
los	zapatos	*shoes*
	de moda	*fashionable*

Higher

la	bata	*dressing gown*
el	camisón	*nightdress*
la	manga	*sleeve*
el	nailon	*nylon*
la	piel	*leather*
el	pijama	*pyjamas*
la	seda	*silk*
la	suela	*sole*
la	talla	*size*

de manga corta (larga) *short (long) –sleeved*
probarse (ue) *to try on*

FOR FOOD AND DRINK SEE THE SEPARATE SECTION ON 'FOOD AND DRINK'

OTHER ITEMS TO BUY
Basic

los	artículos de cuero	*leather goods*
los	artículos de tocador	*toiletries*
el	bolígrafo	*ballpoint pen*
el	bolso	*handbag*
la	bolsa	*(larger) bag, shopping bag*
las	castañuelas	*castanets*
el	cepillo	*brush*
el	cepillo de dientes	*toothbrush*
la	cerámica	*pottery, ceramics*
las	cerillas	*matches*
los	cigarrillos	*cigarettes*
el	champú	*shampoo*
el	disco	*record*
la	guitarra	*guitar*
el	jabón	*soap*
el	juguete	*toy*
el	lápiz	*pencil*
el	libro	*book*
la	loción bronceadora	*suntan lotion*
el	mapa	*map*
el	monedero	*purse*
la	muñeca	*doll*
el	papel	*paper*
el	paraguas	*umbrella*
la	pasta de dientes	*toothpaste*
la	película	*film*
el	perfume	*perfume*
el	periódico	*newspaper*
la	pila	*battery*
la	pluma	*pen*
la	postal	*post card*
el	puro	*cigar*
el	recuerdo	*souvenir*
el	reloj	*clock, watch*
la	revista	*magazine*
el	sello	*stamp*
el	sobre	*envelope*
los	tisús	*tissues*
	algo típico	*something typical*

Higher

el	collar	*necklace*
el	desodorante	*deodorant*
el	encendedor	*lighter*
la	porcelana	*porcelain*
la	pulsera	*bracelet*
el	talco	*talcum powder*

IN THE SHOP
Basic

el	autoservicio	*self-service*

el/la cliente *customer*
el cheque *cheque*
la dependienta *shop assistant (female)*
el dependiente *shop assistant (male)*
la docena (de) *dozen*
la liquidación *(clearance) sale*
la moneda *coin*
el precio *price*
la rebaja *reduction (of price)*
las rebajas *sale*
la tarjeta de crédito *credit card*
el/la tendero/a *shopkeeper*
el/la vendedor(a) *salesperson*
la vuelta *the change*
cambiar *to change*
comprar *to buy*
costar (ue) *to cost*
enseñar *to show*
enviar *to send*
envolver (ue) *to wrap*
gastar *to wear or take (a particular size)*
gustar *to like (see Chapter 12 – Grammar)*
hacer la compra *to do the shopping*
ir de compras *to go shopping*
ir de tiendas *to go shopping*
mandar *to send*
pagar *to pay*
preferir (ie) *to prefer*
querer (ie) *to want*
valer *to cost, be worth*
vender *to sell*
barato *cheap*
caro *dear, expensive*
grande *big*
pequeño *small*
demasiado *too much*

Basic phrases

a) Used by the staff of the shop (Receptive use by candidates)
¿Qué desea? *Can I help you? (What would you like?)*
Aquí tiene *Here you are*
¿Qué número gasta? *What size do you take?*
¿Algo más? *Anything else?*
¿Es todo? *Is that everything?*
¿Se lo envuelvo? *Shall I wrap it for you?*
Por favor, pague en caja *Please pay at the cash desk*

b) Used by the customer (Active use by candidates)
¿A qué hora se abre la tienda? *At what time does the shop open?*
¿A qué hora se cierra la tienda? *At what time does the shop shut?*
Quiero... *I'd like...*
Necesito... *I need...*
¿Tiene un(a)...? *Do you have a....?*
Es demasiado grande (pequeño) *It is too large (small)*
No me gusta el color *I don't like the colour*
Prefiero el amarillo (la amarilla) *I prefer the yellow one*
¿Lo/la tienen más grande? *Do you have a larger one?*
¿Lo/la tienen en rojo? *Do you have it in red?*
¿Tiene otro más barato? *Do you have a cheaper one?*
¿Cuánto es? *How much is it? (price of item or total bill)*
¿Cuánto vale? *How much is it? (price of item)*
Nada más, gracias *Nothing else, thank you*
¿Me lo puede mandar al hotel? *Can you send it to my hotel?*
¿Se puede cambiar? *Can it be changed?*
Aquí tiene *Here you are*
Sólo tengo un billete de mil pesetas *I only have a 1000-pta note*
¿Puedo pagar con tarjeta de crédito? *Can I pay by credit card?*
No funciona *It doesn't work*
Tiene un defecto aquí *It has a fault here*

Higher
el carrito *shopping trolley*
devolver (ue) *to return, bring back*
escoger *to choose*
hacer falta *to be needed*
mostrar (ue) *to show*
costoso *costly, expensive*

Higher phrases
Me hace falta un(a)... *I need a...*
Me lo/la llevo *I'll take it*
Me quedo con éste (ésta) *I'll take this one*
¿Me lo/la puedo probar? *May I try it on?*
¿Tienen suela de cuero (goma)? *Do they have leather (rubber) soles?*

FOOD AND DRINK

MEAT AND FISH

Basic

el biftec/bistec/bisteque *(beef) steak*
la carne *meat*
la carne de vaca *beef*
la carne picada *minced meat*
los calamares *squid*

la cebolla *onion*
el cerdo *pork*
el cordero *lamb*
el chorizo *hard pork sausage*
la chuleta *chop*
el filete *fillet steak*
las gambas *prawns*
la hamburguesa *hamburger*
el hígado *liver*
el jamón (serrano) *cured ham*
el jamón de York *York ham, boiled ham*
los mariscos *shellfish*
la merluza *hake*
el pescado *fish*
el pollo *chicken*
la salchicha *sausage*
las sardinas *sardines*
la ternera *veal, beef*
asado *roast*
cocido *boiled*
frito *fried*

Higher
el bacalao *cod*
los boquerones *(fresh) anchovy*
el conejo *rabbit*
la langosta *lobster, crayfish*
el lenguado *sole*
el lomo *loin*
los mejillones *mussels*
el pato *duck*
el pulpo *octopus*
el solomillo *sirloin*
la trucha *trout*

FRUIT AND VEGETABLES
Basic
la aceituna *olive*
el albaricoque *apricot*
el arroz *rice*
la ciruela *plum*
la coliflor *cauliflower*
los champiñones *mushrooms*
la ensalada *salad*
la ensalada rusa *Russian salad*
la fresa *strawberry*
la fruta *fruit*
los guisantes *peas*
el higo *fig*
las judías *beans*
la lechuga *lettuce*
las legumbres *vegetables*
el limón *lemon*
la manzana *apple*
el melocotón *peach*
el melón *melon*
la naranja *orange*
las patatas *potatoes*
las patatas fritas *chips*
la pera *pear*
el pimiento *pepper, pimiento*

la piña *pineapple*
el plátano *banana*
los tomates *tomatoes*
la uva *grape*
las verduras *green vegetables*
la zanahoria *carrot*

Higher
la cereza *cherry*
la col *cabbage*
los espárragos *asparagus*
las espinacas *spinach*
la frambuesa *raspberry*
la sandía *water melon*

OTHER FOOD ITEMS
Basic
el aceite *(olive/vegetable) oil*
el ajo *garlic*
el azúcar *sugar*
el bocadillo *sandwich (with Spanish bread)*
el bollo *bun*
el caramelo *sweet*
el cocido *stew*
el chocolate *chocolate*
el churro *churro, fritter*
los entremeses *hors d'oeuvres*
el flan *caramel cream*
el gazpacho *cold soup, gazpacho*
el helado *ice cream*
el huevo *egg*
la mantequilla *butter*
la mayonesa *mayonnaise*
la mermelada *jam*
la nata *cream*
la paella *paella*
el pan *bread, loaf of bread*
el panecillo *bread roll*
el pastel *(individual) cake*
el postre *dessert*
el queso *cheese*
la sal *salt*
la salsa *sauce*
el sandwich *sandwich (with sliced bread), toasted sandwich*
la sopa *soup*
el suizo *bun*
la tapa *bar snack*
la tarta *cake, tart*
la tortilla *omelette*
la tostada *slice of toast*
el vinagre *vinegar*
el yogur *yoghurt*

Higher
el consomé *consommé, clear soup*

DRINKS
Basic
el agua (fem.) *water*

el	agua mineral (fem.)	*mineral water*
el	café	*coffee*
el	café con leche	*white coffee*
el	café cortado	*coffee with a little milk*
el	café solo	*black coffee*
la	caña	*glass of draught beer*
la	cerveza	*beer, lager*
la	coca-cola	*Coca-cola*
el	coñac	*brandy*
el	chocolate	*hot chocolate*
el	jerez	*sherry*
la	leche	*milk*
el	licor	*liqueur, spirit*
la	limonada	*lemonade*
la	naranjada	*orangeade*
el	refresco	*(cold) soft drink*
el	ron	*rhum*
la	sangría	*sangria, fruit punch*
el	té	*tea*
el	vermú	*vermouth*
el	vino	*wine*
el	vino blanco	*white wine*
el	vino rosado	*rosé wine*
el	vino tinto	*red wine*
el	zumo	*juice, fruit juice*

Higher

el	batido	*milkshake*
la	horchata	*horchata, tiger nut milk*
la	tónica	*tonic water*

QUANTITIES AND CONTAINERS

Basic

una	bolsa	*bag*
una	botella	*bottle*
una	caja	*box*
una	copa	*glass (of fine wine or spirit)*
una	cucharada	*spoonful*
una	docena (de)	*dozen*
un	gramo	*gramme*
un	kilo	*kilogram*
una	lata	*tin*
una	libra	*pound*
un	litro	*litre*
un	paquete	*packet*
un	pedazo	*piece*
un	poco de	*a little*
una	taza	*cup*
un	trozo	*piece*
una	ración	*portion*
un	vaso	*glass*
	media docena (de)	*half a dozen*
	medio kilo	*half a kilo*
un	cuarto de kilo	*quarter kilo*

Higher

el	cántaro	*pitcher*
la	jarra	*jug, mug*
un	pincho	*small portion on a cocktail stick*

IN THE RESTAURANT, CAFE, BAR OR HOME

Basic

el	almuerzo	*lunch*
el	bar	*bar*
la	bebida	*drink*
el	café	*café, bar*
la	cafetería	*café*
el/la	camarero/a	*waiter/waitress*
la	cena	*evening meal, dinner*
la	comida	*meal, lunch*
la	cuchara	*spoon*
el	cuchillo	*knife*
la	cuenta	*bill*
la	lista de precios	*price list*
la	lista de vinos	*wine list*
la	merienda	*afternoon snack*
la	mesa	*table*
el	menú	*menu*
	menú del día	*set meal, meal of the day*
el	plato	*plate*
el	precio	*price*
la	propina	*tip*
el	servicio	*service*
el	restaurante	*restaurant*
el	tenedor	*fork*
	incluido	*included*
	beber	*to drink*
	cenar	*to have the evening meal, to dine*
	comer	*to eat, have lunch*
	desear	*to want*
	escoger	*to choose*
	preferir (ie)	*to prefer*
	probar (ue)	*to try*
	tener hambre	*to be hungry*
	tener sed	*to be thirsty*
	tomar	*to have (= to eat or drink)*

Basic phrases

¿A qué hora vamos a comer? *At what time are we going to have lunch?*

¿Qué va(n) a tomar? *What would you like?*

¿Qué va(n) a beber? *What would you like to drink?*

¿Qué quiere(n) de postre? *What would you like for dessert?*

¿Hay una mesa libre? *Is there a free table?*

¿Hay una mesa para cuatro? *Is there a table for four?*

Quiero... *I'd like...*

¿Puede traerme...? *Can you bring me...?*

¿Qué recomienda? *What do you recommend?*

¿Qué es...? *What is...?*
¿Cuánto es? *How much is it?*
La cuenta, por favor *Could I have the bill, please?*
¿Está incluido el servicio? *Is the service included?*
Tengo hambre *I'm hungry*
Tengo sed *I'm thirsty*

Higher
el cubierto *place setting*
el merendero *open air snack bar or picnic area*
los palillos *toothpicks*
almorzar (ue) *to have lunch*
merendar (ie) *to have an afternoon snack*

Higher phrases
Quédese con la vuelta *You may keep the change*

DESCRIBING OR COMMENTING ON FOOD AND DRINK

Basic
el gusto *taste*
el sabor *taste*
dulce *sweet*
estupendo *marvellous*
fuerte *strong, rich*
picante *spicy, 'hot'*
rico *tasty*
sabroso *tasty*

Basic phrases
Me gustan mucho los calamares *I really like squid*
Lo siento, pero no me gusta... *I'm sorry, I don't like...*
No puedo comer... *I can't eat...*
¡Qué rica está la paella! *How tasty the paella is!*

Higher
oler (ue) (a) *to smell (of)*
saber (a) *to taste (or smell) (of)*

Higher phrases
Huele a ajo *It smells of garlic*
Sabe a naranja *It tastes (or smells) of orange*

SERVICES

THE POST OFFICE
Basic
el buzón *letter box*
la carta *letter*
el cartero *postman*
Correos *Post Office*
la dirección *address*
el paquete *parcel*
la postal *post card*
el sello *stamp*
el sobre *envelope*
el telegrama *telegram*
la tarifa *tariff, postage rate*
por avión *by air mail*
urgente *urgent, express delivery*
echar *to post*
mandar *to send*
mandar al extranjero *to send abroad*

Basic phrases
Quiero dos sellos de ... pesetas *May I have two ...-peseta stamps*
Quiero mandar este paquete a Inglaterra *I want to send this parcel to England*

Higher
el código postal *postcode*
el giro postal *postal order*
la lista de correos *post restante*
el peso *weight*
entregar *to deliver*
pesar *to weigh*
recoger *to collect*

THE BANK OR EXCHANGE OFFICE
Basic
el banco *bank*
el billete *banknote*
la caja *cash desk*
el cambio *exchange, exchange rate, change*
el cheque *cheque*
el cheque de viajero *traveller's cheque*
el dinero *money*
el duro *5 pesetas, 5-peseta coin*
el empleado *clerk*
la libra (esterlina) *pound*
la moneda *coin*
el pasaporte *passport*
la peseta *peseta (Spanish currency)*
la tarjeta de crédito *credit card*
la ventanilla *position, service window*
cambiar *to change*
cobrar un cheque *to cash a cheque*
firmar *to sign*
pagar *to pay*

Basic phrases
¿Puedo cambiar un cheque de viajero? *Can I change a traveller's cheque?*
Pase usted a la caja *Please go to the cash desk*

Higher
el/la cajero/a *cashier*
las divisas *currency*
rellenar *to fill in (a form)*

Higher phrase

¿A cuánto está el cambio? *What is the exchange rate?*

THE TELEPHONE

Basic

la	cabina telefónica	*telephone kiosk*
la	llamada	*call*
la	telefónica	*telephone exchange*
el/la	telefonista	*telephonist*
el	teléfono	*telephone*

colgar (ue) *to hang up, ring off*
introducir monedas *to insert coins*
llamar *to call, to telephone*
marcar *to dial*
telefonear *to telephone*

Basic phrases

Diga (Dígame) *Hello (when answering a call)*
Oiga *Hello (when the other person answers the call)*
¿Está Luisa? *Is Luisa there?*
¿Tienes teléfono? *Have you a telephone?*
¿Cuál es tu número de teléfono? *What is your telephone number?*
¿Me puedes llamar esta noche? *Can you ring me tonight?*
Por favor, ¿puedo telefonear a mis padres? *May I phone my parents please?*

Higher

el	aparato	*the telephone*
el	prefijo	*dialling code*
la	conferencia	*long distance call*
la	conferencia internacional	*international call*
la	guía telefónica	*telephone directory*
la	llamada a cobro revertido	*reversed charge call*
el	recado	*message*

descolgar (ue) *to lift the receiver*

Higher phrases

¿De parte de quién? *Who (shall I say) is calling?*
Está comunicando *It's engaged*
¿Cuál es el prefijo de Madrid? *What is the dialling code for Madrid?*
Quiero poner una conferencia *I'd like to make a long-distance call*

THE LOST PROPERTY

Basic

la	bolsa	*bag*
el	bolso	*handbag*
la	comisaría	*police station*
el	detalle	*detail*
el	dinero	*money*
el	ladrón	*thief*
la	maleta	*suitcase*
la	máquina fotográfica	*camera*
la	oficina de objetos perdidos	*lost property office*
la	policía	*police*
el/la	policía	*policeman/policewoman*
la	recompensa	*reward*
el	reloj	*watch*
el	robo	*theft, robbery*

buscar *to look for*
contener (ie) *to contain*
dejar *to leave (something)*
describir *to describe*
descubrir *to discover*
encontrar (ue) *to find*
perder (ie) *to lose*
robar *to steal*
valer *to be worth*

Basic phrases

He perdido... *I have lost...*
Me han robado el reloj *My watch has been stolen*
Lo/la dejé... *I left it...*

Higher

el	delito	*crime*
el	informe	*report*
la	sorpresa	*surprise*
el	susto	*shock*

darse cuenta *to realize*
devolver (ue) *to return, give back*
pertenecer *to belong*
recoger *to collect*
sorprender *to surprise*

REPAIRS AND CLEANING

Basic

limpio *clean*
roto *broken*
sucio *dirty*
arreglar *to put right, mend*
funcionar *to work properly*
lavar *to wash*
limpiar *to clean*
reparar *to repair*

Basic phrases

Está roto/a mi... *My... is broken*
Está sucia mi chaqueta *My jacket is dirty*
No funciona el/la... *The... doesn't work*
Lo siento mucho. He roto... *I'm very sorry. I've broken...*
¿Me puede reparar un(a)...? *Can you mend me a...?*

Por favor ¿me podría lavar este jersey? *Could you wash me this sweater, please?*

Higher phrase
¿Cuánto tardará? *How long will it take?*

SEE ALSO 'PERSONAL IDENTIFICATION' AND 'SHOPPING' (for articles that might be lost, damaged or in need of cleaning).

WEATHER

Basic
- el aire *air*
- la brisa *breeze*
- el calor *heat*
- el cielo *sky*
- el clima *climate*
- el frío *cold*
- el grado *degree (of temperature)*
- el hielo *ice, frost*
- la lluvia *rain*
- la niebla *fog*
- la nieve *snow*
- la nube *cloud*
- el sol *sun*
- la sombra *shade, shadow*
- la temperatura *temperature*
- el tiempo *weather*
- la tormenta *storm*
- el viento *wind*
- brillar *to shine*
- llover (ue) *to rain*
- nevar (ie) *to snow*
- agradable *pleasant*
- fresco *cool*

Basic phrases
Hace buen tiempo *It is fine*
Hace mal tiempo *The weather is bad*
Hace calor *It is hot*
Hace fresco *It is cool*
Hace frío *It is cold*
Hace sol *It is sunny*
Hace viento *It is windy*
Hay niebla *It is foggy*
Llueve *It rains, It is raining*
Nieva *It snows, It is snowing*
Como hacía buen tiempo... *As the weather was fine...*

Higher
- la borrasca *squall*
- la escarcha *hoar frost*
- el granizo *hail*
- la llovizna *drizzle*
- la neblina *mist*
- la nevada *snowfall*
- el pronóstico *forecast*
- el relámpago *lightning*
- el rocío *dew*
- el trueno *thunder*
- helar (ie) *to freeze*
- soplar *to blow*
- tronar (ue) *to thunder*

Higher phrases
estar mojado hasta los huesos *to be soaked to the skin*
llover a cántaros *to pour down*
Hará sol *It will be sunny*
Habrá tormenta *There will be a storm*

GETTING STARTED

A **Listening Test** at *Basic Level* is a compulsory part of GCSE Spanish and it is clear that many students tend to worry about it. This chapter aims to ensure that you understand what the test is about and what it requires of you. It also contains some advice on how you can become more confident and more capable in listening. Finally, it provides examples of the questions that have been set by the different Examining Groups.

The cassette that can be bought with this book contains the recordings for the questions and allows you, if you wish, to practise answering the questions just as you would in the examination. It helps you to become familiar with the speed and way of speaking that are normal in the GCSE. The transcripts of all the recordings are included towards the end of the chapter, which will enable you to check carefully the words you have heard. If you have *not* bought the cassette, you could get a friend or relative who speaks Spanish to read the transcripts aloud to allow you to attempt the questions.

CHAPTER 4

LISTENING: BASIC LEVEL

THE BASIC LISTENING TEST

THE RECORDINGS

THE NATURE OF THE QUESTIONS

ANSWERING THE QUESTIONS

IMPROVING YOUR LISTENING SKILLS

TRANSCRIPTS OF THE RECORDINGS

ANSWER KEY TO PRACTICE QUESTIONS

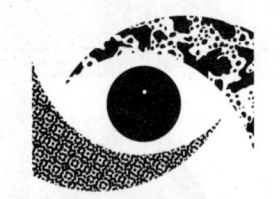

ESSENTIAL PRINCIPLES

1 ▸ THE BASIC LISTENING TEST

❝ Know exactly what is required ❞

Since the Listening Tests of all the Examining Groups involve cassette recordings, it is normal for schools and colleges to arrange for the examination to take place in a comparatively small room, so that you are able to hear clearly. Often a language laboratory is used. It is unlikely that your test will take place in the sort of large hall or gym where most other examinations are taken. So make sure you know where you are supposed to be. If you are using a language laboratory and there are a large number of candidates, you may well find that you have to take the examination in groups, with strict supervision of those who have yet to take the examination or who have just taken it. It is most important that you follow any special instructions about supervision and reporting times, so that your teachers can give the necessary assurances, not just that there was no contact between those who had already taken the test and those who had yet to take it, but that such contact would have been totally impossible.

2 ▸ THE RECORDINGS

❝ Nature of the recordings ❞

The nature of the recorded material you hear in the examination is specified in the National Criteria.

- It is recorded by *native speakers* of Spanish, so that you hear genuine Spanish pronunciation and accents.
- It includes, where appropriate, a limited amount of background noise, such as you would hear in the real-life setting.
- It is restricted to the Topics specified by the Examining Group for Basic Level. (Check that you know which they are.)
- It is restricted to the Settings specified in the syllabus. (A grid of Topics and Settings is included in Chapter 3.)
- It is material that was specifically intended to be heard (i.e. it cannot consist of reading aloud from a text originally intended for silent reading, such as a newspaper or novel).

The *types* of spoken material you will hear are:

❝ Types of spoken material ❞

- announcements (e.g. in shops, stations and campsites)
- spoken instructions
- requests
- broadcast news items, weather forecasts and traffic reports
- recorded telephone messages
- conversations, interviews and discussions

Each recorded item is heard twice in the examination and each item is quite short. Even the 'longer' items are comparatively short and often they are broken into sections the second time you hear them.

3 ▸ THE NATURE OF THE QUESTIONS

❝ What the questions require you to do ❞

- You are expected to demonstrate understanding of specific details. (You will not be required to summarize or draw conclusions.)
- You will be tested only on your understanding of the material. (You will not be required to make any significant use of other skills, such as making calculations.)
- The tests are designed to ensure that they do not place undue emphasis on memory. (This is the main reason why items are kept short.)
- You write your answers on the question paper in the spaces provided.
- The questions are in English (or in Welsh if you take WJEC examinations and choose to be examined in Welsh).

- Answers are expressed either in words in English (or Welsh) or in figures or by ticking boxes or filling in a grid.

(For the IGCSE the questions and answers are in Spanish.)

Two of the most common types of question involve checking whether you can understand:

(a) spoken questions in Spanish (e.g. You are in a restaurant in Valencia and have just ordered a meal when the waiter asks you: *¿Qué quiere beber?* What does he want to know?)

(b) spoken instructions in Spanish (e.g. You are buying an article in a store in Madrid when the shop assistant says: *Por favor, pague en caja.* What is she telling you to do?)

You need to make sure, therefore, that you know your key question words well and that you can understand instructions.

In many other cases the questions will be seeking an answer about

Who?	How long?
What?	How many?
Where?	How much?
When?	Why?

These questions suggest some areas of vocabulary that you would be well advised to make sure you know.

> **Be familiar with these areas of vocabulary**

Who?	– family and friends, jobs,
	– descriptions : physical appearance, size, age, etc.
What?	– almost anything! Check out particularly Shopping, Food and Drink and Free Time and Entertainment
Where?	– position, location of places and buildings, landmarks, countries, directions and distances
When?	– time of day by 12- and 24-hour clock, days, weeks, months, years, dates, frequency, expressions of time (today, yesterday etc.), seasons, important holidays (e.g. Christmas, New Year), beginning, middle, end
How long?	– time, especially duration (*durante* and *hasta* in particular)
How many?	– numbers
How much?	– quantity, numbers
Why?	– reasons

The evidence from the papers set over recent years suggests that you would be well advised to make sure you have a good understanding of the following:

1. Telling the time.
2. Dates and days of the week.
3. Numbers and money. Remember that, because the Spanish peseta is normally valued somewhere in the region of 200 to the pound, prices in Spain involve some quite high numbers. (10 000 pesetas is roughly the equivalent of £50.)
4. Directions (*Tome la primera calle a la derecha, cruce la plaza* etc.) and positions (*delante de la iglesia, enfrente de Correos,* etc.).
5. School subjects.

> **Things you should know**

4 ANSWERING THE QUESTIONS

- Remember that you do not have to understand every word - only the ones relevant to the question. The recordings can contain up to 15% of words from outside the official list, provided that understanding of those words is not needed in order to answer the questions.

- Make use of the opportunity to read the questions before you hear the recording so that you can target your listening specifically on the points being asked.

> **Useful hints on answering the questions**

- If you are confident of your answer, write it straight down in the space for it. There is no real merit it making notes simply to copy them later - that is merely a waste of time. The real value of notes is probably restricted to noting a Spanish word or phrase in the hope of remembering later how to express the idea in English.

- Read the setting carefully. It is there to give you some guidance and help. Quite often it will include a name which might otherwise be unfamiliar and off-putting when you hear it. Often it will point you towards the right answer. Many candidates ignore the setting and make silly mistakes as a result.

> Answer the questions set

- Read the question carefully and make sure what you write actually answers it! If you hear the speaker say, for example, *Mi hermana tiene el pelo largo y moreno*, and the question is 'What colour is her sister's hair?', for goodness' sake don't write 'Long' as the answer. This may seem obvious but many candidates make precisely that sort of mistake.

- Remember to answer in English (or Welsh). Answers in Spanish will almost certainly score no marks (except, of course, in the IGCSE).

- Keep your answers as short as possible (but make sure you do give all the necessary information). Whole sentences are not required. If the speaker says: *¿Qué te parece si vamos a la discoteca?* and the question is 'Where does she suggest you go?', you certainly do not need to write: 'She suggests that we go to the discotheque.' If you do that you will waste a lot of time and may well miss the next point you were supposed to listen for. All that is required in this case is: 'The disco' or even 'Disco'.

> Mark allocations can help

- Check how many marks are awarded for the question. (This is usually shown in brackets at the end of the question.) The number of marks will give you a good indication of the number of items of information that are required. If you are asked what someone will be wearing and the allocation is 4 marks, you may find that he says only that he will be wearing a blue shirt and grey trousers. In this case it will be quite clear that the colours are important and carry one mark each. On the other hand, if the allocation is only 2 marks you would still be well advised to include them, because it could be that each item of clothing scores a mark only if the correct colour is given. Sometimes there are four possible answers and only two marks. In those cases both marks will almost certainly be given for any two correct answers.

> Don't leave a question unanswered

- Always give an answer. Even if you have no idea, make an informed guess, based on what you have understood from the recording and from the setting and the question itself. You never know, you might be right! In multiple-choice questions and true/false questions your chances of guessing the correct answer are particularly good.

- Don't go in for 'blanket bombing' of the target area. If you are asked what colour the car was, pick one colour if you have to guess. Listing every colour you can think of will not be very helpful. The Examining Groups have their own rules for marking such answers. They are likely either to mark the answer wrong straightaway or to mark only the first colour you have mentioned.

5 > IMPROVING YOUR LISTENING SKILLS

In Chapter 2 we looked at some ways of practising listening. The essential message was that there are several sources of listening material available and that you should use them. The more Spanish you hear the better.

Many students do worry about Listening and tend to feel it is the one skill in which they have no control over what happens. They can to some extent control what they say in the Speaking test and what they write in the Writing test. In both Reading and Writing they can go back and review what they have done. In Listening they hear each item twice, at whatever speed, and that is the end of the matter.

> Practice will help

In the examination that is indeed true but, in practising for the examination, you can have far more control. You will certainly need some practice under the sort of conditions that apply in the examination, so, if you have bought the cassette that is available with this book, you will no doubt wish to keep at least some of the recordings for examination practice. If, however, you have real difficulty with listening you could use some of the recordings and any other listening material as outlined below. The first aim must be to ensure you achieve some success in listening.

> Useful hints on practising your listening skills

- Do not restrict yourself to hearing each item twice.

- Before you read the questions (if you are using test material), just listen to the recording and note down any words you recognize. If at first you don't recognize very many, listen again, as many times as you need to, in order to have a reasonable number of the words written down.

- Next, listen again and see how much of what is being said you actually understand. If the answer is 'not much', try it again.

- Only when you are confident you can understand a fair amount should you look at the questions. Then play the recording (or parts of it) as many times as you need in order to answer the questions.

- If, in the end, you have to admit defeat, look at the answer and check the transcript to make sure you can identify the key words.

- Finally, play the recording to make sure you can now recognize the key words when you hear them. If you can't, listen again, if necessary with the transcript in front of you.

In this way, you will ensure that you have an excellent chance of understanding the same expressions next time you hear them. You will also find that, since you have geared yourself to end on a note of success, you will achieve that success slightly more easily next time you practise. If the first time you listen to a recording you find you have to listen twelve times, you should find that the number of hearings you require gradually decreases with recordings you listen to in later practice sessions. Obviously, you must not expect to understand as much of broadcast material as you would of GCSE recordings. But, even with quite difficult material, word-recognition practice is well worthwhile. (If you are having to rely on a friend reading the transcripts to you, it is a good idea to make clear before you begin that you may be asking for things to be repeated several times!)

> Persevere and it will get easier

Regular practice of listening will bring considerable improvement - provided you go about it in a positive way, with the emphasis on what you can do.

> You don't need to understand every word

One final point: Don't forget that you do not have to understand every word. In developing your skills, concentrate first on what you do understand and then on what is needed to answer the questions. In examinations and examination practice concentrate on what you need in order to answer the questions. Ignore the irrelevant words you don't need.

QUESTIONS, STUDENTS' ANSWERS AND EXAMINER'S COMMENTS

In Basic Listening, the tests normally begin with a series of short recordings, with a single question on each. Later there are likely to be some recordings linked to two or three questions. Finally there could be some longer recordings linked to rather more questions. Very often, though not always, the short recordings have links with each other, so that they follow through different stages of a particular incident. All three types are included here in the samples with students' answers. In the Practice Questions that follow, the single-question recordings come first (Recordings 5-9) and the recordings with more questions on each come later.

With each of the first four recordings you are recommended to try the questions yourself *before* looking at the student's answers. *Transcripts* of the recordings are included towards the end of the chapter, so that you can check the wording later. A *key* to the answers follows the transcripts. **Don't be put off by the different question numbers used in the recordings. They correspond with the cassette and are in fact the numbers the questions had when they were used in GCSE examinations.**

Find Recording 1 on the cassette, then attempt the questions before looking at the student's answers that follow. Remember to read the setting and the question carefully. The setting is intended to help you.

CHAPTER 4 LISTENING: BASIC LEVEL

> **COVER UP THE STUDENTS' ANSWERS BELOW EACH SET OF QUESTIONS, THEN TRY THE QUESTIONS YOURSELF BEFORE LOOKING AT THE STUDENTS' ANSWERS AND EXAMINER'S COMMENTS**

RECORDING 1

- Read the questions below then play Recording 1 (or listen to your friend read the transcript on page 68)

Questions 1-5 – *To your great surprise a Spanish friend of yours has just arrived in England and he telephones you to let you know of his arrival.*

Question 1. – Where does your friend say that he is?

.... (1)

Question 2 – You ask him where he intends to stay while he is in England.

2. Why should you already know?

.... (1)

Question 3 – So you ask him again where he is going to stay.

3. In what sort of accommodation is he going to stay?

.... (1)

Question 4 – You ask him what he is going to do during his stay.

4. What sort of work will he be doing?

.... (1)

Question 5 – Finally, you want to know when you will be able to meet him.

5. What does he suggest that you do straightaway?

.... (1)

(SEG)

STUDENT'S ANSWERS

1. Manchester
2. He has written it in his letter.
3. Youth Hostel
4. In an office in the city.
5. Go to the airport straight away.

EXAMINER'S COMMENTS

1. Not enough information. You must also mention the airport.
2. Good answer. Could have been shorter, e.g. 'He told me in letter.'
3. Excellent answer.
4. Good answer. You didn't actually need to add 'in the city'.
5. Good answer, but you certainly don't need to write 'straight away'–that was in the question.

RECORDING 2

- Read the questions below then play Recording 2 (or listen to your friend read the transcript on page 69)

Questions 6 and 7 – *During a visit to Spain with your parents, you arrive at a filling station and need some petrol. The petrol pump attendant comes out and speaks to you.*

6. Why is there no choice as to the petrol you can buy?

.... (1)

7. What else does the attendant offer to do?

.... (1)

Questions 8, 9 and 10 – *Back in the car you have the radio tuned to a Spanish station and you hear this weather forecast.*

8. Who should be especially pleased by this forecast?

.... (1)

9. State **two** reasons why they should be pleased?

.... (2)

10. How long will this situation last?

.... *(1)*

(SEG)

STUDENT'S ANSWERS

6. Because he only has one type.
7. To top up the oil.
8. Those on holiday.
9. Because it is hot and it will be hottest ever this year.
10. Until tomorrow.

EXAMINER'S COMMENTS

6. Wrong. Not enough information. You must make clear that the 2-star (*normal*) has run out OR that they only have 4-star TODAY.
7. Good answer. You could omit 'To'.
8. Perfect answer.
9. Right about it being hot (*1 mark*). For the other mark you need to mention any one of: Good (or fine) weather; Sunny; Very little wind.
10. Wrong. It will last tomorrow and the day after (*Pasado mañana, igual*)

RECORDING 3

- Read the questions below then play Recording 3 (or listen to your friend read the transcript on page 69)

While on holiday in Spain, you meet a Spanish girl called Conchita. She talks about her family. You make notes in English of what she says. There will be pauses so that you will have time to write your answers.

Now read through the questions.

CONCHITA	
1. Age of Conchita's sister	*(1)*
2. What Rosario looks like	*(1)*
....	*(1)*
3. How she describes her flat..	*(1)*
4. What she says about where her flat is	*(1)*
....	*(1)*
5. Her father's job...	*(1)*
6. Her mother's job..	*(1)*
7. What her family does on Sundays	*(1)*
....	*(1)*
	(10)

(MEG)

STUDENT'S ANSWERS

1. 14.
2. Blue eyes.
   Short.
3. It has one dining room.
4. It is quite near to the school.
5.
6. Doctor.
7. They visit their cousins.

EXAMINER'S COMMENTS

1. Age: Good. Expressed as briefly as possible.
2. What Rosario looks like: Blue eyes – Good. Totally misunderstood *Es muy alta*
3. Her flat: Pure guesswork! It is *muy cómodo* – very comfortable.
4. Where flat is: Acceptable (though it should really be 'very' near). The second point (about a park next to it) is completely omitted.

5. Father's job: Don't leave blanks. You just might guess right!
6. Mother's job: Good answer – and brief!
7. Sundays: You missed the first point (*Vamos a la iglesia*). A pity about the second. You were right about the visit but you haven't learnt your family words well enough to get a mark

RECORDING 4

■ Read the questions below then play Recording 4 (or listen to your friends read the transcript on page 69)

Questions 14, 15, 16 and 17 – *You and a couple of Spanish friends decide that you would like to go to the cinema. Your friends show you this advertisement in the local paper and then you listen to them arguing about whether it will be a good film. Study the advertisement and then listen to their conversation.*

14. Why does Juan Carlos want to see the film?
.... *(1)*
15. Why is Chelo less enthusiastic?
.... *(1)*
16. What information is not given in the advertisement?
.... *(1)*
17. What does Juan Carlos suggest they do?
.... *(1)*
(*SEG*)

STUDENT'S ANSWERS
14. He thinks it will be funny and one of his favourite actors is in it.
15. She does not like films like these.
16 It does not say when it starts.
17. Telephone the cinema for the times.

EXAMINER'S COMMENTS
14. Wrong. You seem to have based your answer on Chelo's words.
15. No. She was more specific: She did not like Susan Seidelman's other film.
16. Good. You could omit the first four words of the answer, though.
17. Good answer.

There now follow some practice questions for you to attempt. Answer keys to all these questions (and the ones above) can be found at the end of the chapter.

PRACTICE QUESTIONS

RECORDING 5

- Read the questions below then play Recording 5 (or listen to your friend read the transcript on page 69)

You arrive at a Spanish hotel with your parents. Listen to what the receptionist says and answer the questions below in English. There will be pauses to allow you to write your answers. Now read though the questions.

1. Where are your rooms?
   .... *(1)*

2. What do you learn about your rooms?
   .... *(1)*

3. How much are the rooms per night?
   .... *(1)*

4. What are you told about breakfast?
   .... *(1)*

5. What are you told about the facilities in your rooms? Give **two** details.
   (a) .... *(1)*
   (b) .... *(1)*

6. Where is the lift?
   .... *(1)*

7. What are you told about where the keys are? Give **two** details.
   ....
   .... *(2)*

8. What does the receptionist need to know?
   .... *(1)*

(MEG)

RECORDING 6

- Read the questions below then play Recording 6 (or listen to your friend read the transcript on page 69)

1. You will now hear five questions which you might be asked in Spain.

   (a) In a restaurant – what are you being asked?
   .... *(2)*

   (b) In the street – what does the girl want to know?
   .... *(1)*

   (c) Outside a bank – what does the man ask you?
   .... *(1)*

   (d) At a Spanish Airport – what does the official ask you?
   .... *(1)*

   (e) In a small shop – what does the lady ask you?
   .... *(1)*

(WJEC)

RECORDING 7

- Read the questions below then play Recording 7 (or listen to your friend read the transcript on page 70)

2. You will now hear five announcements which you might hear in Spain.

   (a) You are at a campsite in Spain and hear this announcement on the

64 CHAPTER 4 LISTENING: BASIC LEVEL

loudspeaker system. What are you being told?

.... (2)

(b) At Barajas airport you are a passenger waiting for flight number 268 to Bristol. What are you instructed to do?

.... (1)

(c) You are waiting at a train station in Madrid for a friend who is travelling on the express train from Alicante. What information are you given?

.... (2)

(d) You hear an announcement in a large Department Store. What is the special offer?

.... (2)

(e) Whilst travelling towards Lérida on the N11 you hear a message to motorists on the car radio. What have you been told?

.... (2)

(WJEC)

RECORDING 8

- Read the questions below then play Recording 8 (or listen to your friend read the transcript on page 70)

You are spending a few days in Spain. You have just arrived at the railway station with two Spanish friends, Pedro and Ana.

1. At what time does your train leave?

   .... (1)

2. Where does Ana suggest you go?

   .... (1)

3. What does Pedro think you should do first?

   .... (1)

4. What does Ana want to know?

   .... (1)

5. Where **exactly** do you have to go?

   .... (1)

6. How many tickets do Ana and Pedro decide to buy?

   .... (1)

(NEAB)

RECORDING 9

- Read the questions below then play Recording 9 (or listen to your friend read the transcript on page 70)

You are at the railway station with your friends Ana and Pedro. After buying the tickets you go to the waiting room. Pedro talks about Manuel.

10. Who is Manuel? Mention **two** things.

    (i) ....

    (ii) .... (2)

11. What is Manuel like at the office? Mention **two** things.

    (i) ....

    (ii) .... (2)

12. What is he like with his friends? Mention **two** points.

    (i) ....

    (ii) .... (2)

(NEAB)

RECORDING 10

- Read the questions below then play Recording 10 (or listen to your friend read the transcript on page 70)

While shopping in a department store with your family, you hear some announcements which might help with some ideas for presents.

Question 1 – According to what you are told in the announcement, why are there sales on at the moment?

.... (1)

Question 2 – Why will the music department be worth a visit today?

....

.... (2)

Questions 3, 4 and 5 – The family wishes to visit various departments: note down on this table which departments are on which floors.

Question 3
First Floor .... (1)

Question 4
Ground Floor .... (1)

Question 5
Basement.. (1)

(ULEAC)

RECORDING 11

- Read the questions below then play Recording 11 (or listen to your friend read the transcript on page 70)

On a school exchange visit to Spain, you listen to some Spanish students and teachers talking about their meal times and preferences. You have to note down some details for a report you have been asked to write for your school magazine. Answer the following questions.

Question 6 – When does José have breakfast?

.... (1)

Question 7 – What is Ana's favourite food?

.... (2)

Question 8 – What sort of wine does Don Miguel prefer?

.... (1)

Question 9 – Doña Blanca has been asked whether she likes cooking. Who does the cooking in her house in the evenings during the week?

.... (1)

Questions 10, 11 and 12 – Finally, the headmaster is asked when and where he eats in a normal working day. In the spaces below, fill in where he has the following meals:

Question 10
Breakfast .... (1)

Question 11
Lunch .... (2)

Question 12
Supper .... (1)

(ULEAC)

RECORDING 12

- Read the questions below then play Recording 12 (or listen to your friend read the transcript on page 71)

In this section you will hear five recordings in Spanish. You will hear the first recording twice then the second recording twice and so on. Write your answers in English.

1. You are travelling by car with your family in Spain. You stop at a filling station.

    (a) What question does the attendant ask you?

    .... (1)

(b) What does he then say he will do?

.... (1)

2. Later, you stop at a cafe and order some drinks. The waiter takes your order and then offers you some cakes.

What are the flavours of the cakes that he offers?

(a) .... (1)

(b) .... (1)

3. You want to buy some groceries so you ask the waiter where is the best place to go. However, a second waiter gives another suggestion.

(a) What does the first waiter say about the quality of the supermarket?

.... (1)

(b) What suggestion does the second waiter make?

.... (1)

4. Finally, you arrive at your camp site and book in. You ask about shops on the site. Apart from the food shop on the site, what other services are available?

(a) In the morning.

.... (1)

(b) In the evening.

.... (1)

5. You ask if your friends have arrived.

(a) When did your friends arrive?

.... (1)

(b) Where are your friends now?

.... (1)

(MEG)

RECORDING 13

- Read the questions below then play Recording 13 (or listen to your friend read the transcript on page 71)

4. You are on a cycling holiday in Spain with a friend who speaks no Spanish so you have to explain what has been said.

(a) You arrive at an 'Hostal' and ask about the price of rooms. What is the cost of a room per night?

.... (1)

(b) You feel this is more than you want to pay so you ask if they have anything cheaper. What is the disadvantage of the rooms she offers?

.... (1)

(c) Later you ask the receptionist if she can recommend a good but not too expensive restaurant. On the plan below mark with an X where you would expect to find the restaurant. (2)

(d) You ask how far away the restaurant is. What does the receptionist tell you?

.... (2)

(e) In the restaurant you hear a lady at a nearby table speaking angrily to the waiter. What is she complaining about?
.... (1)

(f) What does she order instead?
.... (1)

(WJEC)

RECORDING 14

- Read the questions below then play Recording 14 (or listen to your friend read the transcript on page 71)

You are on holiday in Spain and one morning you get a phone call from a Spaniard called Alejandro whom you have met during your holiday. Now read through the questions one to eight. There will be pauses so that you have time to write down your answers.

1. **When** did you meet Alejandro?
.... (1)

2. **Where** did you meet Alejandro?
.... (1)

3. What had Alejandro been wearing?
.... (1)

4. When does Alejandro suggest you go to the restaurant?
.... (1)

5. Who will Alejandro bring with him to the restaurant?
.... (1)

6. Give the **two** reasons why Alejandro thinks the restaurant is a good one to go to.
   (a) .... (1)
   (b) .... (1)

7. What are the **two** suggestions that Alejandro makes about where to meet?
   (a) .... (1)
   (b) .... (1)

8. What time does Alejandro think you will be back at your hotel?
.... (1)

(10)

(MEG)

RECORDING 15

- Read the questions below then play Recording 15 (or listen to your friend read the transcript on page 71)

THE CIRCUS COMES TO TOWN!

Questions 20 - 24 are based on a longer passage. This passage is divided into four sections, Question 20, Question 21, Questions 22 and 23, and Question 24. Candidates will hear the whole passage once. Each section will then be heard twice.

One day while you are staying at a campsite in Spain, a car drives around the site broadcasting an announcement over a loudspeaker. Your family wishes to know some details about the announcement.

Question 20 – If you wish to see the circus, why must you go today?
.... (1)

Question 21 – At what time does the show begin?
.... (1)

Question 22 and 23

Question 22 – How much are the **two** types of tickets for adults?
....
.... (2)

Question 23 – Who will be let in free?

.... (1)

Question 24 – Name **two** types of animal which can be seen during the day at this circus.

....

.... (2)

(*ULEAC*)

RECORDING 16

■ Read the questions below then play Recording 16 (or listen to your friend read the transcript on page 72)

2. While waiting in a queue in a post office, you hear the following conversation.

    (a) When does the customer say his letter must arrive?

    ....

    .... (2)

    (b) Where is he told to go?

    ....

    .... (2)

    (c) What is he told to do afterwards?

    ....

    .... (3)

(*NICCEA*)

RECORDING 17

■ Read the questions below then play Recording 17 (or listen to your friend read the transcript on page 72)

4. In a street in Spain, you hear the following conversation between a policeman and a pedestrian.

    (a) Where does the pedestrian want to go?

    .... (1)

    (b) How far away is it?

    .... (1)

    (a) What directions does the policeman give?

    .... (3)

(*NICCEA*)

RECORDING 18

■ Read the questions below then play Recording 18 (or listen to your friend read the transcript on page 72)

3. During your summer holidays you have a temporary job as a waiter/waitress in a restaurant in Cardiff. A Spanish lady and her husband come in and your boss asks you to take their order. You give them the menu and on the notepad you have ready, you jot down their order. You will hear the lady's order first, then the man's.

	LADY	MAN	
Starters			(4)
Main Courses			(3)
Desserts			(3)
Drinks			(3)

(*WJEC*)

6 ▶ TRANSCRIPTS OF THE RECORDINGS

RECORDING 1 (TRANSCRIPT)

Question 1
Hola. Te telefoneo para decirte que ya estoy en el aeropuerto de Manchester.

Question 2
Pues, ¿no has recibido mi carta?
Question 3
Voy a hospedarme en un albergue de jóvenes cerca de tu casa.
Question 4
Voy a pasar un mes trabajando en una oficina en el centro de la ciudad.
Question 5
Pues, si vienes al aeropuerto, nos vamos a encontrar muy pronto.

RECORDING 2 (TRANSCRIPT)

Questions 6 and 7
Hola, buenos días. Siento decirles que sólo tenemos súper hoy. Se nos acabó la normal..... ¿Les pongo algo de aceite también?
Questions 8, 9 and 10
Señoras y señores. Para todos ustedes que están de vacaciones tenemos muy buenas noticias. Mañana va a hacer muy buen tiempo. Hará sol en toda la península. Las temperaturas llegarán hasta un máximo de 32 grados y hará muy poco viento. Pasado mañana, igual.

RECORDING 3 (TRANSCRIPT)

Pues, me llamo Conchita. No tengo hermano pero tengo una hermana. Se llama Rosario. Tiene catorce años. Es muy alta y tiene los ojos azules.

Vivimos en un piso muy cómodo. Está muy cerca de mi colegio y hay un parque al lado.

Mi padre se llama Juan. Es peluquero. Mi madre se llama María. Es médica.

Los domingos vamos a la iglesia y luego visitamos a nuestros abuelos.

RECORDING 4 (TRANSCRIPT)

Questions 14, 15, 16 and 17
Juan Carlos: Mira, Chelo, será estupenda la película «Fabricando al hombre perfecto».
Chelo: ¿Tú crees? Ya sé que será muy divertida, pero no me gustó nada la otra película de Susan Seidelman.
Juan Carlos: ¿Cuál? ¿«Buscando a Susan desesperadamente»? A mí me encantó esa película. Y la vi otra vez en la tele durante las vacaciones.
Chelo: Dice aquí en el anuncio que la nueva película empieza hoy. ¿Por qué no vamos a verla? ¿A qué hora empieza?
Juan Carlos: No vas a creerlo, pero no lo dice. He mirado con cuidado, pero no lo veo. Tendremos que telefonear al cine para preguntárselo.

RECORDING 5 (TRANSCRIPT)

Q.1 Buenas tardes. Ustedes ya tienen habitaciones reservadas ¿no? Las dos habitaciones están en el segundo piso.
Q.2 Las dos habitaciones tienen vista al mar.
Q.3 Las habitaciones cuestan 5500 pesetas por noche.
Q.4 Servimos el desayuno a las ocho.
Q.5 En las dos habitaciones hay agua caliente y un cuarto de baño. En este hotel el agua está siempre caliente.
Q.6 Si ustedes quieren subir, el ascensor está enfrente del comedor.
Q.7 Las puertas ya están abiertas. Ustedes encontrarán las llaves en la mesa cerca de la cama.
Q.8 Perdonen. Una cosa más. ¿Ustedes quieren media pensión o pensión completa?

RECORDING 6 (TRANSCRIPT)

Question 1
a) ¿Quieres vino tinto o blanco?
b) Perdone. ¿Me puede decir dónde está Correos?
c) ¿A qué hora se abre el banco?
d) ¿Tiene usted algo que declarar?
e) ¿Algo más?

RECORDING 7 (TRANSCRIPT)

Question 2

a) Señoras y señores, el supermercado del Camping 'Sol y Sombra' va a cerrar en diez minutos.
b) Señores pasajeros del vuelo Iberia número 268 con destino a Bristol - pasen por la puerta número 9.
c) El expreso Costa Blanca procedente de Alicante viene con veinte minutos de retraso.
d) Señoras y señores, hoy oferta especial para nuestros clientes: Trajes de baño y bikinis... a mitad de precio.
e) La carretera nacional N 11 queda cerrada porque ha nevado mucho entre Lérida y Barcelona.

RECORDING 8 (TRANSCRIPT)

1   F   Bueno, ya hemos llegado.
    M   ¿A qué hora sale el tren?
    F   Sale a las tres y media.
2   M   Ah, entonces todavía falta media hora.
    F   Sí. ¿Por qué no vamos a la sala de espera?
3   M   A la sala de espera podemos ir después. Yo creo que es mejor comprar primero los billetes.
4   F   Vale, los compramos ahora. Oye, y ¿dónde están las taquillas?
5   M   ¿No las ves? Allí . . ., a la izquierda de la escalera.
6   F   ¿Y qué hacemos? ¿Le compramos también un billete a Manuel?
    M   Pero todavía no ha llegado. Si compramos cuatro y no viene ¿qué haremos con el billete? Es mejor comprar sólo tres.
    F   No, estoy segura de que va a venir. Manuel no falta nunca a una cita. Compremos cuatro.
    M   Vale, pues, si tú estás tan segura.

RECORDING 9 (TRANSCRIPT)

10   M   Manuel es un compañero de trabajo mío y también es primo de Ana, él fue quien nos presentó.
11   M   Es un chico que vale mucho. En la oficina es muy trabajador y parece un poco serio. Lo que pasa es que es muy ambicioso y quiere ganar mucho dinero.
12   M   Pero con los amigos, cuando lo conoces, te das cuenta de que es divertido y es un buen amigo.

RECORDING 10 (TRANSCRIPT)

Question 1
Queremos indicar a nuestros clientes que hoy mismo empiezan las Rebajas de Verano. Vendemos todo a precios muy bajos.

Question 2
Hay reducciones en todas las secciones – en la sección de cocina, 20% de descuento; en la sección de música – muchos discos y casetes a precios baratos. En moda femenina – muchas ofertas especiales.

Questions 3, 4 and 5
¿Por qué no visita la sección de juguetes en el primer piso, la sección de libros en la planta baja, y la sección de deportes – en el sótano?

RECORDING 11 (TRANSCRIPT)

Question 6
Bueno, yo desayuno antes de lavarme por la mañana.

Question 7
A mí me gusta todo, pero sobre todo me gusta la tortilla de jamón.

Question 8
En general, prefiero beber vino, especialmente el blanco.

Question 9
A mí no me gusta cocinar – pero a mi marido, sí. Prepara la cena todos los días – pero yo cocino los fines de semana.

Questions 10, 11 and 12
Yo desayuno en un café, a mediodía como en mi restaurante favorito y ceno en casa.

RECORDING 12 (TRANSCRIPT)

Q.1 Lo siento. No puedo llenarle el tanque. Es que no tenemos gasolina. Pero no se preocupe. Hay otra estación de servicio a cinco kilómetros de aquí. Y ¿tienen bastante gasolina para llegar allí? Voy a comprobar los neumáticos..... Sí, están bien.

Q.2 Así que son dos cafés con leche y dos coca-colas. Muy bien, y tenemos unos pasteles riquísimos. ¿No quieren probarlos? Éstos son de fresa y éstos son de piña. Son excelentes.

Q.3 A: Ustedes quieren comprar comestibles? No hay problema. Hay un supermercado a un kilómetro de aquí. Es el mejor que hay. Allí venden de todo.
B: Pero esperen. Esperen. Hoy es martes y todos los martes hay un mercado aquí cerca. ¿Por qué no van allí? Todo será mucho más barato.

Q.4 Sí, tenemos una tienda de alimentación aquí, en el camping. Y además, si ustedes quieren comprar pan por la mañana, no es necesario ir al pueblo. Hay un señor que viene aquí todas las mañanas con un camión. Vende pan y el pan es muy bueno. Y por la tarde el mismo señor vuelve para vender mariscos. Están siempre muy frescos.

Q.5 ¿Sus amigos? Sí, llegaron ayer. Me parece que están en la sala de juegos.

RECORDING 13 (TRANSCRIPT)

Question 4

(a) El precio de una habitación individual con baño es de 2 mil pesetas.
(b) Sí, tenemos habitaciones de 1500 pesetas pero no tienen ni baño ni ducha.
(c) Tome la primera bocacalle a la derecha – . . . después la segunda a la izquierda y el restaurante 'El Molinillo' está a mano derecha cerca de la playa.
(d) Está a 20 minutos a pie.
(e) S   Camarero, esta sopa está fría, no se puede tomar.
    C   Lo siento señora – traeré otra caliente.
(f) S   No, no quiero la sopa . . . tráigame una ensalada.
    C   Sí, señora – ahora mismo una ensalada.

RECORDING 14 (TRANSCRIPT)

Oye. Soy yo, Alejandro, ¿te acuerdas? Te encontré anoche en la discoteca. Yo llevaba la camisa amarilla. Mira, tengo una idea. ¿Por qué no vamos a un restaurante esta noche, tú, yo y mis dos hermanas? Yo conozco un restaurante muy bueno. Es muy barato, ¿sabes? Y está muy cerca de tu hotel. Si quieres, nos veremos en el bar del hotel o delante del restaurante. Me parece que la mejor hora para ir al restaurante es las nueve y media. Y después, quizás, iremos a bailar. A mis hermanas les gusta mucho. Di a tus padres que volverás a la una.

RECORDING 15 (TRANSCRIPT)

Questions 20 - 24 *are based on a longer passage. This passage is divided into four sections – Question 20, Question 21, Questions 22 and 23, and Question 24. Candidates will hear the whole passage once. Each section will then be heard twice.*

Question 20
Señoras y señores, el Gran Circo Canadiense está aquí en Montefrío. Hoy mismo, y para un solo día pueden divertirse con todo lo más divertido y hermoso del circo.

Question 21
Se presenta una sola sesión a las 20.30 en la Plaza de la Iglesia.

Questions 22 and 23
Hay billetes de a seiscientas y de a mil pesetas. Gratis para los niños de menos de cinco años.

Question 24
Durante todo el día pueden visitar los animales: vayan a ver los leones, los tigres, los elefantes, los caballos y los camellos. Vengan hoy mismo a ver el Gran Circo Canadiense.

RECORDING 16 (TRANSCRIPT)

A: Buenos días, señor, ¿qué desea?
B: Quiero enviar esta carta a Madrid y debe llegar antes del miércoles.
A: Pues, mire, usted tiene que ir a la ventanilla número 5. Después, échela al buzón de cartas urgentes allí fuera.

RECORDING 17 (TRANSCRIPT)

A: Oiga, por favor, ¿la estación de ferrocarril está cerca de aquí?
B: Sí, está a quinientos metros, nada más.
A: Y ¿por dónde se va?
B: Pues, vaya todo recto hasta el final de la calle... y la estación está a la derecha.

RECORDING 18 (TRANSCRIPT)

Question 3

Hombre   Bueno Pilar ¿qué vas a tomar?
Mujer   Pues para empezar – sopa de verduras.
Hombre   Y ¿después?
Mujer   A ver... el pescado.
Hombre   ¿Y de postre, querida?
Mujer   Quiero probar el queso.
Hombre   Por favor, para mi esposa: sopa de verduras, pescado y de postre queso... espera... ¿quieres algo de beber, Pilar?
Mujer   Sí, un café con leche.
Hombre   Pues para mí – sopa de champiñones, luego pollo asado y de postre un helado de chocolate... y para beber... a ver... una cerveza.

7 > ANSWER KEY TO PRACTICE QUESTIONS

RECORDING 1 (KEY)

1. Manchester airport.
2. He has written a letter.
3. Youth hostel.
4. Office.
5. Go to the airport.

RECORDING 2 (KEY)

6. They've run out of 2-star OR They've only 4-star today.
7. Put some oil in.
8. holidaymakers.
9. ANY 2 OF: (It will be) good weather;
             sunny;
             hot;
             very little wind.
10. 2 days.

RECORDING 3 (KEY)

Age: 14.
Rosario: Tall (*1 mark*); blue eyes (*1 mark*).
Her flat: (Very) comfortable.
Where: (Very) near school (*1 mark*); next to a park (*1 mark*).
Father's job: Hairdresser.
Mother's job: Doctor.
Sundays: Go to church (*1 mark*); visit grandparents (*1 mark*).

RECORDING 4 (KEY)

14. (He thinks) it will be great.
15. (She) didn't like S. Seidelman's other film.
16. When it starts.
17. Telephone the cinema.

RECORDING 5 (KEY)

1. 2nd floor.
2. (They have a) view of the sea.
3. 5500 pesetas.
4. It's at 8'oclock.
5. Hot water (*1 mark*); bath(room) (*1 mark*).
6. Opposite dining room.
7. On the table (*1 mark*); near the bed (*1 mark*).
8. Half board or full board?

RECORDING 6 (KEY)

a) (Do you want) red wine (*1 mark*) or white (*1 mark*).
b) Where the Post Office is.
c) When the bank opens.
d) (Have you) anything to declare?
e) (Do you want) anything else?

RECORDING 7 (KEY)

a) The supermarket will close (*1 mark*) in ten minutes (*1 mark*).
b) Go through Gate 9.
c) (It is) 20 minutes (*1 mark*) late (*1 mark*).
d) Swimming costumes (*1 mark*) half price (*1 mark*).
e) Road closed (*1 mark*) because of snow (*1 mark*).

RECORDING 8 (KEY)

1. 3.30.
2. Waiting room.
3. Buy tickets.
4. Where ticket office is.
5. To left of stairs.
6. 4.

RECORDING 9 (KEY)

10. ANY 2 OF: Works with Pedro (*1 mark*);
    Ana's cousin (*1 mark*);
    Introduced Ana and Pedro (*1 mark*).
11. ANY 2 OF: Hard-working (*1 mark*);
    (Rather) serious (*1 mark*);
    Ambitious (*1 mark*);
    Wants to earn a lot (*1 mark*).
12. Amusing (*1 mark*);
    Good friend (*1 mark*).

RECORDING 10 (KEY)

1. Summer.
2. Many records and cassettes (*1 mark*) cheap (*1 mark*).
3. Toys.
4. Books.
5. Sports.

RECORDING 11 (KEY)

6. Before washing.
7. Ham (*1 mark*) omelette (*1 mark*).
8. White.
9. Her husband.
10. A café.
11. Favourite (*1 mark*) restaurant. (*1 mark*)
12. At home.

RECORDING 12 (KEY)

1. (a) (Have you) enough petrol to get to next petrol station?
   (b) Check tyres.
2. Strawberry (*1 mark*); pineapple (*1 mark*).
3. (a) The best.
   (b) Go to the market.
4. (a) Bread sold.
   (b) Shellfish sold.
5. (a) Yesterday.
   (b) Games room.

RECORDING 13 (KEY)

a) 2000 pesetas.
b) No bath or shower.
c)

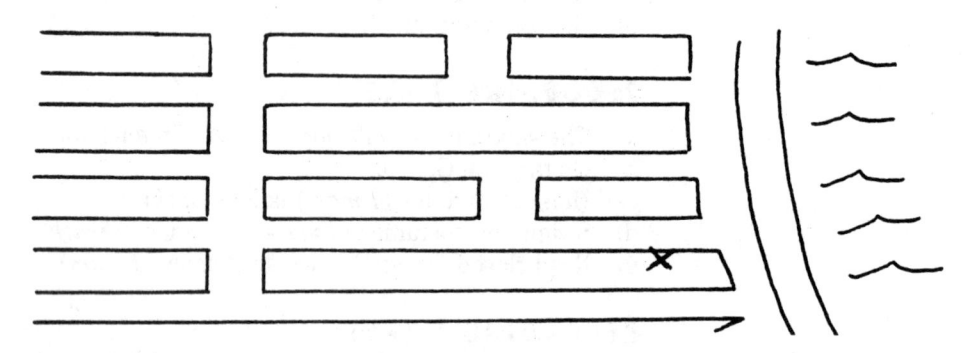

(*1 mark for correct street; 1 mark for correct end and side*)
d) 20 minutes (*1 mark*) on foot (*1 mark*).
e) Soup is cold.
f) Salad.

RECORDING 14 (KEY)

1. Last night.
2. Disco.
3. Yellow shirt.
4. Tonight.
5. His (two) sisters.
6. Cheap (*1 mark*); near the hotel (*1 mark*).
7. Hotel bar (*1 mark*); outside restaurant (*1 mark*).
8. 1 o'clock.

RECORDING 15 (KEY)

20. One day only.
21. 8.30 pm (OR 20.30).
22. 600 pesetas (*1 mark*); 1000 pesetas (*1 mark*).
23. Children under 5.
24. 1 mark each for ANY 2 OF: lions; tigers; elephants; horses; camels.

RECORDING 16 (KEY)

(a) Before (*1 mark*) Wednesday (*1 mark*).
(b) Window (*1 mark*) 5 (*1 mark*).
(c) Post letter (*1 mark*)
    + ANY 2 OF: in letter box (*1 mark*)
                  for urgent (express) letters (*1 mark*)
                  outside (*1 mark*).

RECORDING 17 (KEY)

(a) Railway station.
(b) 500 metres (OR: 500 yards).

(c) Go straight on (*1 mark*)
to end of street (*1 mark*).
It's on the right (*1 mark*).

RECORDING 18 (KEY)

LADY:
vegetable (*1 mark*) soup (*1 mark*)
fish (*1 mark*)
cheese (*1 mark*)
white (*1 mark*) coffee (*1 mark*)

MAN:
mushroom (*1 mark*) soup (*1 mark*)
roast (*1 mark*) chicken (*1 mark*)
chocolate (*1 mark*) ice cream (*1 mark*)
beer (*1 mark*)

A STEP FURTHER

See if you can identify any particular weaknesses in your listening. Many people have difficulty with numbers, prices, times and days of the week. For others the key question words are a problem. Instructions can also cause trouble. Whatever you find is a weakness in your listening, you can enlist the help of a friend to say things to you in Spanish including those particular expressions. The more practice you can be given the sooner you will remedy the weakness. Why not get someone to record a series of your problem expressions for you on a cassette, so that you can practise listening to them on your own?

NB. There is a Review sheet for Basic Listening (and Higher) at the end of Chapter 5

CHAPTER 5

LISTENING: HIGHER LEVEL

- THE HIGHER LISTENING TEST
- THE RECORDINGS
- THE NATURE OF THE QUESTIONS
- ANSWERING THE QUESTIONS
- IMPROVING YOUR LISTENING SKILLS
- TRANSCRIPTS OF THE RECORDINGS
- ANSWER KEY TO PRACTICE QUESTIONS

GETTING STARTED

Higher Level Listening is an optional paper. As with the other optional papers, however, you lose nothing by attempting it. You should have studied the previous chapter on Basic Listening (which you do have to take). The more listening practice you have, the better you will perform, so do take the opportunity to work through the examples in this chapter and recorded on the cassette that can be bought with this book. As with Basic Listening, if you have decided not to buy the cassette, you can ask a friend who speaks Spanish to read the transcripts of the recordings, which you will find towards the end of the chapter.

Doing well in Higher Listening shows you have a good understanding of spoken Spanish.

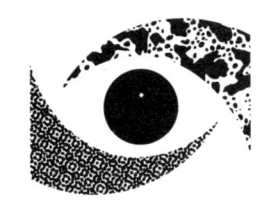

ESSENTIAL PRINCIPLES

1 > THE HIGHER LISTENING TEST

❝ The recordings are longer and cover more topics and skills ❞

The **Higher Listening Test** is similar in form to the Basic Listening, except that the recordings are generally longer, cover a wider range of topics and vocabulary and involve certain extra skills. What was said in the previous chapter about the place where the examination is held applies equally here. Make sure you know where the examination will take place.

There is no substitute for practice in listening, so do make time to use the material in this chapter.

2 > THE RECORDINGS

❝ Native Spanish speakers are used ❞

❝ Sections may be used ❞

As at Basic Level, the recordings are made by native speakers of Spanish, include a limited amount of background noise (in order to sound more realistic), are restricted to the Settings specified in the syllabus and consist of material that was specifically intended to be heard (and was not designed for silent reading). Up to 15% of the words in any recording may be drawn from outside the prescribed list of vocabulary but no questions are set that require understanding of those words.

Although the individual recordings are longer than at Basic level, lasting up to about two minutes (and up to about 150 words), care is taken to ensure that they do not place too much emphasis on memory, and for that reason the longer recordings tend to be split into sections. In some cases you will hear the whole recording first, then each section again with a pause between sections. In other cases the recording is split into sections the first time you hear it, with each section heard twice before you move on to the next. The different Examining Groups tend to have their own preferences about which pattern to use.

What are the other specific features of the Higher Level recordings?

❝ The whole range of the syllabus is used ❞

❝ The speaking is faster ❞

- The Topics covered are from the whole range of the syllabus (where at Basic Level the range was restricted).
- The Vocabulary and Grammar can come fom the whole range of the syllabus.
- The speakers speak faster (and therefore tend to sound more natural).
- There is a variety of 'registers' (the different ways in which people speak, according to the the place they are in and who they are talking to). Examples given in the National Criteria arc the registers used

❝ Different types of 'register' ❞

  – on radio and television
  – in the home
  – in more formal situations
  – by sixteen year olds in Spain

❝ Normal speech is used ❞

Quite often the recordings will include the natural hesitations, repetitions and re-wording that are features of people's normal everyday speech. (Think how often people you know say things like 'um', 'er', 'what I mean is...') Apart from making the speakers sound more natural, these features of speech, when they occur, can in fact be very helpful to you as you listen. Repetition and re-wording obviously are helpful and the hesitations give you more time to note down points you have just heard.

The types of spoken material you will hear are:

❝ Types of spoken material ❞

  – announcements
  – conversations
  – discussions and arguments
  – requests and instructions
  – telephone calls
  – broadcast news items, weather forecasts and traffic reports

– sustained single-voice items (such as tour guides and longer recorded telephone messages)

3 THE NATURE OF THE QUESTIONS

As at Basic Level, the questions are in English (or Welsh) and answers are expressed in English (or Welsh) or by ticking boxes, completing grids or entering the right letter or number in a space.

You are expected to demonstrate understanding of specific details and, in addition, at Higher Level you are expected to be able to

What you are rquired to do

- identify the important points or themes of the material
- identify the attitudes, emotions and ideas of the speakers
- draw conclusions from what you hear
- identify the relationship between ideas expressed

Be selective

These skills imply an ability to select what is relevant and disregard what is irrelevant, when listening to the recordings.

It is obviously a good idea to make sure you know the vocabulary of *emotions and attitudes* (e.g. *triste, alegre, enfadado, le gusta*) but you must bear in mind that a genuine 'Higher Level skills' question does not in fact depend so directly on that vocabulary. If you are asked to identify the emotion of someone who says *Estoy muy contento*, you are really answering a question that tests a specific detail of vocabulary. At Higher Level you may well be asked to identify the emotion expressed in words such as *¡Qué bien! Creí que no te iba a ver*. In this case the word for 'happy' (or possibly 'relieved') has not been said but the emotion has been expressed without it.

Use your imagination

4 ANSWERING THE QUESTIONS

The approach to the questions depends very much on the same principles as in Basic Listening. In summary, you should

You don't need to understand every word

- remember that you do not have to understand every word
- read the settings and the questions carefully before you hear the recordings
- make sure that what you write does actually answer the questions
- answer in English (or Welsh), except in the IGCSE

Be brief and to the point

- answer as briefly as you can while giving all relevant information
- use the mark allocation of each question to work out how much information is required in the answer
- always give an answer

These points are made more fully in Chapter 4.

Remember that the questions about specific detail are normally in the order in which the information occurs in the recording. Questions of the sort that are set only at Higher Level often have to be placed at or near the end of those set on a particular recording, since it is often only when you have heard the whole recording that you can identify the important points, themes, attitudes, emotions or ideas or draw conclusions or identify relationships.

5 IMPROVING YOUR LISTENING SKILLS

The section in Chapter 4 on improving your listening skills is just as valid at Higher Level. If you cope well with Listening at Basic Level but find it difficult at Higher Level, it would certainly be of benefit to you to go back to the section in Chapter 4 and try the techniques suggested there, using the Higher Level recordings for the purpose.

Check back to Chapter 4

QUESTIONS, STUDENTS' ANSWERS, AND EXAMINER'S COMMENTS

Try the questions yourself

Read the setting and questions carefully

You are recommended to try the questions before looking at the students' answers. *Transcripts* of all the recordings are included towards the end of the chapter, so that you can check the wording later. A *key* to the answers follows the transcripts. **Don't be put off by the different question numbers used in the recordings. They correspond with the cassette and are in fact the numbers the questions had when they were used in GCSE examinations**.

Find *Recording 19* on the cassette, then attempt the questions before looking at the student's answers that follow. Remember to read the setting and the question carefully before listening to the recording.

If you do not have the cassette, get a friend to read the transcripts to you for practice

RECORDING 19

■ Read the questions below then play Recording 19 (or listen to your friend read the transcript on page 89).

Your Spanish penfriend's mother tells you about an incident which happened to her last week.

(*a*) What does the mother feel it is important to do when you are in town?
.... (*1*)

(*b*) What happened to her in town last Saturday?
....
.... (*2*)

(*c*) What did she realise when she arrived at the market square?
....
.... (*2*)

(*d*) What comment did the policeman make about incidents of this kind?
....
.... (*2*)
(NICCEA)

STUDENT'S ANSWERS

Section 1

(a) There are a lot of people in the streets.

(b) She had some money stolen.

(c) It was empty

(d) Incidents of this kind are not rare these days.

EXAMINER'S COMMENTS

a) You didn't read the question properly. You were asked what she feels it is important to DO, not to know!
b) You're quite right about something being stolen but *monedero* does not mean 'money' – it means 'purse'. (*1 mark out of 2*)
c) This is fine as far as it goes but what was empty? It reads as though you think the square was empty. (*1 mark out of 2*)
d) Good. You have both the important points (*and both marks*) though you didn't need to write out the first four words of your answer – they are in the question.

CHAPTER 5 LISTENING: HIGHER LEVEL

RECORDING 20

■ Read the questions below then play Recording 20 (or listen to your friend read the transcript on page 89).

You are on an exchange in Spain and you hear a series of conversations over two days between your partner Teresa, and her friend, Rosa.

Listen to their conversations and for each one select from List 1 below, the **topic** which best fits the conversation and write it in the space provided.

(eg The conversation is about **a family illness**.) You will not need to use every word in the list.

Also listen to the conversations and for each one select from List 2 below, the word that best describes the speaker's **attitude**.

(eg The speaker is **happy**.) You will not need to use every word in the list.

You will hear each conversation twice. Now look through the questions.

List 1 – Topics	List 2 – Attitudes
An unexpected journey	happy
A request for help	grateful
A break in routine	worried
A family illness	insistent
A new friend	unsympathetic
An unwillingness to be involved	apologetic
Trouble with parents	jealous

Conversation 1
Rosa is talking to Teresa.
1 Here, Rosa is talking about .... (1)
2 She is .... (1)

Conversation 2
Teresa replies to what Rosa has said.
3 Here, Teresa is talking about .... (1)
4 She is .... (1)

Conversation 3
Rosa replies to what Teresa has said.
5 Here, Rosa is talking about .... (1)
6 She is .... (1)

Conversation 4
The following day, Teresa again talks to Rosa.
7 Here, Teresa is talking about .... (1)
8 She is .... (1)

Conversation 5
Rosa replies to what Teresa has said.
9 Here, Rosa is talking about .... (1)
10 She is .... (1)

(MEG)

STUDENT'S ANSWERS

Conversation 1
Rosa is talking to Teresa.
1 Here, Rosa is talking about *a family illness* .... (1)
2 She is *worried* .... (1)

Conversation 2
Teresa replies to what Rosa has said.
3 Here, Teresa is talking about *unwillingness to be involved* .... (1)
4 She is *unsympathetic* .... (1)

Conversation 3
Rosa replies to what Teresa has said.

5 Here, Rosa is talking about ...... a request for help .... (1)
6 She is ...... apologetic .... (1)

Conversation 4
The following day, Teresa again talks to Rosa.
7 Here, Teresa is talking about ...... a break in routine .... (1)
8 She is ...... apologetic .... (1)

Conversation 5
Rosa replies to what Teresa has said.
9 Here, Rosa is talking about ...... a new friend .... (1)
10 She is ...... jealous .... (1)

EXAMINER'S COMMENTS

1 Presumably you have jumped to a conclusion about why Jaime has not been in touch but he is not in the family and there is no evidence he is ill. We just do not know yet why he is not following the routine.
2, 3, 4 and 5 are fine.
6 People often do apologise when asking for help but listen carefully – Rosa doesn't. But she does repeat herself (*Llámale*) and she does emphasize her past help for Teresa.
7 This is unfortunate. In a sense it is true but you were supposed to use this answer for Q.1! If you had been right on Q.1 you might have given the right answer here. This question is about going to France at short notice (an unexpected journey).
8 Good – but it is just as well on this occasion that you didn't reject 'apologetic' because you had already used it! (Normally you should expect to use each answer once only.)
9 Good.
10 Wrong. You may think Teresa could be jealous that Rosa is going out with Alejandro but you were asked about the attitude of Rosa (the speaker).

PRACTICE QUESTIONS

You can find answers to the following PRACTICE QUESTIONS at the end of the chapter.

RECORDING 21

■ Read the questions below then play Recording 21 (or listen to your friend read the transcript on page 89)

5 Whilst watching television at your friend's house in Spain, you hear a review of a film to be shown later that evening.

   (a) Briefly state the plot of the film.
   ....
   .... (4)

   (b) Is the review favourable or unfavourable? Give a reason for your decision.
   ....
   .... (3)
   (WJEC)

RECORDING 22

■ Read the questions below then play Recording 22 (or listen to your friend read the transcript on page 89).

Question 1, 2, 3, 4 and 5 – *At the beginning of a family visit to Spain your father, who doesn't speak Spanish, asks you to go to a bank to find out about obtaining Spanish* *money. Below is a list of the things he wants you to find out. Listen to what a Spanish bank clerk tells you and write down what your father wants to know.*

THINGS TO FIND OUT		
1.	What is the easiest way of obtaining Spanish money?	(2)
2.	What about travellers' cheques?	(2)
3.	How can I use a credit card?	(3)
4.	When do I pay the credit card bill?	(1)
5.	What if I don't speak Spanish?	(2)

(Sub-total for questions 1-5: 10 marks)
(SEG)

RECORDING 23

■ Read the questions below then play Recording 23 (or listen to your friend read the transcript on page 90).

A group of Spanish schoolchildren who are taking part in an exchange with your school are being asked about their impressions of England by your Spanish teacher.

Look at comments A-F below.

Now listen to each conversation and next to each person's name, write a letter to show which comment applies most aptly to him or her. You will not need to use all the comments. You will hear all the conversations twice. You will hear what María says twice, then what Pablo says twice and so on.

A Could not live in England.
B Admires the English countryside.
C Says that there are not enough facilities for young people in England.
D Says England is preferable to Spain and would like to live here.
E Has not had enough time here to form an opinion.
F Thinks English people are very nice.

1 María ....
2 Pablo ....
3 Teresa ....
4 José ....
5 Conchita ....

(5)
(MEG)

RECORDING 24

■ Read the questions below then play Recording 24 (or listen to your friend read the transcript on page 90).

ANSWER-PHONE

Questions 16–20 are based on a longer passage. This passage is divided into three sections. Questions 16 and 17, Questions 18 and 19, and Question 20. Candidates will hear the whole passage once. Each section will then be heard again.

Your parents have found the following recorded message from a Spanish friend on their answer-phone. The message is quite urgent: you help them to pick out the important points.

Questions 16 and 17

Question 16
Where did Mariano find your home telephone number? Give **two** details.

....
.... (2)

Question 17
Why was Mariano away from home last week?
.... (1)

Questions 18 and 19

Question 18
Where is he being sent to in Madrid?
.... (1)

Question 19
What is the reason for the move?
.... (1)

Question 20

Why can't your parents phone Mariano at his home immediately? Give full details.
.... (1)

(ULEAC)

RECORDING 25

■ Read the questions below then play Recording 25 (or listen to your friend read the transcript on page 90).

While on a camping holiday in Spain you are asked to help another English-speaking family who require the services of a local doctor for one of their children. You listen to what the doctor has to say.

(*a*) What has happened to the boy?
....
.... (2)

(*b*) How does the doctor say he will treat him?
....
.... (2)

(*c*) Why, according to the doctor, are children liable to have this kind of accident?
....
.... (3)

(NICCEA)

RECORDING 26

■ Read the questions below then play Recording 26 (or listen to your friend read the transcript on page 90).

Questions 16, 17, 18, 19 and 20 – *You are staying with a Spanish family in Valencia, and they are considering going out for a meal. They are looking at this advertisement for a restaurant in Playa Estaño and you are listening to their conversation. Study the advertisement and answer the questions which follow.*

Restaurante NOGUERA

CON UNA TERRAZA JUNTO AL MAR Y GRAN SALON PARA BANQUETES (PIDANOS PRESUPUESTO)

LE SUGERIMOS NUESTRAS ESPECIALIDADES EN ARROCES, PESCADO FRESCO Y CARNES.

RESTAURATE NOGUERA
VALENCIA POR LA COSTA
DENIA
NOVA DENIA

PLAYA ESTAÑO
Teléfono 578 01 07 - Denia

16. Why does the mother think this restaurant is so suitable in the present weather conditions?
   ....
   ....
   .... (3)

17. How do you know that the father wants to spend a very relaxed sort of day?
   ....
   ....
   .... (2)

18. Why does the father suggest that his **son** should telephone the restaurant?
   ....
   .... (3)

19. Why ought the family to have known that the restaurant would not suit their daughter?
   ....
   ....
   .... (3)

20. Why do you think the daughter is being sarcastic to her mother when she calls her *simpática*?

CHAPTER 5 **PRACTICE QUESTIONS** 85

....
.... *(2)*

(Sub-total for questions 16-20: 13 marks)
(SEG)

RECORDING 27

■ Read the questions below then play Recording 27 (or listen to your friend read the transcript on page 91).

Your school has invited in three Spanish speakers, María, Juanita and Nicolau to answer a few questions.

Your teacher asks what the speakers think of living in England.

7   (a) How has Nicolau found life in England?
.... *(1)*
   (b) Give **two** reasons for your answer
      (i) ....
      (ii) .... *(2)*

8   What has been María's experience of life in England?
.... *(1)*

9   What were **two** of her problems?
      (i) ....
      (ii) .... *(2)*

10 What **two** reasons does María give for wanting to return to Chile?
      (i) ....
      (ii) .... *(2)*

Now your teacher asks Juanita about her life here.
11 What does Juanita say about her friends? Mention **two** things.
      (i) ....
      (ii) .... *(2)*
(NEAB)

RECORDING 28

■ Read the questions below then play Recording 28 (or listen to your friend read the transcript on page 91).

Your school has invited three Spanish speakers to answer a few questions. Nicolau is from Mallorca.

Your teacher asks Nicolau about life in Mallorca.

13 (a) What overall effect does Nicolau think tourism has on Mallorca?
.... *(1)*
   (b) State **two** of the reasons that he gives.
      (i) ....
      (ii) .... *(2)*

14 Why does he prefer to live in England?
      (i) ....
      (ii) .... *(2)*

15 Nicolau explains what "sobrasada" is. How does he describe it? Mention **two** things.
      (i) ....
      (ii) .... *(2)*

Your teacher has read something about Mallorca in the newspaper and asks Nicolau about it.

16 (a) How do politicians intend to solve the economic crisis in Mallorca?
....
.... (1)

(b) How does Nicolau feel about the politicians' plans?
....
.... (2)

(NEAB)

RECORDING 29

■ Read the questions below then play Recording 29 (or listen to your friend read the transcript on page 92).

Your teacher has received recordings from five Spanish students who are looking for exchange partners. They are called:

María,
Rosario,
Conchita,
Isabel and
Ana

Six pupils at your school are interested. Their names and interests are listed below.

Listen to the recordings and match each Spanish student with the pupil who has the most in common with her.

As there are only five Spanish students, you will have to leave one of the spaces blank.

You will hear each recording twice. You will hear María twice, then Rosario twice and so on. Now read through the questions.

| **Catherine** | Name of Spanish Student |
| Likes pets, exercise and meeting people. | .... |

| **Clare** | Name of Spanish Student |
| Likes travelling and learning Spanish. | .... |

| **Elizabeth** | Name of Spanish Student |
| Likes all sports, going to discos, but hates school. | .... |

| **Caroline** | Name of Spanish Student |
| Likes going out with boys and loves the theatre. She also likes cycling. | .... |

| **Charlotte** | Name of Spanish Student |
| At home, she has her own horse and swimming pool. | .... |

| **Elaine** | Name of Spanish Student |
| Enjoys her school-work, especially English. | .... |

(5)
(MEG)

RECORDING 30

- Read the questions below then play Recording 30 (or listen to your friend read the transcript on page 92).
4. You are on a tour of the north coast of Spain with a Spanish coach company. You have arrived at the town of Castro Urdiales. Your guide, Javier, gives you information and instructions before you leave the coach. At the end of his talk a lady passenger asks him a question. Your father who does not speak Spanish asks you to tell him the main points of the guide's talk. It is divided into two parts.

PART ONE

(a) What does the guide insist on and why?
....
.... (2)

(b) What does he suggest if people lose their way?
....
.... (2)

(c) Why is the cathedral of historic interest?
.... (1)

PART TWO

(d) What may be dangerous and why?
....
.... (3)

(e) What are the reasons for the lady's question?
.... (2)

(f) What will she find in La Calle de la Luz?
....
.... (2)

(WJEC)

RECORDING 31

- Read the questions below then play Recording 31 (or listen to your friend read the transcript on page 93).

PERSONAL PROBLEMS

On Spanish radio, you hear a phone-in programme in which worried teenagers tell an 'Agony Aunt' about their problems. A girl describes her boyfriend problem.

Questions 12 and 13

Question 12
What exactly is Angustias complaining about? Give full details.
....
.... (2)

Question 13
Why does her father treat her like this? Give full details.
....
....
.... (3)

Questions 14 and 15

Question 14
According to the 'Agony Aunt', what might change Angustias' parents' opinion of Andrés?
....(1)

Question 15
What should Angustias' boyfriend do? Give all relevant details.
....
....(2)

(ULEAC)

RECORDING 32

- Read the questions below then play Recording 32 (or listen to your friend read the transcript on page 93).

You are on an exchange in Spain and you hear a series of conversations over two days involving your partner, José Luis, his parents and his friend Rafael.

Listen to their conversations and for each one, select from List 1 below, the **topic** which best fits the conversations and write it in the space provided.
(eg The conversation is about **approval of a new situation**.) You will not need to use every topic in the list.

Also, listen to the conversations and for each one select from List 2 below the word that best decribes the speaker's **attitude**.
(eg The speaker is **helpful**.) You will not need to use every word in the list.

You will hear each conversation twice. Now read through the questions.

List 1 – Topics	List 2 – Attitudes
approval of a new situation	helpful
receiving a present	undecided
a suggested solution	disapproving
a family illness	jealous
work before pleasure	proud
coming to a decision	grateful

Conversation 1
José Luis's mother is talking to you.
1 Here the mother is talking about .... (1)
2 She is .... (1)

Conversation 2
José Luis is talking to his friend, Rafael.
3 Here, José Luis is talking about .... (1)
4 He is .... (1)

Conversation 3
José Luis's mother is talking to José Luis.
5 Here, the mother is talking about .... (1)
6 She is .... (1)

Conversation 4
Rafael is talking to José Luis.
7 Here, Rafael is talking about .... (1)
8 He is .... (1)

Conversation 5
José Luis's mother is talking to her husband.
9 Here, the mother is talking about ....(*1*)
10 She is .... (*1*)
(10)
(MEG)

6 TRANSCRIPTS OF THE RECORDINGS

RECORDING 19 (TRANSCRIPT)

Mira. Quiero decirte algo. Con tanta gente en las calles, es importante tener cuidado. El sábado pasado alguien me robó el monedero, lo que me asustó mucho. ¡Fíjate! Y ¡en el mismo centro de la ciudad! Antes de llegar a la plaza del mercado lo tenía en un bolsillo pero, una vez allí, me di cuenta de que estaba vacío. Cuando fui a la comisaría, un policía me aseguró que cosas así no son raras hoy en día.

RECORDING 20 (TRANSCRIPT)

Conversation 1.
Bueno, Teresa, me parece que las cosas no van bien. Ya sabes que llevo tres meses saliendo con Jaime. Me llamaba cada noche y los viernes y los sábados salíamos a los bares, a un cine, cualquier cosa. Pero el fin de semana pasado no llamó y no salimos. Esta semana no ha llamado, ni una vez. Estoy muy preocupada.

Conversation 2.
Oye, Rosa, lo de tu novio... Mira, yo tengo mis propios problemas con mis estudios y todo. No me aburras. ¿Qué puedo hacer yo? Siempre es igual contigo y tus chicos. Siempre hay drama. Siempre hay algo. Déjame en paz ¿quieres?

Conversation 3.
Pero, Teresa, tienes que ayudarme. Tienes que hacer algo. ¿No te ayudé yo
con tu problema con Enrique? Ya nos conocemos mucho tiempo, amiga. Me debes muchos favores. Ya sabes que conoces a un amigo de Jaime. Conoces a Francisco ¿no? Llámale a ver si él sabe lo que ha pasado, por favor, Teresa. Llámale.

Conversation 4.
Hola, Rosa. Esto... lo que ocurrió ayer... lo que dije, lo siento mucho. Mira, llamé al amigo de Jaime ayer para preguntar qué le pasaba. Jaime se ha ido a Francia. Su tío iba a Francia de negocios. En el último momento invitó a Jaime a ir con él. Jaime no tuvo tiempo para llamar a nadie. ¡Qué tonta soy! ¿Me perdonas, Rosa?

Conversation 5.
Teresa, escucha, una gran noticia. Anoche fui a la discoteca en la calle Mayor ... «La Mariposa» ¿sabes? Y ¿sabes quién estaba allí? Pues, Alejandro. Tú lo conoces: el hermano de Conchita. Pues, cuando entré, me invitó a bailar. Bailamos juntos toda la tarde y esta tarde vamos a un restaurante. ¿Qué dices, Teresa?

RECORDING 21 (TRANSCRIPT)

Question 5.
El Asalto de los Hombres Pájaro
   Esta película trata del secuestro de un hombre de negocios norteamericano en España por un grupo de terroristas.
   El único atractivo de esta película son las espectaculares escenas aéreas. Son emocionantes en el cine pero poco interesantes en la pequeña pantalla.

RECORDING 22 (TRANSCRIPT)

Bueno, aquí en el Banco de Castilla hay tres posibilidades. El método más sencillo es éste. Tu padre puede venir con dinero inglés – es decir, con libras esterlinas – y puede cambiar esas libras en pesetas.
   Si no tiene bastante dinero inglés, supongo que ya habrá obtenido los cheques de viaje en Inglaterra. Pero hay que recordar que con los cheques tiene que traer su pasaporte, porque sin el pasaporte no podrá obtener el dinero español que desea.
   La tercera manera de obtener pesetas en este banco es con una tarjeta de crédito como Visa o Mastercard. Cuando el banco está abierto con una de estas tarjetas puede

obtener pesetas aquí dentro. Otra ventaja de estas tarjetas es que cuando está cerrado hay una máquina donde puede meter la tarjeta y recibir dinero español automáticamente. Y no tendrá que pagar hasta volver a Inglaterra.

Una cosa más. No tendrás que acompañar a tu padre cuando venga a servirse de la máquina automática, porque puede hacerlo todo en inglés.

RECORDING 23 (TRANSCRIPT)

Number 1.
A: Bueno, María ¿cuál es tu opinión de Inglaterra?
M: Pues, lo que más me gusta es lo verde que es el campo. Con el clima que hay aquí, todo parece tan fresco, los árboles, la hierba. En casa todo es tan seco.

Number 2.
A: Y tú, Pablo, ¿cuál es tu opinión de Inglaterra?
P: Pues, a mí me encanta la gente aquí. He hecho muchos amigos y todos parecen muy simpáticos. Todos han sido tan amables con nosotros. Y por eso nuestra visita ha sido un éxito.

Number 3.
A: Y Teresa, ¿cuál es tu opinión de Inglaterra?
T: Bueno, con la lluvia y todo, me parece un país bastante triste. Me hace falta la alegría española. Por dos semanas la vida aquí es tolerable, pero después de dos semanas no puedo más. Tengo unas ganas de volver a España.

Number 4.
A: Bueno, José, ¿qué piensas de Inglaterra?
J: Dos semanas es muy poco tiempo. Conozco a diez o doce ingleses, nada más. Conozco una sola región de Inglaterra. Para conocer Inglaterra y tener una opinión hay que estar en Inglaterra mucho más tiempo.

Number 5.
A: Y Conchita, ¿cuál es tu opinión de Inglaterra?
C: Es que en España salimos mucho mucho. Los jóvenes españoles tenemos muchas cosas que hacer por la tarde: discotecas, clubs, bares, bailes y mucho más. Aquí en Inglaterra los jóvenes se aburren. Aquí hasta los bares están prohibidos a los jóvenes.

RECORDING 24 (TRANSCRIPT)

Questions 16 and 17
Pues, soy Mariano López, y os llamo desde Sevilla. Encontré vuestro número de teléfono en la guía telefónica cuando estaba en Londres la semana pasada en viaje de negocios.

Questions 18 and 19
Lo que pasa es que la empresa donde trabajo – me va a mandar a la oficina central allá en Madrid. En efecto voy a ser jefe de la Sección de Exportación. Os llamo para daros mi nueva dirección para que podáis mandarme los documentos que os pedí.

Mis señas serán: Avenida de Italia – 14, Sexto B, Madrid. No olvidéis el código postal que es – vamos a ver – 28033.

Question 20
Si queréis alguna vez llamarme por teléfono, no me llaméis a la oficina, sino a casa. A partir de la semana que viene mi número personal será el 413–65–82, con el prefijo 91.

RECORDING 25 (TRANSCRIPT)

Mire, afortunadamente, no es muy grave. Se ha cortado el pie, nada más. Le pondré una venda y le daré unas aspirinas. Me parece que ha pisado una botella rota o algo así. Siempre pasa igual. A los niños les gusta quitarse los zapatos cuando juegan.

RECORDING 26 (TRANSCRIPT)

Mamá – Pues yo pienso que sería muy buen sitio adonde ir. El restaurante está en la costa misma, y con este calor que hace, lo mejor para nosotros sería sentarnos a comer al aire libre en la terraza del restaurante.

Papá – Sí, yo estoy de acuerdo con vuestra mamá. Me gusta la idea de estar sentado dos o tres horas pero no en un comedor con mucha gente. Y además, después de comer podemos ir a echarnos la siesta en la playa.

Hijo – Pero, papá, ponen aquí en el papelito las especialidades y no dicen nada de postres. Tú sabes cuánto me gustan. ¿No podemos ir a otro sitio donde ofrezcan postres especiales?

Papá – Mira, hijo, estoy seguro de que los habrá, sólo que no lo ponen en el anuncio. Si te interesan tanto, puedes telefonear al restaurante para preguntarles qué clase de postres tienen. Tienes el número allí al pie del anuncio.

Hija – No vale la pena. Yo no quiero ir allí tampoco. ¿No os acordáis de que anoche decidí que no iba a comer más carne, ni pescado, ni nada que provenga de los animales? Tenemos que buscar un restaurante vegetariano.

Mamá – ¡Qué va! Eso sí que sería difícil. No, si no quieres comer con nosotros, puedes llevarte el traje de baño, y puedes ir a nadar en el mar mientras nosotros comamos en el Noguera.

Hija – ¡Qué simpática eres, mamá!

RECORDING 27 (TRANSCRIPT)

7 F   Bueno, vamos a empezar con las preguntas serias. Me gustaría preguntaros a los tres ¿qué opináis de la vida en Inglaterra?
   M   A mí, desde que he llegado todo me ha ido muy bien. La verdad es que no puedo quejarme de nada. Yo venía un poco asustado, pero nada . . ., la gente es muy simpática y muy educada, todo el mundo te ayuda, . . . tengo muchos amigos, todo parece muy organizado. A mí me encanta todo eso de las reuniones sociales y de tomar el té con galletitas. Si me dejan me quedo a vivir aquí.

8 F   Mi opinión es muy diferente. La verdad es que yo he tenido aquí una vida muy difícil. Creo que yo no he visto la mejor cara de Inglaterra. No me sorprende lo que dice Nicolau, pero para mí la vida aquí ha sido muy dura.

9 F₁ ¿Por qué dices que tenías una vida muy difícil?
   F₂ Mira, al principio vivía del la seguridad social. Mi problema principal era encontrar trabajo. Además, vivía sola con mis dos hijas, y no es fácil, eso lo sabe todo el mundo. Ahora estoy mejor. Mis hijas ya van al colegio y tengo un buen empleo.

10 F₁ Y, a pesar de estar mejor, ¿quieres volver?
   F₂ Sí, siempre me imagino que la vida en Chile debe ser mejor. Y tengo a toda mi familia allí.
   F₁ Entonces, ¿por qué viniste?
   F₂ Fue en 1973, por motivos políticos.

11 F₁ Y tú, Juanita ¿Cómo es tu vida?
   F₂ Voy a un instituto muy bueno en el que hay muy buen ambiente. Estudiamos mucho, pero también salimos mucho. Todos nos llevamos muy bien. Yo creo que la amistad es lo más importante en la vida. Ahora, además, tengo novio y es un momento muy emocionante de mi vida.

RECORDING 28 (TRANSCRIPT)

13 F   Y, oye Nicolau, ¿podrías hablarnos de la vida en Mallorca? ¿Es todo tan fantástico como dicen los folletos turísticos?

fantástico como dicen los folletos turísticos?

    M Claro, naturalmente. Mallorca es el centro del mundo, es extraordinaria. Por eso todo el mundo quiere ir a Mallorca. Y aquí es donde está el problema. Hay desmasiadas urbanizaciones, demasiada gente, demasiada contaminación. Poco a poco se va destruyendo la belleza natural. Es posible que ya no haya solución.

14 F Entonces ¿no te gusta mucho vivir allí?
    M Pues la verdad es que no. Además, Inglaterra tiene un clima maravilloso para la gente a quien le gusta la lectura y el estudio, porque el sitio donde se está mejor es en las bibliotecas. Y aquí las bibliotecas son muy buenas comparadas con las de España... yo me paso la vida allí.

15 F Y no echas de menos nada de Mallorca?
    M Pues la verdad es que no. Bueno, quizás a veces la sobrasada.
    F ¿La sobra... qué?
    M La sobrasada, es una especie de chorizo, es un chorizo más grueso y blando que se puede poner en el pan como si fuese mantequilla.

16 F Oye, Nicolau, yo he leído en los periódicos que la economía de Mallorca está muy mal ¿Es verdad?
    M Pues no sé, dicen que sí, Dicen que hay una crisis bastante grave en el sector turístico. Yo no sé si es verdad. Para que la gente no se asuste y para ganar elecciones, los políticos dicen que van a crear un turismo de gente más rica que dejará más dinero en la isla. Dicen que construirán muchos campos de golf y que vendrá la gente rica de la jet set. Que hagan lo que quieran. Yo con mis libros tengo bastante.

RECORDING 29 (TRANSCRIPT)

1st recording
Hola. Me llamo María. Voy a presentarme. Tengo quince años y tres hermanos. Me gusta el baloncesto y me gusta bailar. No me gustan mis estudios. Prefiero salir.

2nd recording
Hola. Me llamo Rosario. Estoy buscando una inglesa simpática con quien pueda pasar dos semanas. Me gusta le equitación y la natación. Voy al cine cuando tengo dinero.

3rd recording
Buenos días. Me llamo Conchita. Vivo en una casa grande en el campo. Me encanta la lectura. Incluso leo las obras de autores británicos. Me gustan todas mis asignaturas en el colegio. No salgo mucho.

4th recording
Hola. ¿Qué tal? Me llamo Isabel. Tengo ganas de visitar Inglaterra. Me gusta estar al aire libre. Todas las mañanas me levanto temprano y doy un paseo con mi perro. Soy miembro de muchos clubs y conozco a mucha gente. Me encantaría conocer a una inglesa como yo.

5th recording
Buenos días. Me llamo Ana. Lo que más me interesa es aprender idiomas y conocer las culturas de otros países. Mis padres me han llevado a muchos sitios en el extranjero. Ahora quiero conocer Inglaterra.

RECORDING 30 (TRANSCRIPT)

Question 4

PART ONE

Señoras y señores vamos a pasar dos horas aquí en la hermosa cuidad de Castro Urdiales, pero es esencial que vuelvan Vds al autocar a las 4 y media ya que luego nos queda un viaje de 2 horas para llegar a Santander.

Nos encontramos en la Plaza de España y enfrente del parking verán Vds el Ayuntamiento así que, si tienen que preguntar para volver al autocar, sólo hay que buscar el Ayuntamiento, repito el Ayuntamiento.

En Castro Urdiales hay una catedral (Gótica) que se encuentra en la parte vieja de la ciudad. Es de interés histórico porque data del siglo doce. Hay también un museo de arte y el castillo.

PART TWO

Para los jóvenes hay un puerto pesquero y un puerto deportivo y si quieren bañarse la Playa de los Estudiantes se encuentra al final del Paseo Marítimo. Pero – CUIDADO – porque a veces el mar puede resultar peligroso sobre todo cuando hay viento del norte como hoy.

[LADY SPEAKS]
Perdón Javier, yo no tengo ganas de nadar ni de ver monumentos – ¿puedes decirme dónde se encuentran las mejores tiendas, sobre todo las que venden cosas típicas de la región?

[JAVIER]
Sí, señora. Vaya por la Calle de Santiago hasta la Plaza Mayor – tuerza a la izquierda y en la Calle de la Luz encontrará Vd varias tiendas que le pueden interesar y además hoy hay mercado al aire libre. Y no olviden Vds que saldremos a las 4 y media en punto.

RECORDING 31 (TRANSCRIPT)

Questions 12 and 13
Y ahora vamos a escuchar a una chica que tiene un problema – Angustias, que vive en Jaén. Dime, Angustias, ¿qué te pasa?

Buenas tardes, Tía Dolores. Pues, es que mi padre no me deja salir sola con mi novio desde que, sin el permiso de mis padres, mi hermana mayor fue a vivir con un chico que no les gusta. Pero mi novio, Andrés, es un chico formal y trabajador.

Questions 14 and 15
Bueno, ¿por qué no le invitas a tu novio a conocer a tus padres, para que vean cómo es en realidad? El chico puede regalar a tu madre unas flores... o unos caramelos.

RECORDING 32 (TRANSCRIPT)

Conversation 1
Huy, ¿cómo sabías que me gustan tanto las joyas, y sobre todo el oro? ¿De verdad es para mí? Fenomenal. Debe ser de parte de tus padres, ¿no? Voy a escribirles para decirles cuánto me encanta.

Conversation 2
Mira, Rafael. Si no le hablo, si no salgo con ella, sabes qué pasará, ¿no? Va a salir con otro. Y luego habré perdido la oportunidad. Lo que dices es la verdad. Mis padres van a enfadarse, como tengo tantos deberes, pero tengo que hacer algo. Ahora, no sé qué hacer.

Conversation 3
José Luis, no puede ser. ¿No te acuerdas lo que te ha dicho tu padre? Ya sabes que tienes que levantarte muy de mañana para ir al colegio. Y tienes tanto que hacer para tus exámenes. Aún eres muy joven para esto, José Luis.

Conversation 4
Bueno, me parece que tienes problemas, José Luis. Pero, quizás, no son tan grandes. Escucha. Te voy a proponer una cosa. Si tus padres conocieran a esta chica, a lo mejor les encantaría. ¿Por qué no la invitas a tu casa? Puedes decir a tus padres que ella va a ayudarte con tu inglés, como ellos no saben nada de inglés.... Así que puedes estar con ella y tus padres estarán contentos a la vez.

Conversation 5
Oye, ¿sabes una cosa? En lo de anoche, la visita de aquella chica. ¿Sabes? Siento

y divertirse a la vez. Los dos se entienden tan bien. Y ella es tan simpática. Y cuando salieron juntos a la cocina para hablar inglés, me sentí tan orgullosa de mi hijo.

7 › ANSWER KEY TO PRACTICE QUESTIONS

RECORDING 19 (KEY)

a) Be careful (Take care)
b) Someone stole (*1 mark*) her purse (*1 mark*)
c) Her pocket (*1 mark*) was empty (*1 mark*)
d) They are not unusual (*1 mark*) these days (*1 mark*)

RECORDING 20 (KEY)

1 a break in routine
2 worried
3 an unwillingness to be involved
4 unsympathetic
5 a request for help
6 insistent
7 an unexpected journey
8 apologetic
9 a new friend
10 happy

RECORDING 21 (KEY)

a) Kidnapping
   by terrorists
   + ANY 2 OF: (of) American
                   businessman
                   in Spain

b) Unfavourable
   Only one attractive feature
   (Exciting in cinema but) not interesting on TV.

RECORDING 22 (KEY)

1 Change (or take) (*1 mark*) English money (*1 mark*)
2 Cannot be cashed (*1 mark*) without passport (*1 mark*)
   OR can be cashed (*1 mark*) with passport (*1 mark*)
3 To get money in the bank (*1 mark*) or at cashpoint (machine) (*1 mark*) when the bank is closed (*1 mark*)
4 When you return to England
5 Can operate the machine (*1 mark*) in English (*1 mark*)

RECORDING 23 (KEY)

1 B
2 F
3 A
4 E
5 C

RECORDING 24 (KEY)

16 Telephone directory (*1 mark*) in London (*1 mark*)
17 Travelling on business
18 Head office (Central office)
19 To be Head of Exports (Department)
20 The number operates from next week

RECORDING 25 (KEY)

a) Has cut (*1 mark*) his foot (*1 mark*)
b) A bandage (*1 mark*) and some aspirins (*1 mark*)
c) They like to take off *(1 mark)* their shoes (*1 mark*) when playing (*1 mark*)

RECORDING 26 (KEY)

16 It's on the coast
     You can eat in open air (OR It has a terrace)
     The weather is hot

17 Plans 2-3 hours for meal
     (and) siesta (on beach)

18 Son is keen on desserts
     He can ask
     what sort they have (not mentioned in advert)

19 She told them
     she had decided
     to eat no more meat or fish (OR to be a vegetarian).

20 Her mother said she could go to the beach (or not go to the restaurant)
     while they have the meal.

RECORDING 27 (KEY)

7 (a) It's gone well OR No complaints
   (b) ANY 2 OF: People are (very) friendly
                       Everyone helps
                       He has many friends
                       All seems well organized
                       He likes tea parties

8 Very difficult (OR very hard)

9 ANY 2 OF: Had to live on Social Security
              Could not find work
              Lived alone with 2 daughters

10 Thinks life is (must be) better there
     Her family is there

11 ANY 2 OF: They study a lot
               They go out a lot
               They get on very well together

RECORDING 28 (KEY)

13 (a) It is destroying the natural beauty
    (b) ANY 2 OF: Too many housing developments (OR too much building)
                        Too many people
                        Too much pollution

14 Good climate for study
     Good libraries

15 ANY 2 OF: Salami-type sausage
              fatter than others
              soft
              can be spread on bread (like butter)

16 (a) Create tourism for the rich
    (b) He doesn't care (They can do what they like)
        His books are what matter

RECORDING 29 (KEY)

Catherine: Isabel
Clare: Ana
Elizabeth: María
Caroline: –
Charlotte: Rosario
Elaine: Conchita

RECORDING 30 (KEY)

a) Being back at 4.30
    2-hour journey (to Santander)

b) Ask for (OR look for)
    Town Hall

c) (Dates from) 12th century
d) Bathing
   in the sea
   Wind is from the north
e) Not interested in swimming
   nor in (seeing) monuments
f) shops
   (open air) market

RECORDING 31 (KEY)

12 Not allowed to go out alone (*1 mark*) with boyfriend (*1 mark*)
13 Her (elder) sister went to live with a boy (*1 mark*)
    her parents did not like (*1 mark*)
    without their permission (*1 mark*)
14 Meeting him
15 Give her mother (*1 mark*)
    some flowers or sweets (*1 mark*)

RECORDING 32 (KEY)

1   receiving a present
2   grateful
3   coming to a decision
4   undecided
5   work before pleasure
6   disapproving
7   a suggested solution
8   helpful
9   approval of a new situation
10 proud

A STEP FURTHER

In order to deal effectively with questions about attitudes and emotions, it is a good idea to make a list of several different attitudes and emotions. Then note down next to each the Spanish word that describes it (e.g. *simpático, tranquilo, trabajador, contento, triste*). Next, you should think of the sort of sentences that might be used in Spanish by someone displaying each of those attitudes and emotions – but take care *not* to use the specific word you listed before. For example, you might write down 'worried' and then the Spanish word *preocupado*. You then need to write a sentence, or possibly two, such as *¡Ay! ¡Qué problema! Yo no sé lo que va a pasar.*

REVIEW SHEETS: LISTENING (BASIC AND HIGHER LEVELS)

Play each of the first **twenty** recordings again, listen carefully, then try to write some **different questions** of your own. You can then try to answer the questions you have set. You can try these extra questions on a friend; alternatively your friend can write the extra questions and try them on you. (*Note*: Recordings 1 to 18 cover the material in the Basic Listening chapter)

RECORDING 1
Q1 _____
Answer ....
Q2 _____
Answer ....
Q3 _____
Answer ....

RECORDING 2
Q1 _____
Answer ....
Q2 _____
Answer ....
Q3 _____
Answer ....

RECORDING 3
Q1 _____
Answer ....
Q2 _____
Answer ....
Q3 _____
Answer ....

RECORDING 4
Q1 _____
Answer ....
Q2 _____
Answer ....
Q3 _____
Answer ....

RECORDING 5
Q1 _____
Answer ....
Q2 _____
Answer ....
Q3 _____
Answer ....

RECORDING 6
Q1 _____
Answer ....
Q2 _____
Answer ....
Q3 _____
Answer ....

RECORDING 7
Q1 _____
Answer ....
Q2 _____
Answer ....
Q3 _____
Answer ....

RECORDING 8
Q1 _____
Answer ....
Q2 _____
Answer ....
Q3 _____
Answer ....

RECORDING 9
Q1 _____
Answer ....
Q2 _____
Answer ....
Q3 _____
Answer ....

RECORDING 10
Q1 _____
Answer ....
Q2 _____
Answer ....
Q3 _____
Answer ....

RECORDING 11
Q1 _____
Answer ....
Q2 _____
Answer ....
Q3 _____
Answer ....

RECORDING 12
Q1 _____
Answer ....
Q2 _____
Answer ....
Q3 _____
Answer ....

RECORDING 13
Q1 _____
Answer ....
Q2 _____
Answer ....
Q3 _____
Answer ....

RECORDING 14
Q1 _____
Answer ....
Q2 _____
Answer ....
Q3 _____
Answer ....

RECORDING 15
Q1 _____
Answer ....
Q2 _____
Answer ....
Q3 _____
Answer ....

RECORDING 16
Q1 _____
Answer ....
Q2 _____
Answer ....
Q3 _____
Answer ....

RECORDING 17
Q1 _____
Answer ....
Q2 _____
Answer ....
Q3 _____
Answer ....

RECORDING 18
Q1 _____
Answer ....
Q2 _____
Answer ....
Q3 _____
Answer ....

RECORDING 19
Q1 _____
Answer ....
Q2 _____
Answer ....
Q3 _____
Answer ....

RECORDING 20
Q1 _____
Answer ....
Q2 _____
Answer ....
Q3 _____
Answer ....

GETTING STARTED

Everybody has to take a **Basic Level Speaking** test. This is hardly surprising since one of the primary aims of learning a language is to be able to speak to people. If you are not aiming at one of the higher grades (D or above) and are not entered for more than the 'Core' papers (Basic Listening, Speaking and Reading), the Basic Speaking Test counts for a third of your marks. If you are entered for additional papers, the Basic Speaking test still carries as much weight as other papers. So it is worth doing it well.

Candidates who gain good marks in Basic Speaking will be able to cope with straightforward situations likely to be met by a visitor to a Spanish-speaking country. They will also be able to answer simple questions about themselves and their lives and interests. They will pronounce Spanish words well enough to be understood by a 'sympathetic' Spanish speaker – one who is prepared to make some effort, where necessary, to understand.

The Basic Level Speaking test involves taking part in *role-play* and in a *conversation*. We now look at each of these in turn.

The Examining Groups, although they have minor differences, have very similar Speaking tests. (Arrangements are different for the IGCSE.)

- It will be done between March and June at a time to be decided by your school or college.
- It will be conducted by your own teacher.
- It will almost certainly be recorded on cassette so that the Examining Group can check the way it was conducted and whether it was marked to the correct standard.
- Your teacher may well mark the examination, or the recording may be sent away for someone else to mark.
- It will last about ten minutes.
- You will have about ten minutes to prepare the role-play tasks, usually while the previous candidate is being tested.
- It will consist of role-plays and simple questions.

CHAPTER 6

SPEAKING: BASIC LEVEL

ROLE-PLAYS

TOPICS AND SETTINGS

COPING WITH PROBLEMS

APPROACHING THE ROLE-PLAYS

PRACTICE ROLE-PLAY QUESTIONS

POSSIBLE ANSWERS TO PRACTICE ROLE-PLAYS

CONVERSATION

TOPICS COVERED

PREPARING FOR THE TEST

PRACTICE CONVERSATION QUESTIONS

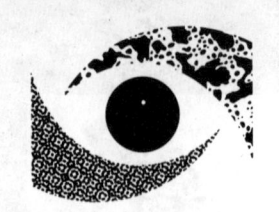

ESSENTIAL PRINCIPLES

1 ROLE-PLAYS

The role-plays will require you to take the initiative, so be prepared to talk! You will need to be able to do things such as the following:

- **buy items**, e.g. in a shop, café or restaurant
- **ask for information**, e.g. in a tourist office
- **give information**, e.g. reporting lost property
- **make bookings**, e.g. for journeys or accommodation
- **make arrangements**, e.g. over the telephone,

Typical role-play tasks

Your teacher will act like a helpful native speaker

You will perform the role-plays with your teacher, who will be asked to take the part of a helpful native-speaker of Spanish. This means that if what you say is not clear, your teacher can give you another opportunity, just as a Spanish-speaker would, by saying something like *¿Cómo?* or *No entiendo*. It can also mean that if you accidentally convey the wrong meaning, your teacher can express surprise, which may give you the chance to correct yourself. For example, if you ask in the restaurant for *una mesa para doce* when you were supposed to ask for a table for two, your teacher could exclaim *¿Para doce?* and, with any luck, you may realize your mistake and correct it. Such a correction is likely to be acceptable, since it is what would happen in real life. Of course this does mean that you have to listen to what your teacher says and not simply move on to the next task on the card! Remember also that your teacher is playing the role of someone who does not understand English, so you cannot ask for the Spanish for certain English words!

Preparing for a role-play

In most cases you will have to do two role-plays. You will be required to arrive at the room for the examination approximately 15 minutes before your test actually begins, to allow for your preparation time. Make sure that you do not have to make a rush at the last minute; it is important to be as calm as you can be in the circumstances. You will be given the role-play cards on which you will be tested, and then you have some 10 minutes to prepare yourself to carry out the instructions on the cards. The instructions will be in English and will indicate clearly what you have to do. You will not be allowed to make notes while you are preparing but you will still have the cards with you during the examination and can refer to them whenever you like.

Keep the conversation going

You are not required or expected to use perfect Spanish. **The main point is to make yourself understood.** That means you need to speak as clearly as you can, to pronounce the words as well as you can, so that the other person can understand. At all stages your teacher will attempt to be as helpful as possible, to allow you to show exactly what you can do. If there are things on the cards that you find difficult, try to work out some way of dealing with them. Above all, do not sit in silence when you come to them in the actual test, leaving your teacher to wonder if you are about to speak. Keep the conversation going, even if the best you can do is to say something you know is wrong, such as asking for wine because you have forgotten the Spanish for beer. At least you will avoid an embarrassing pause, which would only make you feel more uncomfortable and undermine your confidence.

Be positive from the start.

2 TOPICS AND SETTINGS

The role-play situations will be drawn from the *Topic Areas* and *Settings* listed for Basic Level. It is vital, then, that you know the material relevant to you. Check exactly what your Examining Group states and study carefully the Language Tasks and Vocabulary sections in Chapter 3. Remember that material listed in any Topic Area can be tested in a variety of settings.

Some Topic Areas and Settings lend themselves more readily to role-plays than others, so the most common situations you are likely to meet in this section of the examination are listed here.

- asking the way
- shopping
- cafés and restaurants
- hotels, youth hostels and campsites
- trains, buses, taxis and airports
- banks, post offices, customs and tourist offices
- garages and petrol stations
- places of entertainment
- visiting a Spanish-speaking family
- school
- dealing with minor illnesses, injuries and dental problems
- reporting lost property
- making arrangements to meet
- meeting new people

> **Common situations for role-play**

Please remember that this list only represents the most likely situations to be covered. It is not an exhaustive list and you should be prepared to deal with other possibilities.

3 COPING WITH PROBLEMS

If the tasks set require words or expressions that you cannot remember, think how you can get round them:

- **Do you know the opposite expression?**
  If you have to ask if a place is far and you cannot remember *lejos*, why not ask *¿Está cerca?* You would certainly get the information you needed, so you should get your mark. If you cannot remember the Spanish for 'to change trains', ask if the train is direct.

- **Can you explain what you mean without the key word?**
  This involves a definition or description. If you cannot remember the word *hombro* and have to explain to the doctor or chemist that you have a pain in your shoulder, you could try saying *Me duele donde el brazo se une al cuerpo* or *...entre el brazo y el cuerpo*. (In real life, of course, you would point to your shoulder and say *Me duele aquí* but at GCSE you have to show you can communicate with words, not by pointing.)
  If you have to buy carrots and cannot remember *zanahoria*, you could ask for *la legumbre larga y delgada que es color naranja*.

- **Can you explain the function of the item?**
  If you have to ask for a knife and cannot remember *cuchillo*, you could ask for *algo para cortar el pan* (or *algo para cortar la carne*).

It is a good idea to practise these strategies. You can do this on your own but it can work even better with a friend. If your friend can understand what you mean, there is every chance a Spanish speaker (or your teacher) would!

> **Some strategies if you have problems**

4 APPROACHING THE ROLE-PLAYS

Now that you are more confident about what to expect, it is time to look at the role-plays in detail, and how best to prepare for them.

As with all questions, a systematic approach is sensible.

The first thing you need to do is to **read the instructions carefully** and to work out exactly what the tasks are and what you have to say. Let's look at an example.

> **Be systematic**

> You go with a friend to a restaurant in Madrid. Your teacher will play the part of the waiter or waitress.
> a) Ask for a table for two.
> b) Ask for the menu.
> c) Order chicken.
> d) Say you would like chips.
> e) Tell the waiter/waitress what you would like to drink.

The first thing, then, is to work out exactly what you have to say. You do *not* have to translate the exact words on the card. You will almost certainly not use the words for 'ask', 'order', 'say', 'tell', 'waiter' or 'waitress'. You don't have to use the expression 'would like'. You need to identify the key words you will use in communicating each request. If you were performing the role-play in English you would say something like:

❝ In English ❞
a) A table for two, please.
b) The menu, please.
c) Chicken, please.
d) With chips, please.
e) A bottle of wine, please.

❝ In Spanish ❞
So what you will say in Spanish will be something like this:
a) Por favor una mesa para dos.
b) El menú, por favor.
c) Pollo, por favor.
d) Con patatas fritas.
e) Una botella de vino.

Remember that there are many different ways of saying the same thing and it does not matter which you use as long as you get your message across.

Now you try the following situation for yourself.

> You talk to a Spanish friend about what to do for the evening. The role of your friend will be played by your teacher.
> a) Ask whether he/she is free this evening.
> b) Ask whether he/she would like to go out.
> c) Say there is a good film on at the cinema.
> d) Tell your friend it starts at 7.00.
> e) Arrange to meet at the cinema.

❝ In English ❞
If you were performing this role-play in English you would say something like:
a) Are you free this evening?
b) Would you like to go out?
c) There's a good film on at the cinema.
d) It starts at 7.00.
e) Good-bye, until ten to seven at the cinema.

❝ In Spanish ❞
Here is an example of how it could be done in Spanish:
a) ¿Estás libre esta tarde?
b) ¿Quieres salir?
c) Hay una película buena en el cine.
d) Empieza a las siete.
e) Adiós. Hasta las siete menos diez en el cine.

Of course, you did not have to use the word *libre*. If for some reason you could not remember it, you could have said ¿*Estás ocupado esta tarde?* or ¿*Haces algo esta tarde?*. Similarly, if you could not remember the word for 'to start', you could quite simply have said *Es a las siete*. If you could not remember *película*, you might even get away with something like *Hay una cosa muy buena en el cine*, since 'something very good at the cinema' is likely to be understood to be a film!

Remember that there are many ways of getting your message across – you do not always need to use complete sentences; you can take easier solutions. You should, however, make an effort to be polite. If you make a mistake, don't worry or panic, just correct yourself as you would in English.

❝ Look for clues ❞
In some situations what your teacher says may give you the clue to what you have to say next. If may contain a key word you were unsure about. For example, in the role-play you were looking at a moment ago, if you were worried about the word 'starts', you could well have found that, after you said there was a good film on, your teacher asked: ¿*A qué hora empieza?* You could then have used the word *empieza* in your task (d). Alternatively, you could quite reasonably have taken it as understood,

because *A las siete* fully answers the question *¿A qué hora empieza?* So it will pay to listen carefully to what your teacher says. Again, don't panic if there is something you do not understand or hear clearly. Ask for it to be said again, e.g. *¿Cómo?*

The next section will provide a number of different role-plays for you to work through. Get as much practice as you can. Perhaps you can work with a friend or someone at home. Make up your own role-plays and test each other. Whatever interesting ideas you come up with, the easier you will find it to make progress.

5 > PRACTICE ROLE-PLAY QUESTIONS

The following role-play exercises give you an idea of the sort of tasks that have been set at Basic level for different situations. After the role-plays there are suggested ways of dealing with them. There are also comments intended to help you to tackle other similar ones with confidence. Of course, in between each of your tasks your teacher will have to say something, but you will not know what that is until you hear it, so it cannot affect your preparation. Your teacher will also introduce the situation in Spanish, briefly summarizing what you have already found out from the printed English introduction on the card.

Finding the way
After window-shopping in Madrid, you are trying to find your way back to the Hotel Yolanda in time for the evening meal. You go to a newspaper stall to ask for directions. Your teacher will play the part of the stall owner.
1   Say hello. Ask for a plan of the city.
2   Find out where the Hotel Yolanda is.
3   Say you're sorry but you don't understand.
4   Explain you're in a hurry.
5   Say you'll take a taxi.   *(WJEC)*

Shopping
You are looking at towels in a shop in Spain. The assistant (your teacher) asks if he/she can help you.
1   Say you want to buy a towel.
2   Say no, it's for the beach.
3   Say you like the green towel.
4   Ask how much it costs.   *(NEAB)*

In a café
You are in a café in Spain. You find that your bill is wrong. You call the waiter/waitress, who will be played by the examiner, and who will begin the conversation.
1   Say there is a mistake on your bill.
2   Say you had a lemonade and a sandwich.
3   Say it's 500 pesetas.
4   Say it doesn't matter.
5   Ask for the change.   *(ULEAC)*

In a restaurant
You are on holiday in Spain and you go into a restaurant.
Your teacher will play the part of the waiter/waitress.

1   Say you would like a table near the window.
2   Say it is for three people.
3   Ask for three glasses of water.
4   Say that you want the menu of the day.
5   Ask if there is a telephone.   *(MEG)*

At the hotel
You are on holiday in Spain and you arrive at an hotel.
The examiner will play the role of the receptionist.
1   Give your name and say you have reserved a room.
2   Ask if the room has a bathroom.

3 Ask how much the room costs.
4 Ask if breakfast is included.
5 Enquire where the dining room is. (*MEG*)

At a youth hostel
You arrive at a youth hostel in Spain. The role of the warden will be played by the examiner. You begin the conversation.
1 Ask if there is room for tonight.
2 Say there are two of you: your friend and you.
3 Say it's for three nights.
4 Ask if you can cook a meal.
5 Ask when you have to pay. (*ULEAC*)

At a campsite
You are at a campsite in Spain. The role of the receptionist will be played by the examiner, who will begin the conversation.
1 Ask if it's full.
2 Say you have a tent and a bicycle.
3 Say it's for one night. (*ULEAC*)

At the railway station
You are in a railway station in Spain and want to buy a ticket for Toledo. The examiner will play the part of the clerk in the ticket office. You must ask for and give the following information:
1 Say hello to the clerk.
2 You would like a ticket for Toledo.
3 You want to leave at 10.30 a.m.
4 You would like a second class ticket.
5 Ask how much the ticket costs. (*NICCEA*)

At a coach station
You are at a coach station in Spain, enquiring about a coach to Santander. The role of the person at the enquiry desk will be played by the examiner. You will begin the conversation.
1 Ask if there is a coach to Santander.
2 Say you prefer the afternoon.
3 Say you want a single ticket.
4 Ask if you must reserve a seat.
5 Ask if it costs more. (*ULEAC*)

At the customs post
You are at a customs post on the Spanish border. The role of the customs officer will be played by the examiner, who will begin the conversation.
1 State your nationality.
2 Say this is your bag.
3 Say you have nothing to declare. (*ULEAC*)

At the tourist office
You are in Spain and you enter a tourist information office.
Your teacher will play the part of the person behind the desk.
1 Say that you want to go to the museum.
2 Find out if it is open now.
3 Say you are going to Toledo tomorrow
4 Find out if the station is far.
5 Ask for a map of the town. (*MEG*)

At the petrol station
You are on a touring holiday in Spain with your parents and you stop at a filling station.
The examiner will play the role of the attendant.
1 Ask him/her for 20 litres of high-grade petrol.

2 Ask him/her to check the water.
3 Enquire if they sell sweets.
4 Enquire if this is the road to Madrid.
5 Find out how many kilometres it is to Madrid.   (*MEG*)

At the cinema
You are on holiday in Spain and you decide to go to the cinema.
The examiner will play the role of the cashier.
1 Ask if the film is in English.
2 Find out when the film starts.
3 Find out when the film finishes.
4 Say you would like a ticket.
5 Ask how much it costs.   (*MEG*)

Staying with a family – food
You have arrived at your Spanish penfriend's house. The role of your penfriend will be played by the examiner. You will begin the conversation.
1 Ask the time of the evening meal.
2 Say it's different in your country.
3 Say you like Spanish food.   (*ULEAC*)

Staying with a family – planning a shopping visit
You are in the home of your Spanish correspondent who is planning the day's activities. You want to go shopping. The examiner will play the part of your correspondent. You must ask the following questions/give the following information:
1 Ask if you can go shopping.
2 Say you've some presents to buy for your family.
3 Say you've only about 1,200 pesetas.
4 Say you want to go first to a big store.
5 Say you prefer to walk.   (*NICCEA*)

Dealing with a minor illness
You are staying with a Spanish family. One evening you are not feeling very well. Your Spanish friend (your teacher) asks what the matter is.
1 Say you feel ill.
2 Say you have a headache.
3 Ask if he/she has an aspirin.
4 Ask for a glass of water.   (*NEAB*)

Dealing with a minor injury
You are an out-patient in a hospital in Spain, and you wish to obtain treatment for a cut finger. The examiner will play the part of a nurse. You speak first. Your tasks are:
1 To greet the nurse politely.
2 To say you cut your finger.
3 To say it hurts a little.
4 To ask if you have to come back again.
5 To say good-bye and you will see him/her later.   (*SEG*)

Reporting lost property
While on holiday in Spain, you visit a police station to report a lost camera. The examiner will play the part of a policeman/woman. You speak first. Your tasks are:
1 To greet the policeman/woman at the entrance politely.
2 To say you have lost your camera.
3 To say you left it in the Café Universal.
4 To say this morning at 11.00.
5 To say thank you and good-bye.   (*SEG*)

Making arrangements
You are at home and you reply to a phone call from a Spanish friend who is visiting England. The examiner will play the part of your Spanish friend. You speak first. Your tasks are:

1 To answer the phone.
2 To ask when he/she arrived in England.
3 To ask if he/she would like to come to dinner with your family.
4 To ask if he/she can come on Friday.
5 To suggest a suitable time.

(SEG)

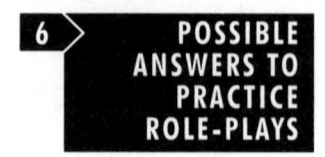

6 > POSSIBLE ANSWERS TO PRACTICE ROLE-PLAYS

The answers given below are possible ways of dealing with the tasks set in the practice role-plays. They are not the only answers that would earn good marks. Getting the message across is what is important.

Finding the way

1 Buenos días. Un plano de la ciudad, por favor.
2 ¿Dónde está el Hotel Yolanda?
3 Lo siento pero no entiendo.
4 Tengo prisa.
5 Voy a coger un taxi.

Notes: 1. You could say 'Hola' and you could say 'Quiero...' or '¿Tiene...?' If you had asked for 'un mapa', it would not really have been the correct word but would have communicated perfectly.
2. You could have asked '¿Por dónde se va al Hotel Yolanda?' '¿Dónde...?' is a key word that you clearly must know. There are ways of getting round it ('Quiero ir al...' 'No encuentro el...') but you really will not get very far without knowing the key question words!
3. Alternatives include 'Perdone' and 'No comprendo'. Again, apologizing and saying you don't understand are essential skills.
4. You could say: 'No tengo mucho tiempo'. Even 'Necesito estar en el hotel a las diez' could get the message across.
5. You don't need to use the Future Tense. At Basic Level, all tasks involving future action should be possible with 'ir a...'. In this case, even that is not essential. 'Cojo un taxi' or 'Tomo un taxi' would work perfectly well. 'Un taxi' on its own would leave some doubt about what you were trying to say.

Shopping

1 Quiero una toalla, por favor.
2 No, es para la playa.
3 Me gusta la toalla verde.
4 ¿Cuánto es?

Notes: 1 Asking for things is an absolutely essential skill. You don't need all the complications of English courtesy ('I should like to buy a...'). In Spanish 'por favor' will provide all that is needed for courtesy. 'Quiero' or 'Deme' are additional extras.
3 'Me gusta' is an important expression that needs to be mastered but in this case 'Prefiero' would work equally well. You could omit 'toalla' in this task. You have already identified what you are talking about in task 1. 'La verde' means 'the green one'.
4 One of the most common expressions used in role-plays.

In a café

1 Hay un error en la cuenta.
2 Tomé limonada y un bocadillo.
3 Son quinientas pesetas.
4 No importa.
5 La vuelta, por favor.

Notes: 1. 'Cuenta' is an important word to know. 'Error' is easy, though you could say 'La cuenta está mal' or 'la cuenta no es correcta'.
4. You could say 'No es importante' or 'No se preocupe' (Don't worry).
5. Yet again 'por favor' makes it a request.

In a restaurant
1   Queremos una mesa cerca de la ventana, por favor.
2   Es para tres personas.
3   Tres vasos de agua, por favor.
4   Queremos el menú del día.
5   ¿Hay teléfono?

Notes: Obviously you don't have to say 'Queremos' in 1 or 4.
¿*Hay...?* is a very useful expression. You can use it to ask about the availability of items of food or drink or, indeed, any items in shops if you wish.

At the hotel
1   Me llamo.... Tengo una habitación reservada.
2   ¿La habitación tiene baño?
3   ¿Cuánto es?
4   ¿Está incluido el desayuno?
5   ¿Dónde está el comedor?

Notes: 1. You could say 'He reservado una habitación.' ('Tengo reserva', though not normal, would communicate). 'Mi reserva una habitación' would not be clear. (Have you done so or do you wish to?)
2. If 'habitación' has already been mentioned, '¿Tiene baño?' would be enough here.
5. You could also call it 'el restaurante'.

At the youth hostel
1   ¿Hay sitio para esta noche?
2   Somos dos: mi amigo/a y yo.
3   Es para tres noches.
4   ¿Podemos preparar una comida?
5   ¿Cuándo tenemos que pagar?

Notes: 2. You were probably asked how many people, in which case 'Dos....' would do.
3. If you were asked '¿Para cuántas noches? you could simply say 'Tres.' but, of course, you could have been asked '¿Para cuánto tiempo?' In that case the word 'noches' would be essential. (In your preparation you must assume you will have to say it.)

At a campsite
1   ¿Está lleno?
2   Tengo una tienda y una bicicleta.
3   Es para una noche.

Note: 1. It would be at least as good, and probably more natural, to say: '¿Hay sitio?'

At the railway station
1   Buenos días.
2   Por favor un billete para Toledo.
3   Quiero salir a las diez y media.
4   Un billete de segunda clase.
5   ¿Cuánto es?

Note: Here again, if you were asked '¿A qué hora quiere salir?', you could say simply 'A las diez y media.' If you were asked '¿Qué clase quiere?' the answer could be as short as 'Segunda.' (However, when you are preparing the role-plays, you cannot be sure what you will be asked, so you should play safe.)

At a coach station
1   ¿Hay un autocar para Santander?
2   Prefiero la tarde.
3   Un billete sencillo, por favor.

4 ¿Hay que reservar asiento?
5 ¿Cuesta más?

Note: 5. ¿Es más caro? is also valid.

At the customs post
1 Soy inglés (inglesa).
2 Ésta es mi bolsa.
3 No tengo nada que declarar.

Stating your nationality is going to be a frequent occurrence when abroad!

At the tourist office
1 Quiero ir al museo.
2 ¿Está abierto ahora?
3 Voy a Toledo mañana.
4 ¿Está lejos la estación?
5 Un plano de la ciudad, por favor.

'Quiero...' and 'Voy a...' are key expressions. For 4 you could ask '¿A qué distancia está la estación?' but that is much more complicated and not really what a Spaniard would say.

At the petrol station
1 Por favor, veinte litros de súper.
2 Compruebe el agua, por favor.
3 ¿Venden caramelos?
4 ¿Es ésta la carretera de Madrid?
5 ¿A cuántos kilómetros está Madrid?

In 4 it would not really matter if you omitted 'ésta'. For 5 you would communicate successfully if you said simply '¿Cuántos kilómetros a Madrid?

At the cinema
1 ¿La película es en inglés?
2 ¿A qué hora empieza?
3 ¿A qué hora termina?
4 Una entrada, por favor
5 ¿Cuánto es?

Tasks 2 and 3 use very important expressions.

Staying with a family – food
1 ¿A qué hora es la cena?
2 Es diferente en Inglaterra.
3 Me gusta la comida española.

It is quite permissible to say 'Inglaterra' instead of 'mi país'.

Staying with a family – planning a shopping visit
1 ¿Puedo ir de compras?
2 Tengo que comprar regalos para la familia.
3 Sólo tengo mil doscientas pesetas.
4 Quiero ir primero a unos grandes almacenes.
5 Prefiero ir a pie.

Dealing with a minor illness
1 Me siento enfermo/a.
2 Me duele la cabeza.
3 ¿Hay aspirina?
4 Un vaso de agua, por favor.

'Me siento...' (I feel) is quite difficult but 'No me encuentro bien' or 'No estoy bien' would do perfectly well.

Dealing with a minor injury
1. Buenos días.
2. Me he cortado el dedo.
3. Me duele un poco.
4. ¿Tengo que volver?
5. Adiós. Hasta luego.

'Tengo que...' is an important expression, as are the greetings.

Reporting lost property
1. Buenas tardes.
2. He perdido mi máquina fotográfica.
3. La dejé en el Café Universal.
4. Esta mañana a las once.
5. Gracias. Adiós.

Making arrangements
1. Diga.
2. ¿Cuándo llegaste a Inglaterra?
3. ¿Quieres venir a cenar con mi familia?
4. ¿Puedes venir el viernes.?
5. A las siete.

'¿Quieres...?' and '¿Puedes...?' are very useful.

7 > CONVERSATION

This part of the test will be fairly brief and will not go into much detail. You will be asked some 10 to 20 straightforward questions (depending on your Examining Group) and you will be expected to provide quite simple answers.

The marks awarded will again depend on your ability to make yourself understood, to communicate some meaning. Your teacher will be trying to help you by taking the role of a sympathetic native-speaker, and, if there is something he or she does not understand, then he or she will react just as if it were a real-life situation. For instance, in real life, if you met a Spanish teenager at a party and asked how old he or she was and you got the reply 'Sixty', you wouldn't just leave it there and go on to another question. You would probably express surprise (!) and say something like 'Sixty? I don't think that is what you mean!' The Spanish teenager would then have a chance to correct the previous answer, 'No, I mean sixteen'. As this is what happens in normal conversation, your teacher is allowed to help you in the same way. Although your teacher has to ask you a particular number of questions, he or she will be trying to make this part of the test as natural as possible by organizing the questions into something like a normal conversation, though the need to cover a certain number of topics may mean some rather sudden changes of subject occur. Try to be as natural as you can and answer each question as it comes.

Your teacher can give some help

The conversation is not a cross-examination! The idea is not to probe into your secrets, but simply to assess your ability to speak Spanish. The conversation will be based on the material you have covered throughout your course. The Speaking test is the equivalent of the Coursework element in other subjects, so the questions and topic areas covered will sample what you have been doing all along in your oral work in class and at home. Your teacher will not be trying to 'trick' you or catch you out and you are most unlikely to be asked a question that has not been asked on a number of occasions during the course. Given that you now know that every effort is made to help you, make sure you help yourself by being prepared to say something!

You will have heard the questions before

Try to avoid one-word answers such as 'Sí' or 'No' or just the name of your home town or village. You really cannot expect to score many marks for showing you can manage that! Always look for the chance to give a whole sentence as the answer - or even more that one. Ideally, the questions will not lend themselves to 'Yes ' or 'No' answers but often you have to be asked, for example, if you have any brothers or sisters before any further questions can be asked about them. If you are asked,

❝ Avoid one-word answers ❞

'¿Tienes hermanos?', rather than simply saying 'Sí', you should anticipate the next possible question by giving more information, saying something like 'Sí, tengo un hermano y una hermana' or 'Sí, tengo una hermana que se llama Tracy.' Even if you have no brothers or sisters, there are still ways of saying more than 'No'. You could, for example, say 'No, pero tengo un perro' or 'No, pero tengo tres primos.'

It is also important to remember that you are not on oath in the witness box! Your teacher is out to assess how well you can speak Spanish – not how truthful you are! He or she will not come round to your house in the evening after the examination to check whether you really do have a dog like the one you have described. He or she is not going to rush off to check the school records to see if they confirm what you have said about any member of your family, so you are free to change the facts, if you need to, to match what you can say in Spanish.

❝ Show off what you can say ❞

Remember also that the aim is to show how much you can say in Spanish, not to avoid making actual mistakes by saying as little as possible. Don't see each question as something to be 'blocked' with great caution, but as an opportunity to show off what you can say. If you are going to change the facts about your family, it will always make far more sense to invent a brother or sister you don't actually have, so that you can say something about them in Spanish, rather than to deny the existence of a brother who does exist, which will only force your teacher to ask you something else, which could well prove a little more difficult.

8 ▸ TOPICS COVERED

The topic areas and vocabulary covered will be those listed for Basic Level only. Again, just check the exact requirements for your Examining Group. In practice, though, some topics lend themselves more to conversation than others. You can talk quite a lot about holidays but it is quite difficult to have a realistic conversation about lost property (unless it has arisen naturally, which is unlikely in the examination).

The topics you are likely to be asked about will include:

- yourself and your family (Personal Identification)
- your home (House and Home)
- your daily routines (House and Home – Life at Home)
- your home town, village or area (Geographical Surroundings)
- your school or college (School and College)
- your free time, interests and hobbies (Free Time and Entertainment)
- your holidays (Holidays)

The conversation will cover a range of these topics and will usually follow a fairly logical sequence. You are likely to be asked two, three or four questions on one topic area before going on to a different one.

9 ▸ PREPARING FOR THE TEST

Students quite often claim that it is not possible to revise or prepare for an oral examination, but that simply is not true.

Once you have checked the topic areas, you can work out small groups of questions for each topic area and make sure that you can answer them. The vocabulary and language tasks in Chapter 3 will help you to do so. See also the examples given in the next section.

❝ Plan your answers for the likely questions ❞

If your teacher gives you a list of possible questions, use it. You cannot be told in advance which of the questions you will be asked, but at least you will have plenty of opportunity to prepare answers to a range of questions, some of which you will be asked.

If there is a question you do not understand, don't panic. Ask the teacher to repeat the question - '¿Cómo?' – or re-phrase it – 'No entiendo.' Make sure you have a few phrases 'up your sleeve' to help you out of such difficulties. Above all, do not sit in silence – it will only make you feel more embarrassed and uncomfortable. If all else fails, if you still do not understand after a question is repeated, think what it might mean and give an answer to that – you might actually be right!

10 > PRACTICE CONVERSATION QUESTIONS

Here are some examples of the kind of questions you can expect in this part of the examination. A possible answer is given after some questions (with italics to show things you will need to adapt to suit your own life). In other cases the beginning of an answer is given, to set you off on a correctly constructed answer, with dots where you have to supply the rest of the answer.

YOURSELF AND YOUR FAMILY:

Questions	Possible Answers
¿Cuántos años tienes?	Tengo *dieciséis años*.
¿Cuándo es tu cumpleaños?	Es el *veinte de junio*.
¿En qué año naciste?	Nací en mil novecientos *setenta y ocho*.
¿Dónde vives?	Vivo en....
¿A qué distancia del colegio vives?	Vivo a *tres* kilómetros del colegio.
¿Qué cosas te gustan?	Me gustan....
¿Cuántas personas hay en tu familia?	Hay *cuatro* personas en mi familia: *mis padres, mi hermana y yo*.
¿Quiénes son?	Son *mis padres, mi hermana y yo*.
¿Tienes hermanos?	*Sí, tengo una hermana*.
¿Cuántos años tiene?	Tiene *catorce* años.
¿Qué hace tu padre?	Trabaja en *un banco*.
¿Qué hace tu madre?	*Es secretaria.*

YOUR HOME:

Questions	Possible Answers
¿Dónde vives?	Vivo en....
¿Cómo es tu casa?	Es *grande y moderna*.
¿Está cerca del centro de la ciudad?	Está a *tres* kilómetros del centro.
¿Cuántas habitaciones hay en tu casa?	Hay...
¿Qué hay en tu dormitorio?	Hay una cama, *una mesa, una silla y un armario*.
¿Dónde haces los deberes?	Los hago en *mi dormitorio*.
¿Qué hacéis en el salón?	Hablamos y vemos la televisión.
¿Tenéis un jardín?	*Sí. Es bastante grande. Hay flores y dos árboles.*
¿Qué se cultiva en el jardín?	Se cultivan *flores y árboles*.
¿Tienes animales en casa?	*Sí. Tenemos dos gatos y un pez rojo.*

YOUR DAILY ROUTINE:

Questions	Possible Answers
¿A qué hora te levantas normalmente?	Me levanto a las....
¿Qué haces luego?	*Me lavo y me visto.*
¿Dónde desayunas?	*Desayuno en la cocina.* OR: *No desayuno.*
¿Con quién desayunas?	Desayuno con *mi hermana*.
¿Qué desayunas?	Desayuno *tostadas y té*.
¿A qué hora cenas?	Ceno a las....
¿A qué hora te acuestas?	Me acuesto a las....

YOUR HOME TOWN, VILLAGE OR AREA:

Questions	Possible Answers
¿Dónde está tu casa?	Está en *las afueras de Leeds*.
¿Dónde está *Leeds*?	Está en *el norte de Inglaterra*.
¿Qué clase de pueblo o ciudad es?	Es *una ciudad industrial*.
¿Qué hay que hacer en *Leeds*?	Hay *cines, piscinas, discotecas y mucho más*.
¿Qué hay de interés en *Leeds*?	Hay....
¿Cómo es *Leeds*?	Es *una gran ciudad industrial*.

YOUR SCHOOL OR COLLEGE:

Questions	Possible Answers
¿Cómo vienes al colegio por la mañana?	Vengo *a pie*.
¿A qué hora llegas?	Llego a las....
¿A qué hora empiezan las clases?	Empiezan a las....
¿Cuántas clases tienes por la mañana?	Hay *cuatro*.
¿Cuánto tiempo dura cada clase?	Dura *treinta y cinco minutos*.
¿Cuánto tiempo dura el recreo?	Dura *un cuarto de hora*.
¿Cuál es tu asignatura preferida?	Es *el español*.
¿Qué asignatura te gusta menos?	Me gusta menos....
Para ti ¿cuál es la asignatura más difícil?	Es....
¿Cuántos alumnos hay en el colegio?	Hay *unos mil alumnos*.
¿Cuántos profesores hay en el colegio?	Hay....
¿Qué haces durante el recreo?	*Hablo con mis amigos.*
¿Qué haces a la hora de comer?	*Como y hablo con mis amigos.*
¿Qué deportes practicas en el colegio?	*Juego al.....*

YOUR FREE TIME, INTERESTS AND HOBBIES:

Questions	Possible Answers
¿Qué te gusta hacer los sábados?	Me gusta *ir de compras con mis amigos/as*.
Si vas al cine ¿a qué hora tienes que volver a casa?	Tengo que volver a las....
¿Cuáles son tus pasatiempos favoritos?	Son....
¿Qué haces en tu tiempo libre?	Me gusta....
¿Con quién juegas al ....?	Juego al.... con *mi hermano*.
¿Con quién vas al ....?	Voy con....
¿Dónde juegas al ....?	Juego en....
¿Dónde tocas el piano?	Lo toco en....
¿Qué deportes practicas?	Juego al....
¿Cuándo?	Juego *los sábados por la mañana*.
¿Con quién?	Juego con....
¿Te gusta la música?	Sí. Me gusta mucho la música pop.

YOUR HOLIDAYS:

Questions	Possible Answers
¿Adónde fuiste de vacaciones el verano pasado?	Fui a....
¿Con quién?	Fui con....
¿Cómo fuiste(is)?	Fui (Fuimos) *en avión*.
¿Dónde os alojasteis?	Nos alojamos en *un hotel*.
¿Cuánto tiempo pasasteis allí?	Pasamos *quince días allí*.
¿Qué tiempo hizo?	*Hizo muy buen tiempo. Hizo sol.*
¿Qué hiciste allí?	*Me bañé y fui a la discoteca.*
¿Visitaste algunos sitios interesantes?	*Sí, visité....*
¿Qué te gustó más allí?	Me gustó más....
¿Te gustaría volver allí?	Sí. *Me gustaría porque lo pasé muy bien.*
¿Has visitado España?	Sí. *Fui allí el verano pasado.* No. *Pero quiero ir un año.*
¿Adónde vas de vacaciones este verano?	Voy a....
¿Has estado allí antes?	No. *Es la primera vez.* OR: *Sí. Fui hace dos años.*

As you can see, there is a good deal of overlap in the kinds of question to expect, but your teacher will use a mixture. There are many other possible questions which could be asked. Make sure you check what you cover during your lessons and listen carefully to what your teacher says about preparation for this section of the examination. In some cases there will be special information about a final selection of topics to be covered shortly before the examination itself.

A STEP FURTHER

There are many ways of improving your fluency. Most come down to actually speaking.

- Speak Spanish whenever you can to anyone who will listen.
- Speak to your pets in Spanish!
- Imagine the conversation – the questions and your answers to them – while on your journey to school or college.
- Prepare the conversation questions carefully. Make sure you know the specialized vocabulary for your parents' jobs and your hobbies.
- Work through the role-plays in this book, your text book and any others you come across.
- Make good use of any mock Speaking test that is arranged for you. It is an excellent opportunity to gain valuable experience. Don't waste it by going in ill-prepared.

The Review Sheets at the end of Chapter 7 cover speaking at both Basic and Higher Levels.

CHAPTER 7

SPEAKING: HIGHER LEVEL

FORM OF THE EXAMINATION

HIGHER LEVEL ROLE-PLAYS

APPROACHING THE ROLE-PLAYS

SAMPLE ROLE-PLAYS

PRACTICE ROLE-PLAY QUESTIONS

POSSIBLE ANSWERS TO THE ROLE-PLAY QUESTIONS

HIGHER LEVEL CONVERSATION

PREPARING FOR THE EXAMINATION

IN THE EXAMINATION

PRACTICE CONVERSATION QUESTIONS

SAMPLE ANSWERS TO CONVERSATION QUESTIONS

GETTING STARTED

The **Higher Level Speaking Test** is optional, but you have nothing to lose by attempting it and, if you are aiming at one of the Higher Grades, you would be well advised to try it. As with the other Higher Level Tests, all candidates have to complete the Basic Level Test as well.

You will almost certainly have to talk about things in the future, you will have to cope with some unprepared elements in the *role-plays* and you will be expected to give rather longer answers in the *conversation*, but remember that, as at Basic Level, the main purpose is to get your message across, (even though the quality of your spoken Spanish will also be assessed) and the skills and knowledge used at Basic Level will still be important.

First of all you need to be familiar with the types of task you will have to do. There is much you can predict and much you can do to prepare yourself.

ESSENTIAL PRINCIPLES

1 > FORM OF THE EXAMINATION

More time is available for the combined test

Check the order with your teacher

As at Basic Level, you will be required at Higher Level to perform *role-plays* and to take part in a *conversation*. (For MEG candidates entering for Higher Level Part 2 there is also a 'Narrator' exercise, in which you have to recount an incident or journey based on notes or diagrams printed on a card you will be given at the start of your preparation time.)

The Higher Level Speaking test is normally linked in with the Basic as one test and the preparation time is increased accordingly. The time allocated to the *combined* test will range from about 12 minutes to a maximum of 20 minutes. It is a reasonable assumption that those correctly entered for Higher Level will both prepare and perform the Basic Level tasks more quickly than those who are taking Basic Level only, so the additional time does not in fact represent the full time you will need for the additional elements.

You may have to do all the Basic Level test and then go straight on to the Higher or you may do the prepared elements – the role-plays for both levels – followed by the conversation for both levels. The order in which the different elements are taken is often up to the teacher, so ask your teacher what the order will be.

For some Examining Groups there must be a clear change from Basic Level to Higher in conversation, with the specified number of Basic Level questions being asked. For other Examining Groups the two are rolled into one conversation, which will begin with some Basic Level questions and move on to more lengthy discussion of topics for the Higher Level. Again, ask your teacher what the format will be. If the two conversation elements are taken separately, find out how you will know when the change occurs. Many teachers will introduce the Basic Level questions with a sentence such as 'Ahora te voy a hacer unas preguntas' and later introduce the Higher Level with a phrase such as 'Y ahora una conversación más general'.

2 > HIGHER LEVEL ROLE-PLAYS

What you are expected to do at the Higher Level

As with Basic Level, *communication* is the key. You should be able to pronounce the sounds of Spanish accurately enough for a native speaker to understand without difficulty, and to speak with a certain degree of correct intonation and stress. Note that at Higher Level the degree of accuracy expected is greater than at Basic Level, but the important thing is still 'getting the message across'.

So what is different about the Higher Level role-play tests?

- You will be expected to cope with tasks from the full range of topics defined in the syllabus.

- The role-plays will contain an element of unpredictability. This means you have to try to anticipate what the problems may be, and be prepared to listen carefully to what the examiner says, and then to think and react quickly.

The role-play cards will normally give a *setting*. Some Examining Groups rely very much on the contents of the setting for the 'unpredictable' elements, so you would be well advised to read it carefully to ensure you are aware of the details that might be relevant to a question you are asked.

The extra topics for Higher Level may well include such things as:

Possible extra topic areas at the Higher Level

- lost property
- repairs and complaints
- more serious medical problems
- accidents and emergencies
- telephoning and more complex situations at the Post Office
- banking and currency exchange
- travel by air or sea

You must remember, though, that Basic Level topics can also be included, but they will be given a different and more demanding emphasis.

The length of the individual role-plays varies from Group to Group in the number and complexity of the tasks required. You can also expect the stimuli or instructions to be more complicated, sometimes presented in an unusual way. In the main, the instructions will be in the form of an outline in English, but could include some kind of a visual stimulus such as a town plan. Again, you must check exactly what your Examining Group requires.

3 > APPROACHING THE ROLE-PLAYS

❝❝ Be systematic ❞❞

So how do you go about preparing for and tackling these Higher Level role-play situations?

As always, a methodical approach will pay dividends. A thorough preparation of the material covered in the Basic Level role-plays is, of course, essential, before you concern yourself too much with the detail of the Higher Level situations. Assuming that you are ready, however, these steps should help you:

1 Make sure you know just what topics are in the syllabus for Basic and Higher Level.

2 Check the settings and language tasks and make sure that you can cope with the Spanish you will need to use and understand. Cross check with Chapter 3 and the details provided by your Examining Group.

❝❝ Some steps in your preparation for Higher Level speaking ❞❞

3 Re-check the section 'Coping with Problems' in Chapter 6. The strategies are just as valid and useful at Higher Level.

4 Study as many role-play situations as you can and get practice. You can practise with a friend and you can test yourself. Use your checklists.

5 Try making up your own role-play situations and then try them out with a friend. This can be fun as well as being good practice. You could try being a 'difficult' shop assistant, hotel receptionist, etc.

When studying the *role-play* instructions, the following points should be helpful:

- Check what the crucial element(s) in each task are and work out what you are going to say. Remember that there are many different ways of saying the same thing.

- Try and work out what you think the examiner might say, and the possible 'twists' to the dialogue. In most cases these will in fact be reasonably predictable. Again the more practice you get, the more predictable they will become.

❝❝ Study the instructions and begin to prepare your role-play ❞❞

- Don't panic! There may well be something that at first you don't understand, but that doesn't really matter. Equip yourself with a series of useful phrases to ask the examiner to repeat something, to ask him or her to say something more slowly, to explain that you didn't quite catch what he/she said. As long as you can do this in Spanish you will not lose credit. But remember, the examiner is playing the part of a Spanish-speaker with no knowledge of English.

- If you have any doubts whether the plan you are adopting in order to carry out one of the tasks will actually work, have a 'fall-back' plan to use if the examiner says something like '¿Cómo? No entiendo.'

4 > SAMPLE ROLE-PLAYS

Now let's look at an example.

1. Lost Property

You are at the lost property office of the Madrid Metro. The role of the person behind the counter will be played by the examiner, who will begin the conversation.

1 Say you have left your bag on a train.

2 Explain that the train was going to Moncloa.

3 State two things about the appearance of the bag.

4   Answer the person's question.
5   Ask if anyone has found it.
6   Say it was about an hour ago.
7   Say you'll fill in a card and come back tomorrow.   (ULEAC)

You will have to deal with most of the tasks exactly as you would at Basic Level, though you will have noticed that they do demand a little more of you.

Commentary and possible responses

1   This is fairly straightforward: *He dejado mi bolsa en un tren.*

2   This looks a little more demanding and involves the Imperfect Tense. You might be asked '*¿Adónde iba el tren?*' but at Higher Level things may well not be quite as simple as that! You will probably have to work out the verb for yourself, after being asked something like: '*¿En qué tren la dejó usted?* So you will need to say: *El tren iba a Moncloa.*

3   No real problems here: *Es una bolsa grande y es azul.*

4   It looks as though you cannot prepare for this one but, if you think about it, there are some fairly good probabilities. The question must make sense in context – so what would you be asked? Your name, perhaps? Possibly, but that seems to be covered in task 7. The most likely is that you will be asked what is in the bag. So be ready to name one or two suitable items – but still listen carefully to make sure you answer the right question!

5   Not too difficult: *¿La han encontrado?*

6   You have obviously been asked '*¿Cuándo la dejó?*' Notice the word 'about'. It will be best to play safe and make sure you include that idea. *Hace una hora aproximadamente.*

7   The Future Tense is clearly needed here – definitely Higher Level. *Rellenaré una ficha y volveré mañana.*

Now try this example:

2. Changing money

You are in a bank in Spain and wish to obtain some Spanish currency. The examiner will play the part of the bank clerk. You speak first. Your tasks are:

1   To greet the bank clerk politely.

2   To say that you would like to change a traveller's cheque.
    *

3   To say you would like to change some bank notes.
    *

4   To ask if you have to sign anything.
    *

5   To say thank you and good-bye.

* The examiner will ask further questions here.   (SEG)

Commentary and possible responses

The tasks set are fairly straightforward but what will the 'further questions' be? After task 2 you can probably work out that you may be asked something about the value, or your nationality or about your passport – so be prepared for that.

After task 3 the most likely possibilities would seem to be the amount and the nationality of the money.

After task 4 it is difficult to predict what may be said. It is probably something quite conversational.

In fact the examiner's script reads as follows:

Bueno. Estamos en un banco y yo soy el empleado/la empleada.

1   –

    Buenos días/ buenas tardes, ¿en qué puedo servirle/la?

2   –

    ¿Es usted inglés/inglesa?

    ¿De qué valor son los cheques?

    ¿Tiene Vd su pasaporte?

    IF YES: *Pues, tenga la bondad de dármelo un momento.*

    IF NO: *Pues, lo siento, sin su pasaporte sólo puede cambiar billetes de banco.*

3   –

    ¿Son libras esterlinas?

    Y otra vez, ¿Cuántas libras?

    Muy bien, pues, tiene que llevar esta hoja a la caja.

4   –

    ¡Ay! Sí, señor(it)(a). Tiene que firmar la hoja. No es ésta su primera visita a un banco español, ¿verdad?

    Ha visitado España antes, ¿no?

    Pues, ¡qué bien habla español!

5   –

The conversation might go something like this:

Examiner: Bueno. Estamos en un banco y yo soy la empleada.

Candidate: Buenos días.
Examiner: Buenos días, ¿en qué puedo servirla?
Candidate: Quiero cambiar un cheque de viajero.
Examiner: ¿Es usted inglesa?
Candidate: Sí.
Examiner: ¿De qué valor son los cheques?
Candidate: Veinte libras
Examiner: ¿Tiene Vd su pasaporte?
Candidate: Sí.
Examiner: Pues, tenga la bondad de dármelo un momento.
Candidate: Aquí tiene. También quiero cambiar unos billetes.
Examiner: Son libras esterlinas?
Candidate: Sí.
Examiner: Y otra vez, ¿Cuántas libras?
Candidate: Treinta.
Examiner: Muy bien, pues, tiene que llevar esta hoja a la caja.
Candidate: ¿Hay que firmar algo?
Examiner: ¡Ay! Sí, señor(it)(a). Tiene que firmar la hoja. No es ésta su primera visita a un banco español, ¿verdad?
Candidate: No. Es la segunda.
Examiner: Ha visitado España antes, ¿no?
Candidate: No. Es mi primera visita.
Examiner: Pues, ¡qué bien habla español!
Candidate: Gracias. Adiós.

The tasks in themselves have not been at all difficult but it has been important for the candidate to listen and make an appropriate response to each question.

5 PRACTICE ROLE-PLAY QUESTIONS

The following role-plays give you an idea of the sort of tasks set at Higher Level by the different Examining Groups. After the role-plays there are suggested answers.

1. At the chemist's

While on holiday in Spain you fall ill and go to the chemist's.

Your teacher will play the role of the chemist.

1   Say that you have a sore throat and a headache.

2   Respond to the chemist's question.

3   Say that you can't eat or sleep, and that you have taken some aspirins.

4   When offered a bottle of tablets, find out how many tablets you are to take every day.

5   Respond to the chemist's question.

The teacher's sheet before task 2 reads '¿Sí? ¿Desde cuándo?'
Before task 5 it reads '¿Cuánto tiempo va a estar en España?' (MEG)

2. In a restaurant

You are on holiday in Spain with a friend in a restaurant. The part of the waiter/waitress will be played by the examiner.

1   Tell the waiter/waitress where you would like to sit.

2   Order any two starters.

3   Tell him/her you haven't made up your mind (about the main course).

4   Complain about the state of the table (e.g. dirty glasses, fork missing etc.).

5   Respond to the waiter's/waitress's suggestion.

6   Order one meat dish and one fish dish.

The teacher's sheet before task 5 has the words: '...Si quieren, pueden sentarse a otra mesa. (Express as a statement.)' (WJEC)

3. At a railway station

You are at a railway station in Spain. You have just arrived there and are met by your Spanish correspondent. You are feeling tired after a 14-hour journey. You have with you a large case and a bag. You would like a cup of coffee as you had nothing on the train for breakfast. You prefer white coffee. Ask how far the house is from the station. Ask whether your correspondent has received the letter you sent last week. The examiner will play the part of your correspondent.

The *examiner's* sheet suggests the following:

1   Greet the candidate.

2   Ask how long the journey has been.

3   Ask how much luggage he/she has.

4   Ask if he/she would like some refreshment.

5   Suggest going to the station cafeteria. Ask what way he/she prefers coffee.

6   Explain that your home isn't far, and that your father will take you.

7   Say you haven't received the letter yet. (NICCEA)

4. At your Spanish penfriend's house

You are staying with your penfriend's family in Spain and you want to travel the following day to Barcelona. You want to call the bus station for information, so you ask your penfriend's parent for some information.

Your teacher will play the role of your penfriend's parent.

1   Ask him/her for the phone number of the bus station.

2   Ask him/her to repeat the number slowly.

3   When he/she says that the bus station is closed now, find out if it is closed all day and what time it opens tomorrow.

4   When he/she shows you the timetable, say that you will take the first bus tomorrow.

5   Be prepared to respond to another question.

The examiner's sheet before task 5 has the following:

'El primer autocar sale a las diez. ¿A qué hora quieres el desayuno?' (MEG)

5. Making arrangements

① SALIDA NACIONAL-INTERNACIONAL
② LLEGADA NACIONAL-INTERNACIONAL
③ PARADA AUTOBUS
④ PARADA TAXI
⑤ APARCAMIENTO DE VEHICULOS
⑥ EDIFICIO SERVICIOS
⑦ MERCANCIAS IBERIA
⑧ IBERIA
⑨ SPANTAX
⑩ EDIFICIO CONTRA INCENDIO
⑪ PISTA DE VUELO
⑫ PISTA DE RODADURA
⑬ PLATAFORMA ESTACIONAMIENTO DE AVIONES
⑭ TORRE DE CONTROL

INSTALACIONES DEL AEROPUERTO DE PALMA DE MALLORCA

You are speaking with your Spanish penfriend in Palma de Mallorca over the phone to plan a meeting at the beginning of a holiday you are going to spend with his/her family. He/she has sent you a plan of the airport so that you can arrange where you will meet when you arrive. The examiner will play the part of your penfriend. Your tasks are:

- To inform your friend of the date and time of your flight to Palma and the name of the airline you will be travelling with.

- To ask your friend which terminal you will arrive at.

- To decide how you will be travelling to the city from the airport.

- In the light of these decisions, to fix a place where you can meet.

- As you don't know each other, to arrange a way by which you will be able to recognise one another.

The only additional information given to the examiner is that you will arrive at Terminal A.

(SEG)

6. At the jeweller's

SITUATION	While you are in Spain your watch falls on the floor and breaks. You take it to the jeweller's where the assistant (your teacher) speaks to you.
YOU MUST	1. Explain to the assistant what happened. 2. Ask how much it would cost to repair it and when it will be ready. 3. Be prepared to make a decision about the watch and give a reason.
REMEMBER	Your watch is an old one and in the shop you have noticed some new watches at around 5,000 pesetas.

The examiner's booklet gives the following instructions
(a) Set the scene by saying:

Estamos en una joyería en España. Yo soy el dependiente/la dependienta.

¿En qué puedo ayudarle?

(b) Allow the candidate to explain what has happened to the watch. Say it's badly damaged.

(c) Say that you could repair it by tomorrow, but it would cost about 4,000 pesetas. Ask the candidate what he/she would like to do. (If he/she is unable to respond, say that you have some nice watches on sale.)

(d) End the conversation by agreeing with the candidate's decision.   (*NEAB*)

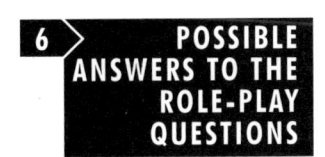

6 — POSSIBLE ANSWERS TO THE ROLE-PLAY QUESTIONS

The answers given below are possible solutions to the questions. They are not the only answers that would earn good marks. Getting the message across is the most important point.

1. At the chemist's

1 Me duele la garganta y me duele la cabeza.

2 Desde ayer.

3 No puedo comer ni dormir. He tomado aspirina.

4 ¿Cuántas tomo cada día?

5 Dos semanas.

Notes: 1 would actually be better expressed: 'Me duelen la garganta y la cabeza.'

4 could certainly be expressed using '¿Cuántas debo tomar...?' *but* '¿cuántas tomo...?' *is quite adequate.*

5 could almost be answered without full understanding. You know that '¿Cuánto tiempo...?' *needs a period of time as an answer.*

2. In a restaurant

1 Buenos días. Queremos sentarnos cerca de la ventana.

2 Por favor, una ensalada y una sopa.

3 Todavía no hemos decidido.

4 Oiga. Estos vasos están sucios... y el mantel también.

5 Pues sí, iremos a otra mesa.

6 Queremos un filete de ternera y una merluza por favor.

Notes: 'Todavía no...' *(not yet) is an important expression. The open-ended task (No.5) had to be expressed as a statement by the waiter/waitress to ensure that you could not simply say* 'sí' *or* 'no'.

3. At a railway station

The conversation might go something like this:

Examiner:	Hola. Buenos días.
Candidate:	Buenos días.
Examiner:	¿Cuántas horas llevas de viaje?
Candidate:	Catorce. Ha sido un viaje muy largo.
Examiner:	Sí. ¿Cuánto equipaje tienes?
Candidate:	Tengo una maleta grande y una bolsa.
Examiner:	¿Quieres tomar algo?
Candidate:	Pues sí. Me gustaría un café, por favor.
Examiner:	Podemos ir a la cafetería de la estación. ¿Cómo prefieres el café?
Candidate:	Me gusta con leche.
Examiner:	Muy bien. ¿Tienes alguna pregunta?
Candidate:	¡Ah! ¡Sí! ¿Está lejos tu casa?
Examiner:	No. No está lejos. Mi padre nos va a llevar.
Candidate:	¿Recibiste mi carta?
Examiner:	¿Qué carta es ésa?
Candidate:	Una que mandé la semana pasada.
Examiner:	Pues, no. Todavía no ha llegado.

Notes: This is a good example of a role-play in which you have to take the information from the outline of the situation. You must accept the invitation to have a drink and you must ensure that you ask for white coffee. (And, of course, you must give the right time for the journey and specify the correct luggage.) With all the other questions you are answering you could easily forget the two questions you have to ask, but your teacher should be able, as in this example, to remind you of that in a perfectly natural way within the conversation.

4. At your Spanish penfriend's house

1 Por favor, ¿cuál es el número de teléfono de la estación de autobuses?

2 ¿Cómo? ¿Puede repetirlo despacio por favor?

3 ¡Ah! ¿Está cerrado todo el día? ¿A qué hora se abre mañana?

4 Bueno. Tomaré el primer autocar mañana.

5 A las nueve, por favor.

Notes: If in 4 you said '... el primer autobús...' you would be understood perfectly, even though the correct word for a bus between towns is 'autocar'.

5. Making arrangements

The conversation might go something like this:

Examiner:	Hola, Sarah. ¿Qué tal?
Candidate:	Muy bien, gracias. Voy a llegar el jueves, 26 de julio.
Examiner:	¿Sí? Pues muy bien. ¿A qué hora llegarás y con qué compañía?
Candidate:	Llego a las once y media con Iberia.
Examiner:	¿Las once y media? ¿De la mañana?

Candidate:	Sí, voy por la mañana.
Examiner:	Bien. Iré al aeropuerto.
Candidate:	¿A qué terminal llegaré?
Examiner:	Si vas con Iberia, será la Terminal A.
Candidate:	Y ¿cómo vamos del aeropuerto a la ciudad?
Examiner:	Bueno, mira, mi padre estará de viaje ese día y no tendremos el coche. ¿Tendrás mucho equipaje?
Candidate:	No. ¿Hay un autobús?
Examiner:	Sí... o podemos coger un taxi si quieres.
Candidate:	Sí, vamos en taxi.
Examiner:	Vale.
Candidate:	¿Dónde nos vemos? ¿En la cafetería?
Examiner:	Sí, buena idea.
Candidate	Soy bastante alta y delgada y soy rubia. Me pondré una blusa amarilla y tendré una bolsa verde. ¿Y tú?
Examiner:	Yo no soy muy alta y soy morena. Llevaré una blusa roja y falda azul.

Notes: Be prepared for the unexpected. You may not have anticipated the question '¿De la mañana?' but you must deal with it if it comes and not rush on to the next thing you have to say. In this case the candidate has taken the initiative very effectively by asking which terminal, suggesting a means of transport when she received no direct response to her own question and suggesting the meeting place. Finally, she has settled the problem of recognition by briefly stating five facts by which she can be recognized and this has really simplified the final task, which she can resolve with the question '¿Y tú?' This has avoided the need for a question involving the verb 'reconocer'. Taking the initiative and suggesting things can really make the whole job more straightforward.

6. At the jeweller's
The conversation might go something like this:

Examiner:	Estamos en una joyería en España. Yo soy el dependiente. ¿En qué puedo ayudarle?
Candidate:	No funciona mi reloj.
Examiner:	¡Ah! ¿Qué le ha pasado?
Candidate:	Cayó al suelo. Está roto.
Examiner:	Bueno, vamos a ver... Pues, está en muy mal estado.
Candidate:	¿Cuánto costará repararlo?
Examiner:	Costará unas cuatro mil pesetas.
Candidate:	Y ¿cuándo lo puede hacer?
Examiner:	Lo puedo reparar para mañana, pero, como digo, costará unas cuatro mil pesetas. Usted verá. ¿Qué quiere hacer?
Candidate:	Es mucho dinero.
Examiner:	Sí. Tenemos unos...
Candidate:	Sí. Voy a comprar otro reloj.
Examiner:	¿Sí?
Candidate:	Sí. Mi reloj es viejo.
Examiner:	Tiene usted razón. Yo creo que no vale la pena repararlo.

Notes: This candidate uses quite straightforward sentences, including just one Future Tense ('costará'). He takes the tasks one at a time and has to be asked why the watch is not working. He does respond quickly when he realizes that he is about to be reminded of the watches on sale and in the end he performs all the tasks very successfully, including giving a reason.

7 > HIGHER LEVEL CONVERSATION

What you are expected to do at the Higher Level

General conversation is a compulsory part of the Higher Level Speaking test for all the Examining Groups. At this level the conversation can cover the full range of vocabulary and topic areas. There are, however, few additional topics at Higher Level that would be suitable for conversation. The most important is the area of your future plans.

The main way in which the Higher Level *conversation* differs from the Basic Level questions is that you are expected to say more! The initiative lies with you much more than it does with the examiner. The questions asked will normally require more than a brief response. Your teacher, as the examiner, will ask questions of a more open nature, giving you a cue to talk on a particular topic. An example could be something like *'Háblame un poco de tu familia'* or *'¿Cómo es tu casa?'*. These questions are a clear invitation to you to say what you can, so at this level you must be prepared to string a number of sentences together on a variety of themes.

> Try to make your answers interesting

Another important feature will be the actual language you use. Communication will still be very important, but there will be some marks for 'quality of language' and this is the chance for you really to 'show off' what you know. You should be looking to make your answers interesting in terms of content, vocabulary, idiom and structure. Remember, if you don't use it, you cannot be awarded credit for knowing it! The examiner will also be aiming to ensure that you have an opportunity to show that you can use a variety of tenses, by asking questions about the past (e.g. your last summer holiday) and the future (e.g. your plans for this year's holidays or your plans for next year).

8 PREPARING FOR THE EXAMINATION

> Prepare thoroughly

The first thing to do is pick out areas of special interest to you. After all, if you are interested in something, you are likely to have something to say! You should then prepare these topics thoroughly. The conversation will not be very long, but it is a good idea to string together some notes and sentences so that you can talk confidently on the individual subjects for at least a minute. In the examination you will not be allowed to give a pre-learnt talk, but you will be expected to volunteer ideas and information.

> You can ask questions

Next you should concentrate on the other possible themes which are perhaps of less interest to you. Remember, though, that you should aim to be interesting in the examination, so pretend, think of ways to convey enthusiasm, e.g. by using particular items of vocabulary and idioms. You are allowed to ask questions also, if you wish. For example, when talking about your holiday in Málaga, you could ask the examiner, *'¿Conoce usted Málaga?'* But do be careful. One, or at most two, questions will be plenty – you don't want to spend your examination time listening to your teacher reminiscing happily about his or her own holiday, only to find there is insufficient time for you to show what you can say!

9 IN THE EXAMINATION

> Don't be too brief in your answers

Try to say a few sentences in answer to every question you are asked. Even the simple question, such as *'¿Dónde vives?'*, can be used as an opportunity to answer at some length, e.g. *'Vivo en las afueras de Birmingham, en un barrio bastante bonito donde hay varias tiendas y una biblioteca. La casa tiene tres dormitorios y un jardín y está a cuatro kilómetros del colegio. Por eso tengo que coger el autobús por la mañana. Llevo cinco años viviendo en esa casa. Antes vivíamos en el norte de Inglaterra.'* Your teacher may interrupt you with another question, because you are not allowed simply to recite a pre-learnt monologue, but if you have to be interrupted in order to stop you talking you are obviously doing well!

10 PRACTICE CONVERSATION QUESTIONS

Below are some open-ended questions of the sort you should be prepared to answer. If your teacher gives you a list of possible questions, use that! At the end of this set of examples, sample answers are given for the first question under each of the first two topics.

YOURSELF AND YOUR FAMILY

Háblame un poco de tu familia.
¿Cómo es tu hermano?
¿Cómo es tu padre/tu madre?

YOUR HOME AND DAILY ROUTINES

¿Cómo es tu casa?
¿Cómo es tu dormitorio?
¿Te gusta tu casa? ¿Por qué?
¿Qué haces por la mañana?

YOUR HOME TOWN, VILLAGE OR AREA

¿Cómo es ....(Nottingham)?
¿Te gusta vivir allí? ¿Por qué?
¿Qué hay de interés en ...(Nottingham)?

SCHOOL OR COLLEGE

Háblame un poco de tu colegio.
¿Cuál es tu asignatura preferida? ¿Por qué?
¿Cómo es tu profesor de (matemáticas)?

FREE TIME, INTERESTS AND HOBBIES

¿Qué haces en tu tiempo libre? ¿Por qué te gusta?
¿Qué hiciste el fin de semana pasado?
¿Qué vas a hacer el sábado por la tarde?
Háblame de tu programa preferido de televisión.
¿Cuál es la última película que viste? ¿Te gustó? ¿Por qué?
¿Cuál es el último libro que leíste? ¿Te gustó? ¿Por qué?

YOUR HOLIDAYS

Háblame de tus vacaciones del verano pasado.
¿Cómo vas a pasar las vacaciones de verano este año.
¿Has visitado España? ¿Qué diferencias has notado entre Inglaterra y España?

YOUR FUTURE PLANS

¿Qué vas a hacer el año que viene? ¿Por qué?
¿Cuando termines por fin tus estudios ¿qué quieres hacer? ¿Por qué?

11 > SAMPLE ANSWERS TO CONVERSATION QUESTIONS

YOURSELF AND YOUR FAMILY

Háblame un poco de tu familia.

Somos cuatro en la familia: mis padres, mi hermana y yo. Mi hermana tiene catorce años y se llama Susan. Tiene el pelo largo y moreno y los ojos negros. Es simpática y bastante viva. Le gusta mucho la música pop y tiene muchos discos en su dormitorio. También le gusta nadar. Mi padre es bastante tranquilo pero a veces se enfada si discutimos mi hermana y yo. Trabaja en un banco. Mi madre es enfermera....

YOUR HOME AND DAILY ROUTINES

¿Cómo es tu casa?

Mi casa es bastante moderna. Tiene tres dormitorios y un jardín. El salón no es muy grande pero es muy cómodo, con dos sillones y un sofá. La cocina es muy grande y a mi madre le gusta mucho. Es mucho mejor que la cocina de la casa donde vivíamos antes. Mi dormitorio es pequeño pero a mí me gusta. Allí tengo mis libros y mis discos. Cuando miro por la ventana veo el parque, donde siempre hay gente....

Notice that you do not have to use long, complicated sentences in order to display your fluency. If you are describing a person, it will always appear more interesting and impressive if you can include: (a) a brief physical description, (b) something about the person's character and (c) something about their likes or dislikes.

12 > MEG HIGHER LEVEL PART 2

If you are taking the MEG Higher Level Part 2 Speaking test you will need special practice and training for the 'Narrator' task that forms this part of the examination. The principles will, however, be the same, in that the stimuli are intended as a basis for you to show what you are able to say.

The object of the exercise is to show that you are capable of giving an account of a journey or incident or day. In order to do that, you will have to turn the printed notes into a series of spoken sentences to give a clear picture of the events. Obviously your use of verbs will be important here. You will not be allowed to tell the whole story in one go – it has to be a conversation – and you must not rush through the account so fast that there is nothing more to say after one minute. The whole task is supposed to last about three minutes. You should use your imagination to add information. You must not contradict what is on the card but you may add anything that could have been included, provided it is reasonably relevant.

Two examples of this type of test are included below.

The notes below give you details of how your family and yourself spent the first day of your holidays in Spain.

On returning to school, you tell the Spanish assistant about your day.

Your teacher will play the part of the assistant.

You need not mention all the details and you may add extra information.

MUCHA LLUVIA
  en el hotel
  lo que hicimos para pasar el tiempo.

EL RESTAURANTE
  ¡qué caro!
  el camarero — lo que dijo
  lo que pasó después

LA PLAYA —
  sol muy fuerte
  incidente con una vieja

EL MUSEO
  cerrado — ¿por qué?

DE COMPRAS — los regalos que compré
  ¡cuánto tráfico!

A conversation on this task might begin something like this:

Examiner: De modo que fuiste a España con tu familia, ¿no? ¿Qué pasó el primer día?

Candidate: Bueno, el primer día por la mañana llovió mucho. Estábamos en el hotel y decidimos no salir. Pasamos la mañana en el bar del hotel haciendo planes. Mi padre tenía unos mapas y hablamos de los sitios que queríamos visitar. Luego miramos los mapas para ver por dónde teníamos que ir.

Examiner: ¿Sí? Y ¿cuándo salisteis entonces?

Candidate: Salimos a la hora de comer para ir a un restaurante. Todos tomamos paella. Fue muy buena. A mí me gusta la paella y también les gusta a mis padres. Bebimos vino tinto. De postre yo tomé un flan y mis

	padres tomaron fruta. Luego mi padre pidió la cuenta... y no le gustó.
Examiner:	¿No? ¿Por qué?
Candidate:	Porque todo era muy caro. Mi padre dijo al camarero que era demasiado. El camarero dijo que la comida buena es cara. Dijo que si no queríamos pagar esos precios debíamos comer en otro sitio. Mi padre se enfadó y llamó al gerente...

Here is another example of this kind of task:

The notes below give an outline of a weekend you had camping and walking in the mountains.

You tell your Spanish exchange partner about your weekend.

Your teacher will play the part of the exchange partner.

You do not need to mention every detail and you may add extra information.

el viaje allí
  medio de transporte

  lo que hicimos al llegar
  donde dormimos la noche del viernes

el sábado
  el desayuno
  lo que había en las mochilas
  el tiempo

  un incidente peligroso
  la persona que ayudó
  nuestro destino
  vuelta al camping

  lo que hicimos por la tarde en el camping
  la persona a quien encontramos

el domingo
  tiempo diferente
  un paseo ¿adónde?
  otro incidente
  la vuelta a casa

A STEP FURTHER

Take a topic from the list for conversation, think about it for a few minutes and then try talking about it in Spanish for a minute to a minute and a half. Try to make it sound interesting. Would a Spaniard actually enjoy listening to you? When you are reasonably happy, try recording it on cassette. Then listen to the cassette and see if you can see ways of improving it. It will always sound more natural if you feel you are actually talking to someone, so it is much better if you don't write it all down and then read it aloud.

You could then make it into more of a conversation by recording on cassette the questions you think you could be asked on that topic and then playing the recorded questions and answering each one as fully as you can.

For role-play, imagine likely situations and think how you would work through them in Spanish. Try to include as many of the 'unexpected' or unprepared questions as you can, so that when you are in the examination there is less chance of being taken completely by surprise. You can imagine role-play situations at all sorts of times, particularly when you are travelling to or from your school or college.

REVIEW SHEETS: SPEAKING: BASIC AND HIGHER LEVELS

1. One of the ways of coping with a role-play when you forget a key word or expression is to use the *opposite* word or expression in an appropriate way. For each of the Spanish words or expressions identify an *opposite* one in Spanish.

   Opposite in Spanish

   - salir..
   - subir..
   - quedarse...
   - mayor..
   - más grande ....
   - llegar...
   - odiar..

   Opposite in Spanish

   - triste..
   - temprano...
   - al final...
   - antes de...
   - de prisa ....
   - de buen humor...................................
   - nunca...

2. Another way of coping with role-play when you forget a key word is to explain what you mean *without using* that key word. Respond in Spanish to each of the following *without using* the Spanish term for the word underlined.

- You have to ask for a <u>fork</u>.
- You must explain to your doctor that you have hurt your <u>hand</u>.
- You must ask the way to the <u>railway station</u>.
- You want the person to open the <u>window</u>.
- You want to know when the <u>gymnasium</u> is open.
- You want the official at the bus station to give you a <u>return ticket</u>.
- You want to know the way to the <u>museum</u>.
- You want to say that you will arrive at the <u>campsite</u> this evening.

3. Think of your *own* responses in Spanish to each of the following questions. Practise speaking your response out aloud.

YOURSELF AND YOUR FAMILY:

Questions

- ¿Cuántos años tienes?
- ¿Cuándo es tu cumpleaños?
- ¿En qué año naciste?
- ¿Dónde vives?
- ¿A qué distancia del colegio vives?
- ¿Cuántas personas hay en tu familia?
- ¿Quiénes son?
- ¿Tienes hermanos?
- ¿Cuántos años tiene tu hermano?
- ¿Qué hace tu padre?
- ¿Qué hace tu madre?

YOUR SCHOOL OR COLLEGE:
Questions
- ¿Cómo vienes al colegio por la mañana?
- ¿A qué hora llegas?
- ¿A qué hora empiezan las clases?
- ¿Cuántas clases tienes por la mañana?
- ¿Cuánto tiempo dura cada clase?
- ¿Cuánto tiempo dura el recreo?
- ¿Cuál es tu asignatura preferida?
- ¿Qué asignatura te gusta menos?
- ¿Para ti ¿cuál es la asignatura más difícil?
- ¿Cuántos alumnos hay en el colegio?
- ¿Cuánto profesores hay en el colegio?
- ¿Qué haces durante el recreo?
- ¿Qué haces a la hora de comer?
- ¿Qué deportes practicas en el colegio?

YOUR FREE TIME, INTERESTS AND HOBBIES:
Questions
- ¿Qué te gusta hacer los sábados?
- Si vas al cine ¿a qué hora tienes que volver a casa?
- ¿Cuáles son tus pasatiempos favoritos?
- ¿Qué haces en tu tiempo libre?
- ¿Con quién juegas al...?
- ¿Con quién vas al...?
- ¿Dónde juegas al...?
- ¿Dónde tocas *el piano*?
- ¿Qué deportes practicas?
- ¿Cuándo?
- ¿Con quién?
- ¿Te gusta la música?

YOUR DAILY ROUTINES:
Questions
- ¿A qué hora te levantas normalmente?
- ¿Qué haces luego?
- ¿Dónde desayunas?
- ¿Con quién desayunas?
- ¿Qué desayunas?
- ¿A qué hora cenas?
- ¿A qué hora te acuestas?

YOUR HOME:
Questions
- ¿Dónde vives?
- ¿Cómo es tu casa?
- ¿Está cerca del centro de la ciudad?
- ¿Cuántas habitaciones hay en tu casa?
- ¿Qué hay en tu dormitorio?
- ¿Dónde haces los deberes?
- ¿Qué hacéis en el salón?
- ¿Tenéis un jardín?
- ¿Qué se cultiva en el jardín?
- ¿Tienes animales en casa?

YOUR HOME TOWN, VILLAGE OR AREA:
Questions
- ¿Dónde está tu casa?
- ¿Dónde está...?
- ¿Qué clase de pueblo o ciudad es?
- ¿Qué hay que hacer en...?
- ¿Qué hay de interés en...?
- ¿Cómo es...?

YOUR HOLIDAYS:
Questions
- ¿Adónde fuiste de vacaciones el verano pasado?
- ¿Con quién?
- ¿Cómo fuiste(is)?
- ¿Dónde os alojasteis?
- ¿Cuánto tiempo pasasteis allí?
- ¿Qué tiempo hizo?
- ¿Qué hiciste allí?
- ¿Visitaste algunos sitios interesantes?
- ¿Qué te gustó más allí?
- ¿Te gustaría volver allí?
- ¿Has visitado España?

HIGHER LEVEL ONLY:

The following tasks are a little more difficult and are more suited to the Higher Level of assessment.

A. Take five of the questions from each of the Topic Areas above and make up suitable answers of *at least four sentences each*.

B. For each of the following situations, think of an appropriate response in Spanish.

1. You've just heard that Juan has lost his job. What do you say to him?

2. You're giving a party. You've just noticed that one of your Spanish guests is standing all alone looking rather lost. What do you say to him?

3. You see something in the window of an antique shop in Spain. You would like to buy it but you don't know what it's called in Spanish. What do you say?

4. Your Spanish exchange partner's neighbour has just come back from holiday abroad. He now has his leg in plaster. What do you say?

5. You are alone in your Spanish exchange partner's house. You know their neighbours are on holiday. You hear noises coming from their house. You ring the police. What do you say?

6. Some Spanish friends have asked you to babysit for them. Their children are not very well-behaved. Say no, but nicely.

7. You are watching television with some Spanish friends who are staying with families near your home. You go to the kitchen to make coffee for them. When you come back, they've changed over from the programme you wanted to see. What do you say?

GETTING STARTED

Basic Level Reading is one of the tests that everyone has to do, so it is only sensible to make sure you know what to expect and how to deal with it. Reading is probably the easiest of the four skills for most candidates, since it does not require you to produce any Spanish and you can work at your own pace, going back a number of times over the parts you are unsure about. It is also an easy skill to practise on an individual basis. It does not require special equipment, can be done almost anywhere and in long or short sessions. There is usually plenty of reading material available in schools, colleges, bookshops and libraries. On the other hand, it is a good idea to make sure you know what sort of reading matter you need to practise with for the Basic Level test.

The nature of the reading material you are expected to deal with is specified in the National Criteria.

- It is material of the sort you would have to cope with in a Spanish-speaking country or when in contact in this country with Spanish-speaking people.
- It is restricted to the Topics specified by the Examining Group for Basic Level. (Check that you know which they are.)
- It is restricted to the Settings specified in the syllabus. (A grid of the Topics and Settings is included in Chapter 3.)

CHAPTER 8

READING: BASIC LEVEL

READING MATERIAL

NATURE OF QUESTIONS

ANSWERING QUESTIONS

UNDERSTANDING SIGNS AND NOTICES

UNDERSTANDING LONGER ITEMS

COPING WITH WORDS YOU DO NOT KNOW

ANSWER KEY TO PRACTICE QUESTIONS

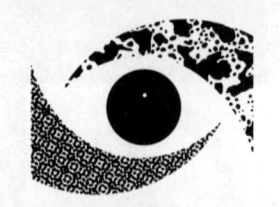

ESSENTIAL PRINCIPLES

1 > THE READING MATERIAL

❝ Be familiar with these types of reading materials ❞

The types of reading material you will be expected to understand include:

- public signs and notices
- simple instructions likely to be found in public places or on items bought in shops
- menus, price lists and labels on food and drink
- timetables (for school and public transport)
- advertisements and publicity handouts
- brochures and guides
- town plans, simple maps and tickets
- magazine articles likely to be of interest to a sixteen year-old
- post cards, notes and messages
- informal letters (from penfriends or from acquaintances of parents or friends)
- formal letters (e.g. about accommodation or town twinning arrangements)
- imaginative writing of the sort likely to be read by a sixteen year-old

❝ The materials will look realistic ❞

The material will be printed in as realistic a form as can reasonably be expected within the limits of an examination paper. Signs will look like signs – not free-standing words – and quite often they will be presented in photographs. (One Examining Group even includes some colour photographs.) Brochures will look like brochures and usually will be direct copies of the originals. Letters will look authentic – and that means that informal letters will be handwritten, so you need to be able to read Spanish handwriting. (Don't get too worried – the Examining Group will make sure they are legible!)

2 > THE NATURE OF THE QUESTIONS

❝ What you must be able to do ❞

- You are expected to demonstrate understanding of the main point of short items.
- You are expected to show understanding of specific details of longer items.
- You are expected to extract relevant specific detail from texts.
- You will *not* be required to show any other skills, such as the ability to summarize or to draw conclusions.
- Usually you write your answers on the question paper in the spaces provided. (At present the exception is SEG, which requires answers to be written in a separate answer booklet.)
- The questions are in English (or in Welsh if you take WJEC examinations and choose to be examined in Welsh).
- Answers are expressed either in words in English (or Welsh), in figures, by ticking boxes or by filling in grids.

(For the IGCSE the questions and answers are in Spanish.)

❝ You will know the setting ❞

In each case you will be told in English the *setting* in which you would be reading the item. This can be very helpful information in understanding the item and it also means you cannot be asked questions such as 'Where would you be if you saw this sign?'

❝ Types of setting or situation ❞

All the situations are of the sort that a British 16-year-old might realistically have to deal with when

- in a Spanish-speaking country
- reading a letter, post card or message from a Spanish-speaking person

- interpreting for someone who does not know Spanish well enough to understand the material for himself/herself

- reading material published in a Spanish-speaking country.

You are not allowed to use a dictionary or any other reference books in the examination.

3 > ANSWERING THE QUESTIONS

> Answer the question actually set

> The setting can guide you

> Keep to the point

> Always make an attempt

- **Remember that you do not have to understand every word** – only the ones relevant to the question. Items may contain up to 15% of words from outside the official list, provided that understanding of those words is not needed in order to answer the questions.

- **Make sure you read the question and that what you write does actually answer it.** If you are looking at a small advertisement and you are asked what you should do if you are interested in buying the article advertised, don't write down what the article is. What is almost certainly needed is a statement that you should ring a particular telephone number or go to a particular place (possibly at a particular time).

- **Read the setting carefully.** It is there to give you some guidance and help and it will often point you towards the right answer. If you are told, for example, that you see a particular notice in your hotel bedroom, it is hardly likely to be telling you that this is a one-way street or that may not park your car there!

- **Remember to answer in English (or Welsh).** Answers in Spanish will almost certainly score no marks (except in the IGCSE).

- **Keep your answers as short as possible** (but do make sure you give all the necessary information). Whole sentences are not required. If you are looking at a sign that reads *Se prohibe fumar* and the question is 'What are you told not to do?', you certainly do not need to write: 'I am told not to smoke'. All that is required in this case is 'Smoke'.

- **Check how many marks there are for each question.** (This is usually shown in brackets at the end of the question.) The number of marks will give you a good indication of the number of items of information required. Look for the extra points but make sure you find them in the text! There could be three marks for saying 'He bought (*1 mark*) an interesting (*1 mark*) book (*1 mark*)', so make sure you include the details. (Sometimes there are more points to be made than marks allocated. In such cases it is quite common for, say, 2 marks to be given for any two of three possible points.)

- **Always give an answer.** Even if you have no idea, make an informed guess, based on what you have understood from the setting, the question and the Spanish words themselves. You never know, you might be right! Your chances of guessing the correct answer are particularly good in multiple-choice and true/false questions.

- **Don't list every possibility you can think of.** If, when looking at a shop sign, you are asked what sort of shop it is, there is no point in listing every sort of shop you can think of. The examiner is likely either to mark your answer wrong straightaway or to mark only the first answer. (The Examining Groups have their own rules for marking such answers.)

- **Remember to use your common sense.** If the answer you have given seems totally unlikely or ridiculous, it is almost guaranteed to be wrong. In the Students' Answers – Examiner's Comments section later in this chapter there is a good example of what can happen if you fail to apply common sense and bear in mind the setting and the question. The answer was actually written by a candidate under examination conditions.

4 UNDERSTANDING SIGNS AND NOTICES

Signs and **notices** are often very brief, consisting of one, two or three words only. It is then important to understand those words. They normally do one of the following:
(a) tell us what something is or where it is (by pointing towards it)
(b) tell us what to do
(c) give us further information

SIGNPOSTS AND SIGNBOARDS

It is a good idea to make sure you know the Spanish for the places that are often **signposted** in towns or inside public buildings and hotels and also the Spanish for places that have notices on them to inform us what they are.

❝ Types of signposts in towns ❞

The sort of signposts you will see in *town* include:

AYUNTAMIENTO	*Town Hall*
BIBLIOTECA	*Library*
CASTILLO	*Castle*
CATEDRAL	*Cathedral*
CORREOS	*Post Office*
ESTACIÓN	*Station*
MERCADO	*Market*
OFICINA DE TURISMO	*Tourist Office*
PARQUE	*Park*
PISCINA	*Swimming Pool*
PLAYA	*Beach*
PLAZA MAYOR	*Main Square*
PLAZA DE TOROS	*Bull Ring*
PUERTO	*Harbour*

❝ Types of signposts in commercial settings ❞

The sort of signposts you will see in *hotels*, *offices* and *shops* include:

ASCENSOR	*Lift*
COMEDOR	*Dining Room*
CAJA	*Cash desk*
CAMBIO	*Exchange, bureau de change*
RECEPCIÓN	*Reception*
SERVICIOS	*Toilets*

There are others that you will find in the vocabulary lists. It is well worth while making sure you will be able to recognize the names of different departments on a store guide.

The signs that tell you what something is include the different types of shops and also banks and any of the places that may be signposted in the town. It is useful to remember that the names of most shops have the ending *-ería*, e.g.

a shop selling *libros* is *una librería*
a shop selling *pescado* is *una pescadería*

INSTRUCTIONS

It is also useful to be able to recognize an **instruction** when you see one!

Perhaps rather surprisingly, there is no agreed way in which the readers of public notices are to be addressed in Spanish. You will therefore find, often quite close together, signs that address you in the singular and others that address you in the plural; signs that address you in the familiar forms (*tú, vosotros*) and signs that address you more formally (*usted, ustedes*). Finally there are signs that issue instructions quite simply by using the infinitive of the verb (e.g. *Bajar con cuidado* – Go down carefully).

❝ Certain verb endings suggest instructions ❞

You therefore need to be aware that any verb ending in

-a	-an	-ar
-e	-en	-er
		-ir

<u>could</u> be an instruction. What is absolutely certain is that any verb ending in

-ad	-ed	-id

<u>is</u> an instruction.

> **Ways of giving 'pull' as an instruction**

Thus the instruction 'Pull' on a door or handle could be given in any of the following ways

TIRE	(*addressing the reader as* usted)
TIRA	(*addressing the reader as* tú)
TIREN	(*addressing the readers as* ustedes)
TIRAD	(*addressing the readers as* vosotros)
TIRAR	(*using the infinitive*)

> **Ways of giving the instruction not to smoke**

Instructions *not to do something* often include the word 'No' (e.g. *No fumar*) but they very frequently use the verb *prohibir* in some form or other. Thus the instruction *not to smoke* is likely to be expressed in one of the following ways:

Se prohibe fumar
Está prohibido fumar
Queda prohibido fumar
Prohibido fumar

More forcefully it may be linked with the word *terminantemente* (strictly):

Queda terminantemente prohibido fumar (Smoking strictly prohibited)

If all this sounds confusing, don't worry! You don't have to be able to reproduce all of these in Spanish. You simply have to recognize them as instructions and work out what they mean.

FURTHER INFORMATION

> **Other types of information given in signs**

Signs giving *further information* can deal with a whole range of matters but among the most frequent are notices that
 – state that a place is open or closed
 – state hours, days or dates of opening
 – give instructions on how to get there
 – state what is for sale
 – publicize special offers
 – publicize the specialities of restaurants and bars

It is important, therefore to know the days of the week, the months, the seasons of the year and the words for the different parts of the day - and it is worth making a special point of checking very carefully all answers about these. It is surprising how many candidates make silly mistakes over days and seasons.

You also obviously need to know expressions such as

> **Some useful expressions**

abierto *open*	cerrado *closed*
se abre *opens*	se cierra *closes*
de.. a.. *from.. to..*	desde.. hasta.. *from.. until..*
se vende *for sale*	vendo *for sale* (= I am selling)
descuento *discount*	liquidación *clearance sale*
rebajas *price reductions* (= sale)	

The words for items of food and drink, clothing and other things you could be interested in buying are likely to be important

You also need to be fully aware of expressions telling you *where* places are, e.g. *enfrente de Correos* (opposite – not in front of – the Post Office), *al lado del cine*.

5 UNDERSTANDING LONGER ITEMS

The *longer items* do not depend so much on your understanding of individual words. You have more text to help you. On the other hand you do have to identify the key points and you are more likely to have to understand the verbs that are used.

> **Hints for reading letters**

In **reading letters**, for example, it is quite important that you can tell whether the writer is telling you of something that regularly happens, is going to happen or has happened. For that reason you really do need to be able to identify the main tenses (Present, Future, Preterite). You may well receive help in this from the inclusion of other expressions such as *todos los sábados, el año que viene* or *la semana pasada* but you cannot be sure that there will always be help of this sort.

> **Look at the verb endings**

It is also important to look at the **endings of verbs** in order to be sure who it is that does, did or will do the action. Do be careful here of verbs that end in *-ó. Llegó*, for example, means 'He (or she) arrived' – <u>not</u>, as all too many candidates decide under the pressure of the examination, 'I arrive(d)'.

> **Subjects of verbs are often omitted**

You have to remember also that the **subject of the verb** (the person who does the action) is regularly omitted in Spanish. In particular, it is important not to let yourself be misled by object pronouns (*me, te, le, lo, la, nos, os, les, los, las*) coming before the verb. *Me dio...* means 'He (or she) gave me...' <u>not</u>, as many candidates decide, 'I gave...' If you are in the habit of making mistakes of that kind, it is a good idea to make a special point of checking for them in every piece of reading work you do and to make a mental note to check for them in your examination answers.

In many cases the questions will be seeking an answer about

Who?	How long?
What?	How many
Where?	How much
When?	Why?

These questions suggest some areas of vocabulary that you would be well advised to make sure you know.

> **Some useful vocabulary**

- Who? – family and friends, jobs.
  – descriptions: physical appearance, size, age etc.
- What? – almost anything! Check out particularly Shopping, Food and Drink and Free Time and Entertainment
- Where? – position, location of places and buildings, landmarks, countries, directions and distances.
- When? – time of day, days, weeks, months, dates, frquency, expressions of time (today, yesterday etc.), seasons, important holidays (e.g. Christmas, New Year), beginning, middle, end
- How long? – time, especially duration (*durante* and *hasta* in particular)
- How many? – numbers
- How much? – quantity, numbers
- Why? – reasons

6 COPING WITH WORDS YOU DO NOT KNOW

In coping with *unknown words* there are a number of strategies that can be used:

- Check if they are important for you to be able to answer the questions you have been asked. If they are not, don't worry about them!

- Are they similar to any words in English (or any other language you know)? If they are, does that lead you to a meaning that makes sense in the context?

- Do the other words and the meaning of the sentences around them give you a clue to their possible meaning?

- Does the question or the setting give you an indication of possible meanings?

> **Some techniques to help when you come across unfamiliar words**

- Does the word begin with a common prefix, e.g. *des-* or *in-* (which are the equivalent of the English 'dis-', 'un-', 'in-')? For example, *desagradable* means 'unpleasant'.

- Does the word end in a common *suffix*? At Basic Level you need to be aware of the following:

  -mente is the equivalent of the English *-ly* (as in *desafortunadamente*: unfortunately).

  -ito (*-ita*) means 'little' (as in *casita*: little house).

  -ería usually means 'shop' (as in *pastelería*: cake shop).

> **The suffix may help you**

  -ero (*-era*) means either 'person who deals with..' or 'container for..' (as in *camionero:* lorry driver; *florero*: vase).

  -ista usually means 'person who deals with or is involved in...' (as in *maquinista*: machinist or engine-driver; *futbolista*: footballer; *taxista*: taxi-driver).

- Will a change of one or two letters make the word look more like an English word that will make sense in the sentence? At Basic Level the following are worth trying:

  f – change to *ph* (as in *farmacia*: pharmacy; *foto*: photo).

  t – change to *th* (as in *tema*: theme).

  qu – change to *ch* (as in *máquina*: machine; *arquitecto*: architect).

-ción – change to *-tion* (as in *nación*: nation).

-cia – change to '*-cy*' or '*-ce*' (as in *agencia*: agency; *esencia*: essence).

It is also worth trying an exchange of *g* with *j* or *j* with *g* and an exchange of *b* with *v* or *v* with *b*.

STUDENTS' ANSWERS WITH EXAMINER'S COMMENTS

The first items in the examination are usually very short. There is often only one word to read. Typically the early sections will deal with signs and notices.

SHORT ITEMS

Q1 You are on holiday in a Spanish town with a group of friends who don't know any Spanish. At mid-day on your first day, you are looking for somewhere to have a snack. Outside a bar you see this sign.

What two types of snack are available?

Hamburgers

Sandwiches (2)

> Good. Both right.

(ULEAC)

Q2 While taking a walk in a park, you see the notice below.

$$\boxed{\text{AGUA NO POTABLE}}$$

> ❝ No. 'Potable' means 'drinkable'. It is not drinking water. ❞

What warning does it give you?
...Don't put water in pots................................. (1)
(ULEAC)

Q3 You take a bus to the town-centre. Inside the bus you see a sign.

⟨ PROHIBIDO HABLAR CON EL CONDUCTOR ⟩

> ❝ No. 'Conductor' means 'driver'. In any case the first four words of your answer were unnecessary ❞

What are you told not to do?
...You're told not to speak to the conductor. (1)
(MEG)

Q4 Later, you enter a dry-cleaner's. You see their price-list on the wall.

LISTA DE PRECIOS

Abrigo	540
Blusa	225
Camisa	300
Chaqueta	500
Corbata	120
Falda	400
Pantalón	450
Vestido	510

> ❝ Wrong. 'Vestido' is a dress. A skirt is 'falda'. So the answer is '400 pesetas' ❞

How much does it cost to have a skirt dry-cleaned?
...510.. (1)
(MEG)

Q5 You see this advertisement for a drink called Sinsa.

¡SED! ¡CALOR! ¡FATIGA!

beba **Sinsa**

CON SABOR NARANJA

* * *

Apropiado para todas las edades
De venta en farmacias

Necesario disolver el contenido del sobre en agua fría.

CHAPTER 8 STUDENTS' ANSWERS WITH EXAMINER'S COMMENTS

(a) What advice is given on line 2?

💬 Good 💬 .....Drink Sinsa.. (1)

(b) What flavour is the drink?

💬 Good 💬 .....Orange.. (1)

💬 No. 'Todas las edades' means 'all ages' 💬

(c) For what ages is the drink recommended?

.....Adults.. (1)

💬 Yes. (Most people would say 'chemist's') 💬

(d) Where can you buy the drink?

.....Pharmacy.. (1)

(e) What advice is given about dissolving the contents of the envelope?

.....Dissolve in cold soapy water.. (1)

(MEG)

💬 Really! This is a drink — have you forgotten that? Everything is right except for 'soapy' but you really can't expect a mark if your interpretation of the instructions would lead you to do something quite so ridiculous! Incidentally, 'sobre' means 'envelope' 💬

LONGER ITEMS

Q6 On a visit to another town you are given this publicity.

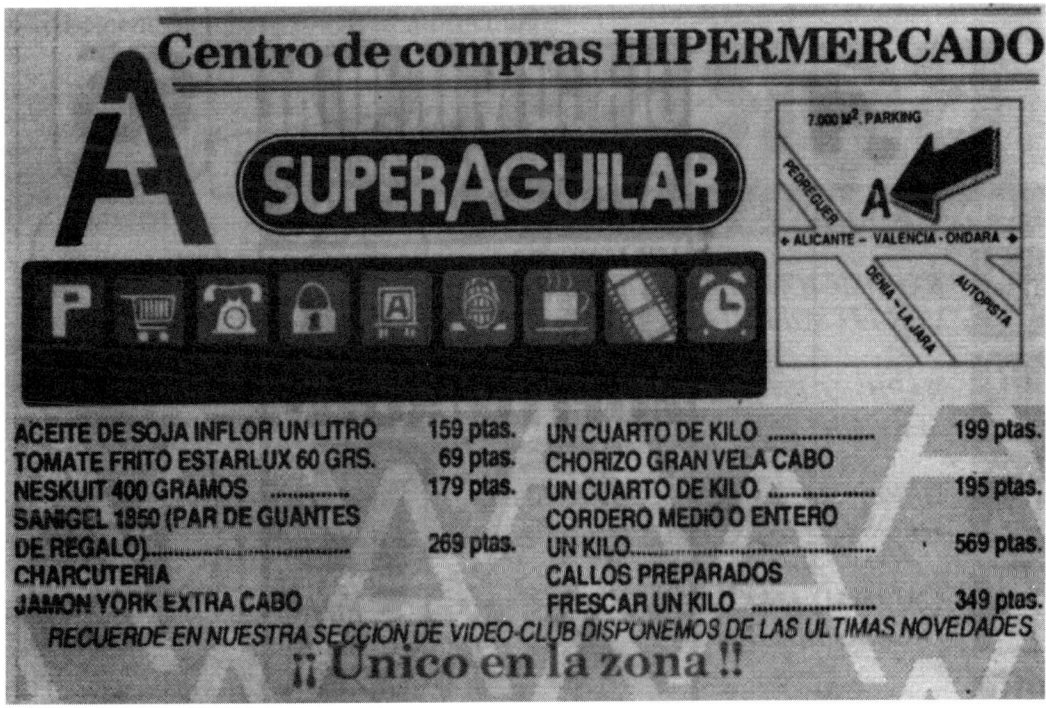

💬 Yes. It's a hypermarket, really, but 'supermarket' is acceptable 💬

(a) What sort of shop is it advertising?

.....Supermarket... (1)

(b) What two types of meat could you buy there?

.....York ham and Veal... (1)

💬 York ham, or just ham is right; a pity you have confused 'cordero' (lamb) with 'ternera' (veal) 💬

(c) What item of clothing is being given away?

.....A tee-shirt.. (1)

(SEG)

💬 No. I don't know where you got that from — presumably it is just a guess based on the sort of free gift often handed out — in which case it was a good idea... but not right! The right answer is 'a pair of gloves' — 'un par de guantes'. 'de regalo' means 'as a gift' 💬

CHAPTER 8 **READING: BASIC LEVEL**

Q7 Your family is thinking of going to Spain next year and this advertisement for a new holiday development caught your eye recently in a Spanish magazine.

PUERTO SHERRY

EN PUEBLO SHERRY CUALQUIER CASA TIENE, ADEMAS, 200.000 m²

Porque PUEBLO SHERRY es un lugar único, diferente, con más de 200.000 m² llenos de atractivas posibilidades. Para tener en familia mucho más que una casa a orillas del Atlántico.

Barco, pesca, piscinas al aire libre y cubierta, gimnasios, baños turcos, saunas, terrazas, salones... En el sitio excepcional de Puerto Sherry.

Locales comerciales y apartamentos sencillos o dúplex, con chimenea, acceso directo y los más excepcionales acabados. En el puerto en el corazón de la bahía, con el clima, las playas y la tradición de Andalucía.

Invertir en Pueblo Sherry es tener la visión de futuro de los que en su día lo hicieron en la Costa Azul o en la Riviera...

Courtesy of Brent Walker España, S.A.

(a) Apart from size and location, give two reasons why Pueblo Sherry is so attractive.

There are many possible attractions much more than a house by the sea (2)

❝ This a little vague. You qualify for one mark. You really need any two of: It is unique OR different; There are many possible things to do; It is good for families; It is much more than a house by the Atlantic. ❞

> 3 marks out of 4. Turkish baths are not a sport! You needed to mention 'boating' for the fourth mark.

(b) Name four sports available in Pueblo Sherry.
   ....Fishing..., swimming..., gymnastics............................
   .....Turkish bath.. (4)

(c) Where precisely is Pueblo Sherry located?
   ....In the corner of the bay...
   .... (3)

> 1 mark for 'the bay'. *El corazón* is not the corner but the heart. You could get marks for any 3 of: – on the Atlantic coast; – by the harbour – at the heart of the bay

(d) What three features of Pueblo Sherry are typical of Andalucía?
   ....climate, beaches and tradition...
   .... (3)
   (NICCEA)

> A perfect answer. 3 marks

PRACTICE QUESTIONS

SHORT ITEMS

Q1 Here are some signs and notices you are likely to see in Spain. Look at each one carefully and answer the questions.

(a) If you saw this notice in a shop window what would it tell you?

CERRADO

.... (1)

(b) You might see this sign on a door – what should you do?

EMPUJEN

.... (1)

(c) Travelling along a main road you are likely to see this sign – what does it warn you of?

OBRAS

.... (1)

CHAPTER 8 **READING: BASIC LEVEL**

(d) At a campsite you might see this sign – what does it tell you?

> AGUA POTABLE

.... (1)

(e) In a shop you might see this notice – what is it telling customers?

> GRAN LIQUIDACION

.... (1)

(f) Why might you follow this sign?

> ◀ CORREOS

.... (1)
(*WJEC*)

Q2 You are travelling in Spain by train and have picked up this brochure for a Hotel in Cartagena.

hostal
los habaneros

☎ 968 - 50 52 50 (5 lineas)
SAN DIEGO, 60
CARTAGENA

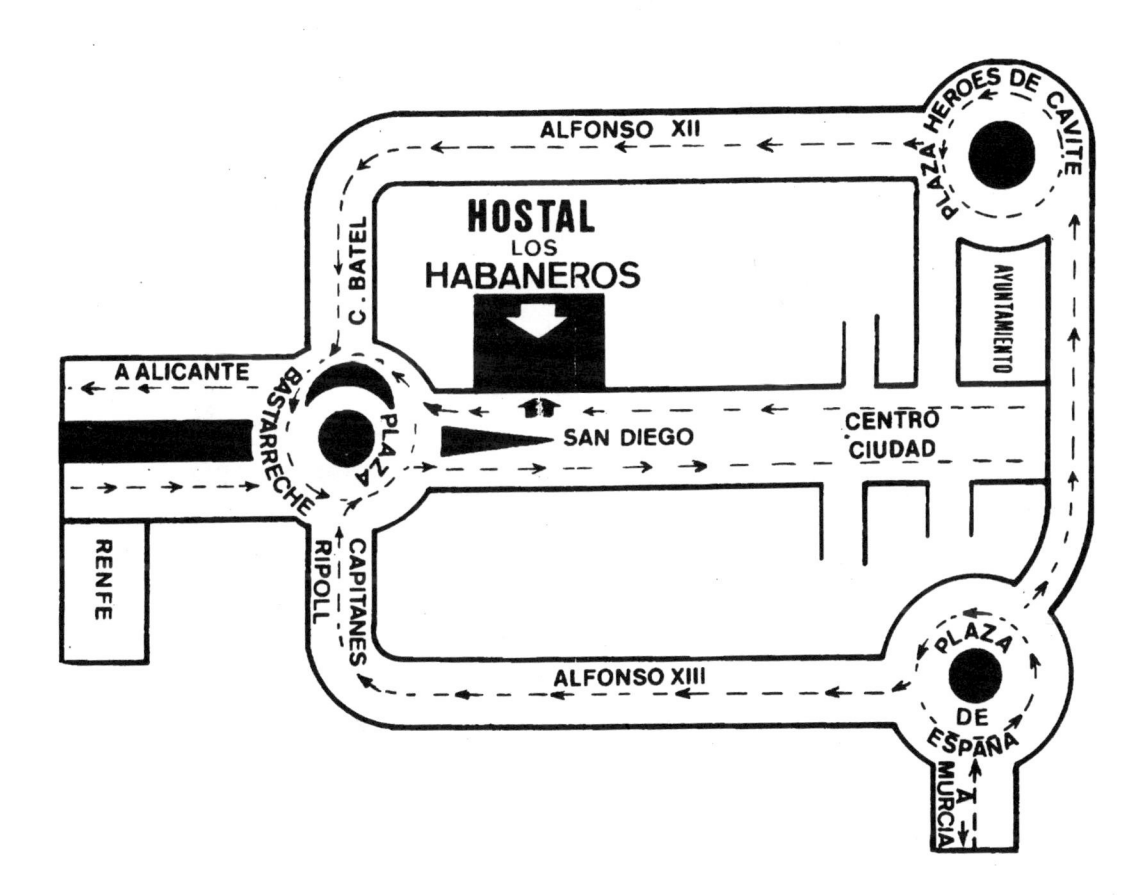

(a) On the plan above, show with a cross the situation of the Railway Station.
.... (1)
(WJEC)

Q3 You see this advertisement in the newspaper.

LIBRERIA

Núñez

- PRENSA EXTRANJERA.
- METODO DE ESPAÑOL PARA EXTRANJEROS.
- DICCIONARIOS.
- LITERATURA EXTRANJERA.
- NOVEDADES.
- PAPELERIA.

RUA MAYOR, 13

What kind of store is this?

.... (1)

(*Bahamas GCSE*)

Q4 You are going on holiday to Mallorca. Your plane ticket comes in a folder with this message on the front.

Buen viaje

What does it say?

.... (1)

(*NEAB*)

Q5 When you get to your hotel you see this sign.
What does it tell you about?

```
HORARIO  COMIDAS
    DESAYUNO      08.00 - 10.00
    ALMUERZO      13.00 - 15.00
    CENA          18.30 - 21.15
```

.... (1)
(*NEAB*)

Q6 Later, you take the lift to your hotel room. What does the instruction inside the lift say?

PROHIBIDO
SUBIR MAS DE TRES PERSONAS

.... (1)
(*MEG*)

Q7 You go out into the street and you see a bar.

DESAYUNOS BAR ESTEBAN
APERITIVOS

Which meal of the day does the bar specialise in?

.... (1)
(*MEG*)

Q8 Later, you decided to go to the market. You see the following signposts. Which sign would you follow?

[Signpost image: Plaza de toros, PLAZA MAYOR, Biblioteca, mercado]

Tick one box only.

(1)
(MEG)

Q9 While browsing through some newspapers in your Spanish department, you come across this advertisement.

> **Vendo** por traslado mesas, armarios, sillas. Teléfono 233221. Seis a nueve.

What three articles are for sale?

....
....
.... *(3)*
(NICCEA)

Q10 Next you visit Salamanca where a shop has some biscuits from Ledesma on the counter. You are interested in the contents of this packet, but have never heard of *rosquillas*.

> Especialidad en
> Rosquillas típicas
> de Ledesma
> y otros productos
>
> LEDESMA (Salamanca)
> Teléfono 57 00 08
> Fórmula Cualitativa:
> harina, huevos, azúcar y mantequilla
> Peso 250 gr.

What are **two** of the ingredients of these biscuits?

.... *(2)*
(SEG)

Q11 Flicking through the newspaper you notice this announcement.
How might you be able to help, and what should you do if you can?

> **PERDIDO RELOJ**
>
> OMEGA en oro blanco, cuadrado y rodeado de brillantes, el domingo, 24 de mayo, en las proximidades de la Clinica Delfos o en calle Balmes-Mitre
>
> Por favor, llamar al teléfono 200-44-49
> Se gratificará

.... *(2)*
(SEG)

Q12 As you tour the city where you are staying, you come across a building you would like to visit, but there is a notice on the gate.

> **PROHIBIDO EL PASO**
> MONUMENTO en RESTAURACION
> ZONA de OBRAS

What does the notice tell you?

.... *(2)*
(SEG)

Q13 One of your friends has to go home early to the U.K., and gets this leaflet from a travel agent's.

> **Condiciones**
>
> - Billete válido 6 meses.
> - Fecha de vuelta abierta o cerrada.
> - Niños de   0 a 4 años GRATIS.
>   4 a 12 años 50% reducción.
> - Estudiantes, menores de 27 años
>   y 3.ª Edad: 10% descuento.
> - Equipaje: 2 maletas gratis por pasajero.

(a) What discount is available for students?
.... *(1)*

(b) What are the arrangements for luggage? Give full details.
....
.... *(2)*

(Please note that in the original GCSE paper the leaflet was printed in colour, with black print on a yellow background.)

(ULEAC)

Q14 In the restaurant, you decide to have the set meal menu.

SNACK RESTAURANTE El Molino

Sopa de Tomate	Bistec	Tarta de Manzana
Ensalada Mixta	Bistec Pimienta	Helado Variado
Cóctel de Gambas	Merluza	Tarta Helada
Sopa de Pollo	Chuleta	
	Tortilla Española	
	Pollo	

Select a meal for one of your friends who is a vegetarian, and does not eat fish or ice-cream. Note (in English) below what each course is.

First course: ....
Main course: ....
Dessert: .... *(3)*

(ULEAC)

Q15 In a café, two of your friends take sugar in their coffee. They ask you about their horoscopes on the back of the sugar sachets:

CANCER
del 21/6 al 21/7

Prepare las maletas. Va a hacer el viaje de sus sueños.

VIRGO
del 22/8 al 22/9

¿Tiene el corazón fuerte? Hoy va a vivir una romántica aventura.

(a) What can **Cancer** expect?
.... *(1)*
(b) What will happen to **Virgo** today?
.... *(1)*

(ULEAC)

Q16 In your room you read about your hotel.

HOTEL ·· DELFÍN AZUL

MALLORCA
Tels. (971) 54 53 50/54/58

Ideal para familias. El Hotel Delfín Azul está situado a sólo 200 metros de la playa de Alcudia. Zona juegos y piscina para niños. Guardería. Entretenimientos varios en el hotel. Aire acondicionado (ver símbolos).
270 Habitaciones.

(a) Why is it ideal for families? Mention two things.
   (i) ....
   (ii) .... (2)
(b) Why will the rooms be cool?
   ....
   .... (1)
   (*NEAB*)

CHAPTER 8 READING: BASIC LEVEL

LONGER ITEMS

Q17 After you have returned to England, you receive this note from the friend you met in Mallorca.

> ¡Hola! Estoy pasando unos días en Canarias con mis padres. Me quedé muy triste cuando te fuiste pero puedo ir a visitarte el próximo verano ¡Fenomenal! ¡Ah! encontré tu reloj ¿Te lo mando o te lo llevo cuando te visite? Escríbeme pronto. Recuerdos a tus padres, fueron muy amables
>
> tu amiga española
> Ana

(a) Why was your friend sad?
.... (1)

(b) What is your friend going to do next summer?
.... (1)

(c) What **two** suggestions does she make about your watch?
(i) ....
(ii) .... (2)

(d) What does she say about your parents?
.... (1)

(NEAB)

Q18 Your Spanish assistant in school has just returned after a visit to Spain. She shows you this ticket.

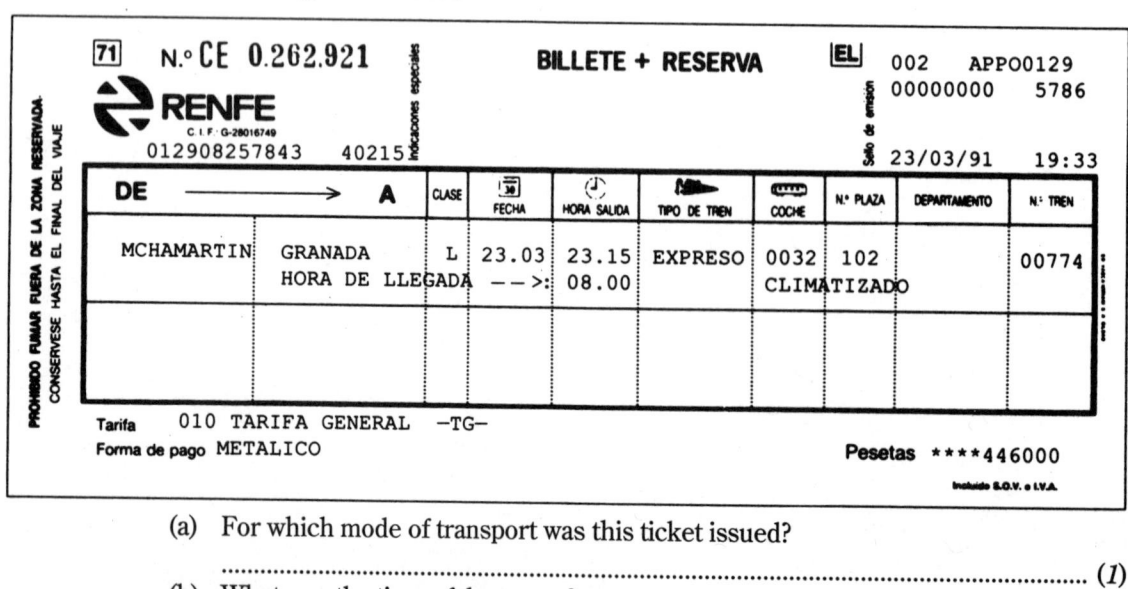

71	N.° CE 0.262.921		BILLETE + RESERVA		EL	002 APP00129				
	RENFE C.I.F: G-28016749					00000000 5786				
	012908257843 40215					23/03/91 19:33				

DE → A	CLASE	FECHA	HORA SALIDA	TIPO DE TREN	COCHE	N.º PLAZA	DEPARTAMENTO	N.º TREN
MCHAMARTIN GRANADA	L	23.03	23.15	EXPRESO	0032	102		00774
HORA DE LLEGADA -->:			08.00		CLIMATIZADO			

Tarifa 010 TARIFA GENERAL —TG—
Forma de pago METALICO   Pesetas ****446000

(a) For which mode of transport was this ticket issued?
.... (1)

(b) What was the time of departure?
.... (1)

(c) What was the assistant's seat number?
.... (1)
(d) According to the ticket, where is smoking not permitted?
.... (1)
(NICCEA)

Q19 You are in Spain and you are making drinks for a party. Your Spanish friend shows you a recipe for making party drinks.

COCKTAIL DE FRUTA

Pon 800 mls. de zumo de piña en una jarra grande y luego añade 200 gramos de azúcar. Echa un litro de zumo de uva.

Antes de servir, pon el cocktail en la nevera durante dos horas.

Sirve tu *COCKTAIL DE FRUTA* con hielo.

(a) What **three** ingredients do you need in order to make the drink?
   (i) .... (1)
   (ii) .... (1)
   (iii) .... (1)
(b) What should you do **before** serving the drink?
.... (1)
(c) How should you serve the drink?
.... (1)
(MEG)

Q20 You leave your friend and go back to your hotel. You need to get some clothes washed. The hotel has a laundry service. Here are the instructions.

SERVICIO DE LAVANDERIA.

Por favor, deje la ropa con esta lista. La ropa tiene que estar delante de la puerta de su habitación a las 10:45 de la mañana. Puede recoger su ropa a partir de las 6:30 de la tarde del día siguiente.

	Vestidos
	Pañuelos
	Pantalones Cortos
	Pijamas
	Camisas
	Faldas

NOMBRE
HABITACION
FECHA

(a) Put a tick in the box on the list next to
   (i) shorts
   (ii) shirts
   You should put only TWO ticks. *(1)*
(b) Where do you leave your washing at 10.45?
   .... *(1)*
(c) When **exactly** can you collect your washing?
   .... *(1)*
(d) What **three** pieces of information do you have to write on the bottom of the form?
   (i) ....
   (ii) ....
   (iii) .... *(3)*

(NEAB)

Q21 Your friend Tim has just received the letter below from his Spanish penfriend. He asks you to help him understand it.

Valladolid, 22 de mayo

Querido Tim:

¿Cómo estás? Yo muy bien. Y mi familia también. En esta carta, voy a decirte lo que me gusta hacer. Es más fácil decirte lo que no me gusta hacer; no me gustan los deportes, no me gustan mis estudios, no me gusta la música clásica.

¡A mí me encanta cocinar! Me gusta cocinar platos de todos los países del mundo. Mi madre dice que mis platos son muy ricos; pero a veces mis padres no están muy contentos. ¿Sabes por qué? Pues dicen que los ingredientes son muy caros.

¿A ti qué te gusta hacer?

Un abrazo,

Elena.

(a) What is Elena's favourite pastime?
.... (1)
(b) Why are Elena's parents unhappy sometimes?
.... (1)
(MEG)

Q22 Here are three advertisements for restaurants which appeared in the same issue of a local paper.

CAFETERÍA RESTAURANTE Riofrío

LES DESEAN FELICES FIESTAS

Les recordamos que permaneceremos abierto el día 31 hasta las 2 de la madrugada

RESERVE SU CENA

Teléfonos 319 29 77 - 78
Calle Génova, 28
Centro Colón

RESTAURANTE
Servicio de Cafetería

MEDITERRANEO

Feliz Navidad y próspero Año Nuevo

Mohamed Ben Omar Ben Mimón

La más alta cocina ARABE y ESPAÑOLA en el mejor ambiente

AIRE ACONDICIONADO

O'Donnell, 28 - Arturo Reyes, 6
Teléfonos 681688 - 681927 - MELILLA

RESTAURANTE-CHINO
SHANGHAI
Menú especial para Navidad
AUTENTICA COMIDA CHINA
COMIDA PARA LLEVAR A CASA
Abierto todos los días desde 12,30 a 16 y 19 a 23
FELIZ NAVIDAD
Avda. Miguel Bueno s/n. Telf. 470201
Dirección Jymmy   FUENGIROLA

(a) Which restaurant offers a 'take-away' service?
.... (1)

(b) In which restaurant are you advised to book in advance?
.... (1)

(c) Apart from food what facility does the MEDITERRANEO offer?
.... (1)

(d) What do all the restaurants wish their customers?
.... (1)

(*WJEC*)

Q23

ANUNCIOS POR PALABRAS

Inmobiliarias

■ **MANSILLA** San Francisco del Lagarillo - Blanco. Locales comerciales. Facilidades pago. Teléfonos 297304 - 380383.

■ **MANSILLA** en Torremolinos Mirador de las Palmeras III, casas adosadas, de 2 y 3 dormitorios, garaje, jardín, piscina, cocina amueblada, solarium. Teléfonos 386525 - 380289.

■ **MANSILLA** en Torremolinos Coto de Rosas. Casas adosadas de 2 y 3 dormitorios, jardín, piscina, cocina amueblada y solarium. Teléfonos 371046 - 380289.

■ **ATABAL** chalet, 1.000 m². terreno, 250 m². construidos, piscina, extraordinarias vistas. Telf. 307856 - 280158.

■ **VENDO** piso en Málaga 153 m² con garage. Razón Melilla. Tfno: 685880.

■ **MARBELLA** local 350 m². C/. Principal, esquina 30 m. escaparate, renta baja, terminado e instalado. Telf. 307856 - 280158.

■ **ALAMEDA** Prolongación, venta de locales, o alquiler, a elegir metros fachada principal. Telf. 307856 - 280158.

■ **NAVES** en venta, varias zonas y distintas condiciones. Telf. 319844 - 339766.

■ **VELEZ - MALAGA.** Vendo piso estrenar 3 dormitorios, 2 baños, parabólica, puerta blindada, garaje, facilidades 13 años. Ptas. 5.757.000. Sr. Romero. Telf. 542900 (24 horas).

■ **TORRE DEL MAR.** Vendo apartamento estudio semi amueblado, vista al mar, 100 m. de playa, piscina, tenis. Ptas. 2.700.000. Sr. Romero. Telf. 542900 (24 h.).

■ **TORRE DEL MAR.** Vendo piso 3 dormitorios, 4ª. planta sin ascensor, muy céntrico. Sr. Romero. Telf. 542900 (24 h.).

The above advertisements give firstly the location and then details of property for sale.

(a) Where would you find properties that have a swimming pool? Name **three** places.
....
.... (3)

(b) Where would you find a 3 bedroom apartment with 2 bathrooms and a garage?
.... (1)

(c) What attractions does the property at ATABAL offer?
.... (1)

(*WJEC*)

Q24 Someone sends you this clipping, knowing that there is a new baby in your household. You decide to indicate some interesting facts for the other members of your family.

> ¿Cómo es, en líneas generales, la evolución del bebé en su primer año? Observe la guía que le damos.
>
> **A LOS 2 MESES.** Ya sonríe, y comienza a emitir algunos sonidos para expresar sus estados de ánimo.
>
> **A LOS 4 MESES.** Le gusta que lo levanten en el aire y que lo llevan de un lado a otro.
>
> **A LOS 5 MESES.** Puede entretenerse sólo por cortos períodos de tiempo.
>
> **A LOS 6 MESES.** Trata de asir su imagen si la ve en un espejo.
>
> **A LOS 8 MESES.** No le gusta que lo dejen solo, y hace oír su protesta cuando esto ocurre.
>
> **A LOS 10 MESES.** Se abraza a la mamá y a las personas que muestran afecto.
>
> **A LOS 11 MESES.** Comienza a imitar las acciones de las personas que ve a su alrededor.
>
> **A LOS 12 MESES.** Sigue con el cuerpo el ritmo de la música.

Your information happens to be out of order. Next to each description of babies' behaviour, write the age in months at which the behaviour is displayed.

BEHAVIOUR	NO. OF MONTHS
Does not like to be left alone.	..................(1)
Shows awareness of rhythm.	..................(1)
Responds to affection by hugging.	..................(1)
Tries to grab mirror image.	..................(1)
Likes to be lifted and swayed.	..................(1)

(*Bahamas GCSE*)

Q25 You look at the advertisement page in a magazine.

BUENAS OCASIONES

- Desearía intercambiar postales de todo el mundo. Escribir a Antonio Juan. Les Agudes, 58, C 5°1.ª.08033 Sevilla.

- Deseo hacer amigos o amigas, para alquilar piso en Benidorm. Teresa Teruel. Burgos, 9, 1° B. 01002 Vitoria Alava.

- Vendo falda de cuero, por sólo 4,000 pesetas. Carmen. (93) 437 10 23. Hospitalet, Barcelona.

AMIGOS

- Deseo saber algo de un amigo que conocí hace años en Torrejón de Ardoz. Se llama Marcelo Quiles y vivió en la calle Campiña, 6. Si le conocéis, decidle que María sigue viviendo en el mismo sitio en Guadalajara. Gracias. María. (911) 21 42 07. Guadalajara.

- Quisiera tener correspondencia con chicos y chicas de 10 a 11 años. Si es posible de Barcelona. Hago patinaje sobre ruedas. Noemí Ruiz Fontés. Menorca, 120, 1.°-2.ª 08020 Valencia.

BOLSA DE TRABAJO

- Soy un chico de 17 años, responsable y serio, y me ofrezco como jardinero los fines de semana. Pedro Estefanía. (91) 687 61 84. Leganés, Madrid.

(a) What does Antonio Juan want to exchange?
.... (1)

(b) Why does Teresa Teruel want to meet people?
.... (1)

(c) What is Carmen selling? Give full details.
.... (2)

(d) Why is Maria advertising?
Tick one box only.

To tell someone she has moved house. ☐

To meet up with an old friend. ☐

To find a new friend. ☐

To try and trace a relative. ☐
(1)

(e) What pastime does Noemí mention?
.... (1)

(f) What service is Pedro offering?
.... (1)

(*MEG*)

Q26 This article, entitled *"An interview with the dolphins"*, attracts your attention. You decide to use it as the basis of a piece of English GCSE coursework, and your Spanish teacher gives you some questions to help you pinpoint the main elements of the article.

UNA ENTREVISTA CON LOS DELFINES

Concha Galán y Goyo González, los presentadores de «En verano», uno de los programas de la tarde de TVE-1, son aficionados a los animales y a la aventura. Recientemente, los dos jóvenes reporteros decidieron hacer la entrevista más difícil de su vida: fueron al delfinario del Zoo de Madrid para «entrevistar» a unos animales simpáticos: «Lizzy», «Mary» y «Guarina» – tres delfines nacidas en el mar cerca de Cuba hace seis años. Pronto van a dejarlas en libertad en el Mar Caribe.

– Me gustan todos los animales – nos comentó Concha –, excepto las serpientes y los insectos. Los delfines me gustan mucho. Son unos animales muy inteligentes. En mi casa hemos tenido animales: pero, desde hace unos años, cuando murió nuestro perro y quedamos muy tristes, decidimos no volver a tenerlos.

– Me gustan mucho los delfines – explica Goyo –, porque se parecen a las personas. Me gustan todos los animales. Bueno, me resultan desagradables todos los insectos. En este momento tengo en casa dos canarios.

– ¿Con qué animal puedes comparar a Goyo?
– Un gatito. Tranquilo y amable; pero que, a veces, necesita estar solo.
– Y tú, Concha, ¿a qué animal te pareces tú?
– Me veo como una coneja. ¡Tímida y dulce!

(a)	At what time of day is «En verano» shown?	*(1)*
(b)	What did Concha and Goyo feel about this 'interview'?	*(1)*
(c)	Where do the dolphins live?	*(1)*
(d)	How old are the dolphins?	*(1)*
(e)	Where do they come from?	*(1)*
(f)	What does Concha like about dolphins?	*(1)*
(g)	How long is it since she had any animals at home?	*(1)*
(h)	Why does she no longer have any animals at home? Give full details.	*(2)*
(i)	Why does Goyo particularly like dolphins?	*(1)*
(j)	What does Goyo feel about insects?	*(1)*
(k)	Why does Concha think Goyo is like a cat? Give two details	*(2)*
(l)	What animal does she think she is like, and why? Give three details.	*(3)*

(ULEAC)

7. ANSWER KEY TO THE PRACTICE QUESTIONS

SHORT ITEMS (ANSWER KEY)

1. (a) Closed
   (b) Push
   (c) Roadworks
   (d) Drinking water
   (e) (There is a) sale (on)
   (f) To go to the Post Office (OR to post a letter OR to buy stamps etc.)
2. Your cross should be on the left in the rectangle marked 'RENFE'.
3. Bookshop
4. (Have a) good journey
5. The times of meals
6. No more than 3 people allowed to go up (at a time)
7. Breakfast
8. Mercado
9. Tables, cupboards and chairs (*1 mark each*)
10. ANY TWO OF: flour, eggs, sugar, butter (*1 mark each*) (*2 max.*)
11. Might have found the watch OR could look for the watch (*1 mark*)
    Telephone the number (200-44-49)
12. No entry OR You can't go in (*1 mark*)
    EITHER: The building is being restored
    OR: Work in progress (OR work area) (*1 mark*)
13. (a) 10%
    (b) 2 suitcases; free; per passenger
        (*2 elements = 1 mark; 3 elements = 2 marks*)
14. Tomato soup OR (mixed) salad;
    Spanish omelette;
    Apple cake (OR apple gateau OR apple pie) (*1 mark each course*)
15. (a) A journey
    (b) A romantic adventure (OR a romance)
16. (a) ANY 2 OF: (It is) near the beach (OR only 200 metres from the beach)
                  (It has a) games area
                  (It has a) children's swimming pool
                  (It has a) creche
                  (It has a) variety of entertainments
    (b) (It has) air-conditioning

LONGER ITEMS (ANSWER KEY)

17. (a) Because I left
    (b) Visit me
    (c) Send it (*1 mark*); Bring it (when she comes) (*1 mark*)
    (d) They were very nice (OR kind OR likeable)
18. (a) Train
    (b) 11.15 p.m. or 23.15
    (c) 102
    (d) Outside the reserved area
19. (a) pineapple juice (*1 mark*)
    sugar (*1 mark*)
    grape juice
    (b) Put it in the refrigerator (for 2 hours)
    (c) With ice
20. (a) You should put ticks against the 3rd and 5th items:
        Pantalones cortos AND Camisas (*1 mark if both correct*)
    (b) Outside your door OR Outside your room
    (c) From 6.30 p.m. the next day
    (d) Name (*1 mark*)
        Room number (*1 mark*)
        Date (*1 mark*)
21. (a) Cooking
    (b) The ingredients are expensive
22. (a) Shanghai (C)

(b) Riofrio (A)
(c) Air conditioning
(d) Happy Christmas
23 (a) Mansilla
Atabal
Torre del Mar   (*1 mark each*)
(b) Vélez – Málaga
(c) Swimming pool; excellent (extraordinary) views
24 8
    12
    10
    6
    4
25 (a) Post cards
(b) To rent a flat (in Benidorm)
(c) Leather (*1 mark*) skirt (*1 mark*)
(d) To meet up with an old friend
(e) Roller skating
(f) Gardening
26 (a) Afternoon (OR early evening)
(b) The most difficult of their life
(c) Madrid Zoo (in the dolphinarium)
(d) 6 (years)
(e) Near Cuba (OR The Caribbean)
(f) They are (very) intelligent
(g) A few years
(h) Their dog died (*1 mark*)
    They were very sad (*1 mark*)
(i) They are like people
(j) He doesn't like them
(k) ANY 2 OF: Calm
                   Likeable
                   Sometimes needs to be alone   (*1 mark each – max.2*)
(l) A rabbit
    Timid
    Sweet (OR gentle)   (*1 mark each*)

A STEP FURTHER

Make a list of any more buildings in a town that might be signposted or have signboards on them. Check that you would understand the Spanish if you saw those signs. Look through your text book for any more signs that you might see displayed in Spain. Then find half a dozen signs giving instructions and see if you can write down the other ways those instructions could have been expressed (addressing the people in the singular or plural, in familiar or formal ways, or using the infinitive).

Look in a Spanish newspaper for some advertisements, particularly restaurant advertisements and small ads of items for sale. Can you understand the key points? Note down any phrases you find that you think might be helpful in understanding other similar advertisements in the future.

The review sheets at the end of Chapter 9 cover reading at both Basic and Higher levels.

CHAPTER 9

READING: HIGHER LEVEL

- READING MATERIAL
- NATURE OF QUESTIONS
- ANSWERING QUESTIONS
- UNDERSTANDING HIGHER LEVEL TEXTS
- COPING WITH WORDS YOU DO NOT KNOW
- ANSWER KEY TO PRACTICE QUESTIONS

GETTING STARTED

Like all the Higher papers, **Higher Level Reading** is an *optional* paper. However, if you are aiming to achieve one of the higher grades, you should certainly consider attempting it. As we mentioned in Chapter 8, many students find reading Spanish easier than the other skills. You can work at your own pace and take more time to work out the parts that are causing you problems.

As we have seen, whether you take Higher Reading or not, you do have to take Basic Reading and, even if it seems straightforward, you must take it seriously. It counts just as much towards your final grade.

Don't forget that it is comparatively easy to get practice in reading.

As at Basic Level, the reading material is of the sort you would have to cope with in a Spanish-speaking country or when in contact in this country with Spanish-speaking people. It is restricted to the Settings specified in the syllabus. At this Level the full range of topics and vocabulary will be covered, so you need a good knowledge of the vocabulary specified for Higher Level. Up to 15% of the words in any item may come from outside the official list published by the Examining Group but no questions will be set that require you to understand those words.

CHAPTER 9 READING: HIGHER LEVEL

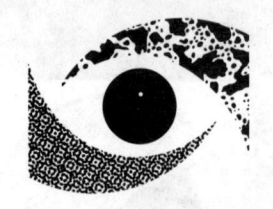

ESSENTIAL PRINCIPLES

1 > THE READING MATERIAL

Types of reading material at the Higher Level

A list of the types of reading material you can expect to encounter in the tests was included in Chapter 8. At **Higher Level** the extracts will be longer (ranging up to about 250 words). There are more extended pieces from magazines and newspapers. Any letters and advertisements tend to be longer. Where small ads, cinema guides and horoscope items are included, they tend to occur in groups, rather than individually, so that an individual question can be based on information taken from several or can require you to select the appropriate item or items from the group. There are not likely to be any signposts or signboards.

The material will look authentic and is very often photocopied directly from Spanish newspapers and magazines.

2 > THE NATURE OF THE QUESTIONS

What you are expected to do at the Higher Level

1. You will be expected to demonstrate the skills listed under Basic Reading over the wider range of clearly defined topic areas – check what is applicable in your case. Those skills involve

- understanding specific details
- extracting relevant specific detail from texts

2. In addition you will be expected to show that you can

- identify the important points or themes within extended texts
- identify the relationship between ideas expressed
- draw conclusions from what you read

The conclusions you are expected to draw are likely to refer to

- the attitudes and emotions expressed in the texts (or likely to be felt by the people involved)
- the ideas implied (but not directly stated) in the texts

As in Basic Reading, the questions are in English (or Welsh if you have chosen to be examined in Welsh by the WJEC); the answers are expressed in words in English (or Welsh), in figures, by ticking boxes or by putting letters in boxes or completing grids. (For the IGCSE the questions and answers are in Spanish.)

Usually you write your answers on the question paper in the spaces provided. (At present the exception is SEG, which requires the answers to be written in a separate answer booklet.)

The setting can guide you

In each case you will be told in English the *setting* in which you would be reading the item.

All the situations are of the sort that a British 16-year-old might realistically have to deal with.

You are *not* allowed to use a dictionary or other reference books in the examination.

3 > ANSWERING THE QUESTIONS

How to answer the questions

The way in which you should go about answering the questions was set out fully in Chapter 8. The same principles apply at Higher Level. They are summarized below (but for fuller details you can refer back to Chapter 8):

- You don't have to understand every word.
- Read the question carefully and make sure that is the question you answer.
- Read the setting carefully and use any help it gives you.
- Remember to answer in English (or Welsh).
- Keep your answers short (but give all relevant information).
- Use the number of marks as a guide to how much information you need to give.

CHAPTER 9 ESSENTIAL PRINCIPLES

- Always give an answer.
- Don't list every possibility you can think of.
- Remember to use your common sense.

Questions about specific facts will normally be set out in the order in which the information is given in the texts but the questions testing your ability to identify the important themes, to identify relationships between ideas and to draw conclusions will come nearer the end, since they require you to look at the text as a whole.

4 UNDERSTANDING HIGHER LEVEL TEXTS

The points made in Chapter 8 about understanding *longer texts* at Basic Level are equally valid at this level:

- Identify the tense from the verb ending.
- Identify who does, did or will do the action, also from the verb ending.
- Remember that the subject of the verb is regularly omitted in Spanish sentences.
- Do not be misled into thinking that an object pronoun (*me, te, le, lo, la, nos, os, les, los, las*) is the subject of the verb.

❝ Hints to help your understanding of longer texts ❞

At Higher Level it is worth spending some time looking at two other key features of Spanish sentence-structure:

- the flexibility of Spanish word order
- the personal 'a'

THE FLEXIBILITY OF SPANISH WORD ORDER

Consider the following sentences and work out what you think they each mean:
a) Mis padres compraron una mesa.
b) Compraron mis padres una mesa.
c) Compraron una mesa mis padres.
d) Una mesa la compraron mis padres.

If you have applied the principle of using the verb ending to decide *who* did the action, you will have realized that all four sentences mean 'My parents bought a table.' In English the word order is critical: 'My parents' must come before 'bought' and 'bought' must come before 'a table'. Any variation in that will produce either a different meaning or complete nonsense. What would any of us make of a sentence such as 'Bought a table my parents'? Yet in Spanish the **word order** can be much more flexible and we have to make use of other 'markers', such as the verb ending, in order to understand the sentence.

❝ The word order is flexible in Spanish ❞

Now consider these four sentences and decide what they mean:
a) El hombre ve el perro.
b) Ve el hombre el perro.
c) Ve el perro el hombre.
d) El perro lo ve el hombre.

In this case, as in the previous set of sentences, they all have the same meaning: 'The man sees the dog.' And yet, while we all know that a table cannot buy people, it is quite clear that a dog is capable of seeing a person. So why does none of the four sentences mean that the dog sees the man? The answer lies in the use of the personal 'a'.

THE PERSONAL 'A'

Because of the flexibility of Spanish word order, an extra 'marker' is needed in order to make clear whether a person is the *subject* of the verb (the person who does the action) or the *direct object* of the verb (the person who is seen, helped, heard etc.). That 'marker' is the use of the word 'a' before the direct object if the direct object is a *person*. So, if we wish to say that the dog sees the man, the possibilities are:

❝ Look out for the 'marker' ❞

a) El perro ve al hombre.
b) Ve el perro al hombre.
c) Ve al hombre el perro.
d) Al hombre le ve el perro.

The same principle applies to nadie, alguien and ¿quién?.

No vio a nadie	= *He/she saw nobody*
No vio nadie	= *Nobody saw*
¿A quién vio?	= *Who(m) did he/she see?*
¿Quién vio?	= *Who saw?*

It is perhaps worth mentioning that the personal 'a' is also sometimes used when the direct object is an animal, in order to make the meaning clear:

'Atacó el perro el gato' does not make clear which animal attacked the other. 'Atacó el perro al gato' clearly means 'The dog attacked the cat'. The use of the personal 'a' has ensured clarity.

> **Be familiar with flexible word order and the personal 'a'**

A sound understanding of these two related points (flexible word order and the personal 'a') will help you to avoid the sort of confusion that many candidates seem to have with some sentences at Higher Level.

5 > COPING WITH WORDS YOU DO NOT KNOW

> **Useful strategies to help with unfamiliar words**

The strategies outlined in Chapter 8 are all valid at Higher Level as well. In addition the following points are worth knowing:

- *-ura* is often the equivalent of the English *-ness*
    e.g. blancura: *whiteness*
    (Note also: hermosura: *beauty*)
  -izo is the equivalent of the English *-ish*
    e.g. rojizo: *reddish*
  -illo / *-illa*
  -ecillo / *-ecilla*   all mean 'little', e.g. mesilla: *small* table
  -ecito / *-ecita*   panecillo: *bread roll* (= *little loaf*)

- In the case of fruit, trees and orchards/groves the following pattern is common:
    -a is the ending for the fruit (which is a feminine word)
    -o is the ending for the tree (which is a masculine word)
    -ar / *-al* is the ending for the orchard or grove
    Thus: manzana: *apple*   naranja: *orange*
              manzano: *apple tree*   naranjo: *orange tree*
              manzanar: *apple orchard*   naranjal: *orange grove*

- Additional letter substitutions that can be tried, in order to find a similarity with a word in English, French or other European language, include:
    ue – change to *o* as in *puerto:* port;
              fuerte: strong (French: *fort*)
    ie – change to *e* as in *hierba:* grass (French: *herbe*)
    ll – at beginning of word change to *pl* as in *llover* (French: *pleuvoir*)
              or to *fl* as in *llamas:* flames
    h – at beginning of word change to *f*

Sometimes two of these substitutions will work together. Thus, if you take the word *hierro* and apply the two suggested changes you find you now have *ferro*, which you may well recognize as having to do with iron. (*Hierro* means 'iron'.)

STUDENTS' ANSWERS WITH EXAMINER'S COMMENTS

Here are two examples of Higher Level Reading texts, followed by students' answers and examiner's comments on the answers.

Q1 You are on holiday in Spain with your family and it is raining. You decided to go to the cinema and your family asks you to look at the film guide below and say which kind of film is showing at each cinema.

Guía de los cines

COLISEUM. 'El tren.' Problemas en el oeste. El ferrocarril se acerca .... y los vaqueros no están contentos.

LICEO. 'Recompensa.' Se declara un incendio forestal de tanta magnitud que no hay más remedio que utilizar explosivos para cortarlo. Ofrecen una recompensa a quien se arriesgue a transportarlos.

ARCADIA. 'Voces de muerte.' La verdadera historia de Edward Chapsan, un agente doble que trabaja sin descanso contra los rusos.

ASTORIA. '¿Quo vadis?' Adaptación de la novela de Henry Sinkiewicz sobre el encuentro entre un radiante soldado romano y una frágil cristiana.

FILMOTECA. 'Mi hermana Elena.' Está muerta ... pero vuelve a medianoche.

MODERNO. 'Providencia.' Historia relacionada con los vuelos espaciales del futuro.

WALDORF. 'La cocina.' Chistes y risa entre estudiantes.

Your family tells you that they are particularly interested in
- comedy films
- adventure films
- horror films
- spy films
- science-fiction films
- westerns
- romantic films

Write in the spaces provided the type of film being show in each cinema. The first has been done for you.

(a) At the Coliseum, there is a ...... *western* ...... film.

(b) At the Liceo, there is a ...... *comedy* ...... film. (*1*)

🔴🔴 Wrong. It is not at all clear why you chose this answer. It looks like a process of elimination. The correct answer is 'adventure' 🔴🔴

🔴🔴 Correct 🔴🔴 (c) At the Arcadia, there is a ...... *spy* ...... film. (*1*)

CHAPTER 9 **READING: HIGHER LEVEL**

❝ Correct ❞   (d) At the Astoria, there is a ……romantic…… film. (1)

(e) At the Filmoteca, there is a ……horror…… film. (1)

❝ No. It does involve adventure but space travel is normally seen as science-fiction. If you had given the right answer to Q1, you would probably have chosen correctly here ❞

❝ Good. You have clearly identified this as a ghostly return! ❞

(f) At the Moderno, there is a ……adventure…… film. 1)
(MEG)

❝ General comment: These questions may seem comparatively easy but they do all involve drawing conclusions from the text (a specific Higher Level skill). Notice that the words for 'adventure', 'spy', 'romance', 'horror' and 'science-fiction' do not occur in the film guide. ❞

Q2 You notice this advertisement for a new 'magazine' which looks interesting. Your friend asks you about some details.

No leas esta revista.

Nace «Lourdes a las cinco». Una nueva revista diaria que no debes leer.

Escúchala de 5 a 7, de lunes a viernes, en cualquiera de las 70 emisoras de la Cadena Rato.

Lourdes Zuriaga dedica su gran experiencia periodística en televisión y otros medios, para presentar dos horas diarias de radio-revista.

El mundo de la cultura y de los pasatiempos. Las últimas noticias en cine y teatro y música. Entrevistas a los personajes de mayor actualidad. Conexiones en directo a través de unidades móviles…

Todo esto es «Lourdes a las cinco». No te pierdas ni un minuto de esta nueva revista.

(a) What seems to you to be contradictory about the instruction in the heading of this advertisement?

❝ A very good answer ❞   It's an ad for a magazine but it says not to read it. (1)

(b) When can you enjoy this new 'magazine'? Give full details.

❝ Another good answer – and suitably brief ❞   Between 5 and 7 Mon-Fri (2)

(c) What explanation are you given for the odd instruction in the heading?
It says it's a new daily newspaper that you don't have to read. (1)

❝ No. You've missed the point here. 'Escúchala' and 'emisoras' were meant to show you it is a radio magazine programme ❞

(d) What qualifications did Lourdes Zuriaga need for her job? Give two details.

She needs experience in journalism on TV (2)

> Fine. You've mentioned two details, as required. You could have added 'other media' but that was certainly not required. You already have both marks

(e) What sort of people will be attracted to this new 'magazine'? Give any two details.

People of older age (2)

> No. 'Mayor' doesn't always mean 'older'. The answer is: 'People interested in ...' and you then need to mention any two of: culture, entertainment, cinema, theatre, music

(f) What final recommendation does the advertisement make?

It says don't miss a minute of this new magazine. (1)

> Good. But you don't need too many words. 'Not to miss a minute of it' is enough

(ULEAC)

PRACTICE QUESTIONS

Q1 You see an article about traffic accidents at Christmas.

65 muertos en accidentes de tráfico durante el 'puente' de Navidad

EL PAÍS, Madrid

Sesenta y cinco personas resultaron muertas en los 49 accidentes ocurridos en las carreteras españolas desde las tres de la tarde del pasado viernes, en que comenzó la *operación Navidad*, hasta las ocho de la tarde del pasado domingo, según datos provisionales facilitados por la Dirección General de Tráfico. Otras 45 personas sufrieron heridas graves y 31 de carácter ligero.

Las carreteras de la red principal registraron durante la mañana del sábado un intenso tráfico e importantes retenciones debido al masivo desplazamiento de vehículos por las vacaciones de Navidad y a la huelga de maquinistas de Renfe.

La normalidad volvió a la red viaria en la noche del pasado sábado y durante la jornada del domingo y lunes, aunque en diversas provincias (Albacete, Badajoz, Lérida, Madrid, Navarra y Teruel) una fuerte nubosidad impidió una visibilidad correcta.

Las causas principales de los accidentes fueron la invasión de la calzada izquierda, velocidad inadecuada, salidas de la vía por exceso de velocidad o distracción, según las fuentes informantes.

(Calzada - lane)

(a) Give **three** details of traffic accidents over the Christmas period.

....
....
.... (1)

(b) When was traffic at its heaviest?

.... (1)

(c) What problem did drivers face in certain provinces such as Albacete?

.... (1)

(d) What were the main causes of accidents?

....

....
....
....
....
.... (4)
(WJEC)

Q2 You are travelling in Spain with your penfriend Carmen. She buys a Spanish magazine to read on the journey. You read this letter from the mother of a teenage girl.

Quiere estudiar, pero necesitamos que trabaje

Correo

Una hija mía termina este año el COU y tiene empeño en estudiar una carrera universitaria. Su profesor dice que está muy capacitada. El problema es que en casa tenemos una mala situación económica y necesitamos otro sueldo. Yo quiero que busque un trabajo. ¿Es la mía una proposición egoísta?

OPINION

Su hija podría buscar alguna pequeña ocupación a tiempo parcial, que suelen realizarse fuera del horario de estudios: clases particulares, cuidar algún niño..., así la carrera de su hija no supondría una carga para la economía familiar y realizar estudios superiores le permitiría, en el futuro, acceder a algún puesto de trabajo de mayor categoría.

(a) What does the daughter want to do when she leaves school?
.... (1)

(b) What would her mother prefer her to do?
.... (1)

(c) Why?
.... (1)

(d) Do you think the answer is biased towards the daughter or the mother or neither?
.... (1)
Give a reason for your answer.
....
.... (2)
(NEAB)

Q3 The teacher who runs the annual ski trip at your school is wondering where to go next year. He/she is particularly interested in bob sleighing, tobogganing and slalom. You show him/her the following article and summarise the information in it under the headings listed below.

Un deporte de España

El esquí

El deporte del esquí no cuenta todavía en España con tantos aficionados como en otros países europeos, pero es uno de los que se están popularizando con mayor rapidez.

Hace algunos años existían en España muy pocas pistas apropiadas para este deporte. Las razones eran varias. En primer lugar, aunque España es un país montañoso, sus montañas no son muy altas y en muchos sitios no había transportes adecuados, lo que dificultaba la afluencia de deportistas.

Hoy día todo ha cambiado. Se han «descubierto» y acondicionado muchos lugares adecuados para esquiar y se han multiplicado los hoteles y albergues de montaña. Debido a ello, las competiciones nacionales e internacionales son cada vez más numerosas.

El deporte del esquí, procedente de Noruega, comenzó a practicarse en España en 1908 a través de la influencia de aquél y otros países europeos que ya lo practicaban. La región donde mejor arraigó es Cataluña, que cuenta con buenas condiciones en los Pirineos (donde hay montañas que sobrepasan los 3.000 metros de altura). Actualmente hay también gran actividad, durante la temporada de invierno, en las sierras centrales de la Península, como Gredos y Guadarrama, y empieza a «descubrirse» la Sierra Nevada, donde se encuentran las montañas más altas de la Península y las pistas de esquí más cercanas a las playas mediterráneas de Europa.

En España se practican todas las especialidades de este deporte: saltos, carreras de fondo, carreras de velocidad, etc. El único que no se practica es el «tobogán», debido a que la nieve no es bastante dura para este tipo de pruebas.

(a)	Current state of skiing in Spain	....	(2)
(b)	2 reasons why there were few adequate ski slopes some years ago.	1.. 2..	(2)
(c)	2 reasons why this state of affairs has now changed.	1.. 2.	(2)
(d)	2 things to be found in the Sierra Nevada.	1..	(2)
(e)	1 type of skiing speciality practised in Spain.	....	(1)
(f)	Why are this teacher's particular interests not catered for in Spain?	....	(1)

(MEG)

Q4 Someone you met while in Spain said that he lived in Serradilla del Llano. As you read this news report, your family wonders why you are so concerned. You explain about your friend and they begin to bombard you with questions.

Un incendio forestal en Serradilla del Llano

Sobre las seis de la tarde de ayer se registró un incendio forestal en el término municipal de Serradilla del Llano en un paraje denominado «Lombollano» situado a unos veinticinco kilómetros de Ciudad Rodrigo.

El fuego, que al parecer fue intencionado ya que se constató la existencia del mismo en cuatro puntos diferentes, afectó a un total de 10 hectáreas de una propiedad particular, y aunque hasta el momento no se han evaluado los daños, se sabe que ha afectado a pinos de unos 20 años.

En la extinción del fuego han participado la Guardia Civil, brigadas de Icona así como personal civil procedente de los pueblos limítrofes con la zona. También tuvieron que ser empleados dos helicópteros y un hidroavión que en un momento dado se dirigió a repostar en el pantano del Agueda y ante los problemas de espacio, tuvo que trasladarse al pantano de Gabriel y Galán de Cáceres.

En el momento de redactar esta información se sabía que el fuego fue controlado sobre las ocho y media de la tarde y que afortunadamente no se había producido ningún herido.

(a) What kind of fire was this?
.... (1)

(b) Where in Serradilla is Lombollano?
.... (1)

(c) What does the article say about the damage caused?
....
.... (2)

(d) What is said about the civilians from neighbouring villages?
....
.... (1)

(e) How long did it take to get the fire under control?
.... (1)

(f) How many persons were injured?
.... (1)

(Bahamas GCSE)

Q5 You notice this letter to the editor in a Spanish newspaper while you are on an exchange visit to Spain.

El mal estado de los parques infantiles

He leído en su periódico que los parques infantiles madrileños se encuentran en muy mal estado. La noticia es totalmente cierta. Todas las tardes bajo con mis dos nietos pequeños a un parque próximo a mi casa para que jueguen un rato al aire libre.

No entiendo cómo el Ayuntamiento no dedica algo de dinero a arreglar estos problemas de los parques infantiles. Desde mi punto de vista no todo es arreglar calles para mejorar el tráfico de la ciudad, que parece que es lo único importante para los responsables municipales.

Este problema de que me quejo en sus páginas no sólo se produce en el parque de mi barrio, que se encuentra en la zona norte de Madrid. He podido comprobar que en otros barrios ocurre lo mismo. Mi petición como la de tantas otras personas que son contrarias al deterioro de los parques es que se adopten soluciones urgentes.

No se puede consentir que estos lugares de diversión, cada día más difíciles de encontrar, se mueran por falta de atención de quien corresponda.

María Jiménez

(a) What is the writer complaining about?

.... (3)

(b) What personal knowledge has she of this problem?

.... (3)

(c) As far as the writer can see, what business takes priority in the municipal council?

.... (2)

(d) How do you know that her district is not the only one with this problem?

.... (3)

(e) What does she say must not be allowed to happen to these parks?

.... (1)

(NICCEA)

Q6 You are in Spain and are reading a magazine in the company of Spanish friends. You decide to look at the horoscopes.

INFORMACION
HOROSCOPO

ARIES (Marzo 21 - Abril 20)

Se sentirá pesimista y poco decidido a seguir adelante en el trabajo que tiene actualmente entre manos. Por otro lado, en su tiempo libre sentirá grandes deseos de divertirse.

TAURO (Abril 20 - Mayo 20)

Es posible que su salud sufra un poco debido a las muchas actividades que querrá realizar, por eso le recomendamos que tome las cosas con mucha más calma.

GEMINIS (Mayo 21 - Junio 20)

Evite amistades que le hagan perder su tiempo. Sus ideas están muy bien para ciertos momentos y ciertas situaciones. Hoy eso le puede traer problemas en su habitual lugar de trabajo.

CANCER (Junio 21 - Julio 21)

Tendencia a olvidarse un poco de los seres que le quieren. Cuidado, lo puede lamentar.

LEO (Julio 22 - Agosto 21)

Haga planes para mejorar las rutinas del día. Está inclinado a tomar decisiones o iniciativas de efectos negativos para su bolsillo.

The statements below summarise the messages given in the horoscopes. Write down the letter of the message in the box beside each star sign.

For instance, if you think that the message for **Aries** people is that they must keep their promises, write **A** in the box beside **Aries**.

You will not have to use all the messages.

- **A** You are told to keep your promises.
- **B** You are told to be cautious at work and to avoid certain people.
- **C** You are told that you will not feel positive about your work and will want to enjoy yourself.
- **D** You are advised not to overstretch yourself.
- **E** You are warned about taking your family for granted.
- **F** You are told to organise yourself and to be careful about money.

(a) Aries ☐ (*1*)
(b) Taurus ☐ (*1*)
(c) Gemini ☐ (*1*)
(d) Cancer ☐ (*1*)
(e) Leo ☐ (*1*)

(*MEG*)

Q7 You find this clipping from a magazine and, in the company of your friends, use it to recall events which took place in Spain.

En la Base Naval de Cartagena

La Infanta Elena, madrina de la carabela «La Niña»

La Infanta Elena, hija mayor de los Reyes de España, fue la madrina de la carabela «La Niña», réplica de la nave que, junto a «La Pinta» y la «Santa María», descubrieron el Nuevo Mundo.

Desde un atril preparado al efecto, la Infanta lanzó una botella al casco de la carabela, mientras ésta se dirigía al agua.

A su llegada al Arsenal de Cartagena, Doña Elena fue recibida por el Capitán General del Departamento Marítimo y por el Presidente de la Junta de la Comunidad Murciana.

Tras escuchar el himno nacional, una Compañía rindió honores y, ya desde el pódium, Doña Elena presenció un desfile, terminado el cual, tuvo lugar la botadura.

Por iniciativa de la Comisión Nacional «Quinto Centenario», se han construido las tres réplicas de las carabelas que Colón utilizó en 1492 en la expedición que descubrió América.

Las carabelas han sido construidas en roble y pino silvestre. La madera de «La Niña» se consiguió tras una larga búsqueda en Galicia, siendo la edad media de los árboles entre 140 y 150 años. Diecisiete meses fueron necesarios para terminar «La Niña».

En 1990, las tres naves serán expuestas en países europeos antes de partir para América, recordando la gesta colombina. Tras el viaje, las tres naves se instalarán en un museo norteamericano mientras otras tres réplicas, que ya se están construyendo, se exhibirán en el Monasterio de Santa María de la Rábida, donde podrán ser admiradas por el público español.

(a) When did Princess Elena throw the bottle against the hull of the ship?

.... (*1*)

(b) What happened on her arrival at the Cartagena Dockyard?

.... (*1*)

(c) Describe the building of the replica <<La niña>> in the following terms:

Type of wood: .... (*1*)

Age of wood: .... (*1*)

Construction time: .... (*1*)

(d) After sailing to America, where would the three ships be kept?

.... (*1*)

(e) In which country would the other three replicas be displayed?

.... (*1*)

(*Bahamas GCSE*)

Q8 Your penfriend Carmen has done this quiz in the magazine she bought. You look at her answers, which she has marked with crosses.

¿TE GUSTA DARTE UN CAPRICHO?

1. ¿Cuántas horas te pasas delante de la televisión?

- ☐ Para mí la televisión es algo secundario.
- ☐ De dos a tres horas diarias.
- ☐ La veo pocas veces, como mucho seis horas a la semana.
- ☒ La televisión me aburre a muerte.
- ☐ Soy bastante adicta y veo casi todo lo que puedo.

2. ¿Podrías alimentarte exclusivamente de comida rápida (hamburguesas, pizzas, perritos calientes, patatas fritas, coca-cola)?

- ☐ Es la comida más rica que conozco.
- ☐ No, me resultaría demasiado monótona.
- ☐ No, intento alimentarme de modo sano y natural.
- ☐ Como mucho la tomaría una vez a la semana.
- ☒ No tendría ningún problema si no fuera por el dinero o por la oposición de mis padres.

3. ¿Fumas?

- ☐ Aún no he probado el tabaco.
- ☐ No más de diez pitillos.
- ☐ Sólo en fiestas o cuando salgo.
- ☐ En momentos tensos de estrés.
- ☐ Lo he probado, pero no me llama.
- ☒ ¡Qué pregunta! Intento que a mi alrededor todo el mundo lo deje.

4. ¿Por qué te gusta salir?

- ☐ Me gusta estar con la pandilla.
- ☒ Por miedo a perderme algo bueno.
- ☐ Porque si no mi chico se buscaría a otra.
- ☐ Porque me aburro en casa.
- ☐ Siempre que falto, salta la bomba.
- ☐ Para no separarme de mi chico.

(a) What effect does television have on her?

.... (1)

(b) Your penfriend does not eat as much fast food as she would like. Why not? Give **two** reasons.

(i) ....

(ii) .... (2)

(c) What does she do where she sees her friends smoking?

.... (1)

(d) Why does she like going out?

.... (1)

(e) Look at your friend's answer to question number 5:

> **5.**
> ¿Sientes el deseo de ser siempre la número 1 (por ejemplo, en el deporte, la clase, el trabajo, con los chicos, en la pandilla...)?
>
> ☐ Me basta con ser la número 2.
> ☒ No me he parado a pensarlo.
> ☐ Nunca podría ser la número 1 en nada.
>
> ☒ Yo soy la número 1.
> ☐ Siempre pongo un límite a mis ambiciones.
> ☐ Mi lema es «más diversión y menos angustia».

What does it tell you about her personality?

.... (2)

(*NEAB*)

Q9 You read a letter to the editor of a newspaper.

Cartas al director

Las multas del Metro

El pasado 28 de agosto fui víctima en la estación de Sants, como tantos otros usuarios del *metro*, de lo que considero un robo organizado por parte de la compañía, pues tuve que pagar 500 pesetas como multa por no poder enseñar un billete que realmente había pagado. Es lógica la existencia de revisores en los trenes, porque es fácil subirse a ellos sin haber pagado el billete, pero no en el *metro* barcelonés, donde en todas las entradas hay taquillas imposibles de eludir. Entonces, ¿para qué poner revisores? Pues muy sencillo: para robar a los viajeros, porque saben muy bien que la persona que no lleva billete no es que no lo haya pagado, sino que lo ha perdido, y con este fútil pretexto hacen pagar una multa que consiste en 15 veces el precio del billete. Es triste que algunos trabajadores de la compañía se presten a esa función revisora e injustamente sancionadora.

[**Manuel Sánchez.** Sant Joan Despí, Barcelona.]

(a) What happened to Manuel Sánchez on August 28th?

....
.... (2)

(b) What is the point he makes about inspectors on the 'metro' as opposed to inspections on trains?

....
.... (2)

(c) Why is he so angry at the treatment he has received?

....
.... (2)

(*WJEC*)

Q10 During your visit to Spain you read an article about an event which took place in Madrid during the *puente festivo* (holiday weekend).

Cerca de 300.000 personas acudieron a la fiesta de la bicicleta

Cerca de 300.000 personas, según la organización, participaron ayer en la undécima edición de la fiesta de la bicicleta de Madrid. El alcalde de la capital, Juan Barranco, que un año más completó en bicicleta los 28 kilómetros de recorrido, dedicó la carrera a Emiliano Revilla. Desde las nueve de la mañana hasta mediodía, numerosas calles del centro de la ciudad estuvieron cortadas, aunque, a diferencia de años anteriores, los conductores esperaron con más calma el paso de los participantes.

La fiesta de la bicicleta no pudo superar el récord del año pasado cuando 350.000 personas, según la organización, recorrieron las calles de Madrid pedaleando. El puente festivo y la lluvia impidieron superar esta participación, que en esta ocasión se acercó a los 300.000 ciclistas. En la primera, celebrada hace 11 años, participaron 25.000 personas. El alcalde de Madrid, Juan Barranco, quiso dedicar la presente edición a Emiliano Revilla, cuya liberación había sido anunciada a las cinco de la madrugada.

Los ciclistas pasearon por las calles de Madrid por espacio de tres horas a un ritmo que fue más lento que el de otros años a causa de la lluvia, que provocó varias caídas durante el recorrido.

Barranco fue uno de los ciclistas que se cayó a la altura del paseo de Rosales, cuando introdujo el tubular delantero de su bicicleta en una grieta del asfalto. Sin embargo, el alcalde terminó la carrera en el grupo de cabeza, aunque con el impermeable destrozado a la altura del muslo. Pero el alcalde sacó media hora de ventaja a sus dos amigos que le acompañaron, y cuando vio llegar al primero de ellos le dijo: "Se tiene que notar que soy el alcalde, ¿no?"

Los primeros participantes llegaron a la meta a las 10.45, cuando todavía otros muchos pedaleaban por la Ciudad Universitaria.

(a) When precisely did the event take place?
.... *(2)*

(b) What did the participants have to do?
.... *(2)*

(c) In what way has the event affected motorists and how does the article suggest they have reacted in the past?
....
.... *(3)*

(d) Write down **three** ways in which rain affected the event.
....
.... *(3)*

(e) In what way did Juan Barranco tease one of this two friends?
....
.... *(3)*

(f) What makes you think Juan Barranco is a determined sort of man?
....
.... *(3)*

(g) How much time elapsed between the arrival of the first and the last participants at the tape?
.... *(1)*

(SEG)

Q11 UN ESPAÑOL QUE HACE HISTORIA SOBRE RUEDAS
An English friend of yours who is keen on motor sport wants some help in understanding this article from a Spanish magazine.

UN ESPAÑOL QUE HACE HISTORIA SOBRE RUEDAS

Hace muchos años en Madrid, un jovencito de diez años llamado Carlos Sainz usó una casual relación familiar para entrar en el fabuloso mundo de los coches: su hermana mayor se casó con Juan Oñoro, ex campeón de España de *rallies*. A los 13 años, Carlos le acompañaba en las prácticas. Se colocaba detrás de él y su copiloto, Juanjo Lacalle, en el asiento trasero del coche. Al principio, los padres no aprobaron estas aventuras de su hijo, que iba a ser campeón de *squash* y querían verle con la carrera de abogado.

La carrera de Carlos Sainz ha sido fenomenal, pero ha tenido que esperar varios años para el éxito internacional hasta los 28 años. Los problemas de El Matador, como se le conoce entre sus amigos, pues controla el volante de un coche como un torero controla a un toro, continuaron hasta los 18 años. Nadie en su familia dejaba el coche con las llaves puestas, ya que Carlos Sainz se ofrecía siempre para hacer los recados. Poco después de obtener el carnet de conducir ganó la Copa Renault para principiantes. Pero también tuvo el primer accidente con su coche particular. Ese golpe le hizo tomar una decisión, pues no quería estar cuatro meses sin coche. Así que decidió dedicarse completamente a las carreras.

Hoy es el piloto oficial del equipo Toyota, al que llegó como segundo del campeón del mundo finlandés, Juha Kankkunen, ahora en el equipo Lancia. Cerca de 140 personas dependen de él tanto como Carlos de ellas. Más de 200 días al año vive lejos de casa, dentro del coche en el que devora 600 kilómetros diarios desde hace muchos años. Es reservado. Es amigo sólo de sus amigos. Pero este hombre silencioso ha sido el primer español en conseguir el campeonato del mundo de rallies.

Moya y Sainz (arriba) y Cardús (abajo), a punto de lograr su primer campeonato.

(a) What makes the author think Carlos Sainz only became a rally-driver by chance? Give full details.
   ....
   .... (2)
(b) What was the attitude of his parents to his new hobby?
   .... (1)
(c) What hopes did they have for his future? Give two details.
   ....
   .... (2)
(d) Why do his friends call him El Matador? Explain fully.
   ....
   .... (2)
(e) What precaution did his family have to take when he was young, and why?
   ....
   .... (2)
(f) What do you find strange about the event which made Carlos Sainz decide to become a rally-driver?
   ....
   .... (2)
(g) How many people are needed to run the Toyota rally team?
   .... (1)
(h) Why should Spanish people be particularly proud of Sainz?
   .... (1)

(ULEAC)

Q12 While in Spain visiting your penfriend, his family takes you out to a restaurant in Plasencia. Later, this article appears in the paper. You have kept it as a souvenir of your meal out.

Francisco Javier Dávila

Desde los 14 años llevando la cocina de Extremadura a otras regiones

Francisco Javier Dávila Martín, un joven de treinta y cuatro años de edad, casado y padre de dos niños, lleva dedicado a la profesión de cocinero veinte años de su vida. Comenzó a los catorce años en la cocina de un hotel salmantino y hasta llegar hace año y medio a la cocina del restaurante KM-4 de Plasencia, donde trabaja actualmente, ha recorrido restaurantes de muy diversos y apartados puntos de la geografía española, llevando a todos ellos la cocina típica de Extremadura. Aunque le encanta su profesión reconoce que es muy dura y espera que sus hijos nunca sigan su camino.

(a) Give three personal details about Señor Dávila.

....
....
.... (3)

(b) What would suggest that cooking has always interested him?

.... (1)

(c) For how long has he been working in his present position in Plasencia?

.... (1)

(d) What has been Señor Dávila's speciality in all the restaurants in which he has worked throughout Spain?

.... (1)

(e) Señor Dávila admits that his work is very hard. What evidence suggests that this is the case?

....
....
.... (3)

(NICCEA)

Q13 You read the following article in a Spanish magazine.

LA CAIDA DE MARTA PONS

Ni siquiera "Dallas" se atrevió a inventar un monstruo semejante. Un monstruo de la avaricia, claro. Reina del mercado petrolero norteamericano, Marta Pons es dura, arrogante, riquísima ... y si el Juez Johnson se sale con la suya, tendrá que cumplir una pena de cinco años por no haber pagado impuestos. La verdad es que hace falta un talento excepcional para despertar tanta hostilidad entre gente que normalmente respeta a los ricos.

Las historias terribles sobre esta millonaria de sesenta y nueve años abundan. Cuando murió su único hijo de un ataque cardíaco a los treinta años, Marta pidió el anillo de oro a su viuda.

Hija de inmigrantes pobres de Brooklyn, Marta Pons empezó a trabajar como secretaria en una empresa de muebles nada más salir del colegio. Sus superiores notaron su fuerza de carácter del tipo bulldozer y su sentido de organización. In 1985, tuvo suerte. Encontró al propietario de una cadena de hoteles, Walter Jackson. Marta necesitó menos de un mes para persuadir a este príncipe encantador, casado desde hacía años a dejar a su mujer.

Marta y Walter, dueños de una fortuna, vivían juntos como estrellas. Los montones de dólares se acumularon. Vivían en todo lujo. Un empleado, Juan Gómez contó que tenía que dar vueltas constantemente alrededor de la piscina con una bandeja de plata e inclinarse para que Marta pudiera comer unas gambas mientras nadaba. Otra empleada, Pilar Díaz contó que Marta, para comprobar la industria de las limpiadoras, depositaba fragmentos de pan en la alfombra y luego caía sobre ellas si no habían desaparecido en el cuarto de hora siguiente.

Naturalmente, el principal enemigo de Marta era el Estado. Transformó sus gastos personales en cuentas profesionales. Ningún americano puede perdonar a Marta porque dijo a los periodistas: <<Nosotros no pagamos impuestos. Eso queda para los desgraciados.>>.

(a) (i) What change many soon occur in Marta's life-style?
.... (1)

(ii) What has Marta done wrong?
.... (1)

(b) Why does the writer say that Marta must have exceptional talent?
.... (1)

(c) What incident in paragraph 2 suggests that Marta is mean?
....
.... (1)

(d) What precisely was Walter Jackson's occupation? Give full details.
.... (1)

(e) How did Walter Jackson's life change within a month of meeting Marta?
.... (1)

(f) Why might their employee Juan Gómez feel tired after his day's work? Give full details?
....
....
.... (2)

(g) From what another member of their staff Pilar Díaz says, which statement best describes Marta's attitude to her employees? TIck one box only.
   (i) She underpays her staff ☐
   (ii) She ignores her staff ☐
   (iii) She makes her staff work hard ☐
   (iv) She makes her staff work long hours ☐ (1)

(h) Why could no American ever forgive Marta?
....
.... (1)

(MEG)

ANSWER KEY TO THE PRACTICE QUETIONS

1 (a) ANY 3 OF: 76 people died
                   45 were seriously injured
                   31 were slightly injured
                   There were 49 accidents   *(1 mark each)*
   (b) Saturday morning
   (c) Poor visibility
   (d) Going into the left hand lane
       Inadequate speed
       Excessive speed
       Being distracted   *(1 mark each)*

2 (a) Go to university (Study a university course)
   (b) Get a job
   (c) They need the money
   (d) Neither
       It allows both what they want   *(1 mark each)*

3 (a) Not as many skiers as other countries
       One of the sports gaining popularity fastest *(1 mark each)*
   (b) ANY 2 OF: The mountains are not very high
                   Inadequate transport
                   made it difficult for people to get there   *(1 mark each)*
   (c) ANY 2 OF:
       Many suitable ski centres (slopes) discovered (developed)
       Increase in mountain hotels (and hostels)
       More and more national/international competitions *(1 mark each)*
   (d) Highest mountains in the peninsula (OR Spain)
       ski-slopes nearest to Mediterranean beaches   *(1 mark each)*
   (e) ONE OF: Ski jump
                  Downhill (OR speed) races
                  Long distance races
   (f) The snow is not hard enough

4 (a) A forest fire
   (b) About 25 km from Ciudad Rodrigo
   (c) ANY 2 OF: 10 hectares affected
                   Damage not yet evaluated
                   20-year-old pines affected   *(1 mark each)*
   (d) They took part in the firefighting
   (e) About two and a half hours
   (f) None

5 (a) The bad condition
       of children's
       playgrounds (OR parks)   *(1 mark each point)*

(b) ANY 3 OF: She goes to one
near her home
every afternoon
with her grandchildren (*1 mark each point*)
(c) Repair of streets
to improve the traffic (flow) (*1 mark each*)
(d) She has been able to find out
that the same happens
in many other districts (*1 mark each point*)
(e) Disappear (die) through lack of care

6 1 C   2 D   3 B
    4 E   5 F

7 (a) As the ship was going towards the water
    (b) She was greeted by officials
    (c) EITHER oak OR pine
        140-150 years
        17 months

    (d) An American museum
    (e) Spain

8 (a) Bores her (to death)
    (b) (Lack of) money
        Parents' opposition (*1 mark each*)
    (c) Tries to stop them
    (d) For fear of missing something good
    (e) She is competitive
        and confident (*1 mark each*)

9 (a) He was fined 500 pesetas
        for not being able to show his underground ticket (*1 mark each*)
    (b) It is impossible to enter the underground without a ticket
        It is easy to get on trains without one (*1 mark each*)
    (c) The company knows perfectly well
        that anyone without a ticket has lost it
        (OR has paid for one) (*1 mark each*)

10 (a) Yesterday (OR the previous day)
     From 9 till 12 (*1 mark each*)
    (b) Cycle
        28 kilometres (*1 mark each*)
    (c) It closed many streets
        in the city centre (OR the centre of Madrid).
        Angrily OR with impatience (*1 mark each*)
    (d) It reduced the number of participants
        (OR prevented a record entry)
        It made the pace slower
        It caused many riders to fall (*1 mark each*)
    (e) He suggested
        that he had to beat him
        because he was the Mayor (*1 mark each*)
    (f) He completed the race
        in spite of falling
        and in spite of his cape being torn (*1 mark each*)
    (g) One and a quarter hours

11 (a) (It happened because) his sister married
       a rally driver (*1 mark each*)
    (b) They disapproved

(c) He was to be a squash champion
   They wanted him to be a lawyer (OR study Law) *(1 mark each)*
(d) He controls a car (steering wheel)
   as a bullfighter controls a bull *(1 mark each)*
(e) Never to leave the keys in the car
   He always offered to go on errands *(1 mark each)*
(f) It was the result of an accident in his car
   It was his only way to have a car to drive
(g) nearly 140
(h) He is (the first Spaniard to be) the world rally champion

12 (a) He is 34
   married
   with 2 children *(1 mark each)*
(b) He began when he was 14
(c) A year and a half
(d) Typical dishes (cooking) from Extremadura
(e) He hopes
   that his sons (children)
   will not follow the same career *(1 mark each)*

13 (a) (i) She will go to prison
      (ii) Not paid her taxes
(b) She has aroused so much hostility (in spite of being rich)
(c) She asked for her daughter-in-law's wedding ring when her son died
(d) Owner of a chain of hotels
(e) He left his wife
(f) He had to keep walking round the swimming pool
   and bending down so she could eat prawns while swimming

(1 mark each)

(g) (iii)
(h) She said tax-paying was only for the unfortunate

A STEP FURTHER

Using the advice given in this chapter and Chapter 8, make sure you can recognize the different verb tenses.

Then it is a good idea, from time to time, to take a Spanish newspaper or magazine, look at a few pages, particularly advertisements and news items (and possibly letters to the editor), and see how much you can understand without using a dictionary. Make a list of, say, 20 words that you had never seen before but that you were able to understand, simply from the context, the pictures, similarity with other words you know or by applying other techniques suggested in these two chapters. Then look for about half a dozen sentences in which the subject comes after the verb (see Flexibility of Spanish Word Order) and half a dozen sentences in which you can see the personal 'a' being used.

CHAPTER 9 READING: HIGHER LEVEL

REVIEW SHEETS: CHAPTERS 8 AND 9

BASIC LEVEL

- Write down the *Spanish* for each of the following items you might read on signposts in a town.

    library...
    station...
    post office..
    tourist office.....................................
    beach..
    swimming pool..................................
    park...

    cathedral..
    market...
    town hall...
    castle..
    bull ring...
    harbour...
    main square.......................................

- Write down the *Spanish* for each of the following items you might read on signposts in a hotel or shopping area.

    dining room.....................................
    toilets..
    lift...

    reception..
    cash desk...
    bureau de change............................

- Write down the *Spanish* for each of the following words or phrases you might read in shops or offices.

    open..
    discount...
    from... to..
    for sale..

    closed..
    sale (price reductions)....................
    next to..
    opposite (place)...............................

- Write down 6 useful strategies for dealing with words you don't recognise.

    1. ....
    ....
    2. ....
    ....
    3. ....
    ....
    4. ....
    ....
    5. ....
    ....
    6. ....
    ....

HIGHER LEVEL

- Write down the *English* meaning of each of the following suffixes.

    -ero.......................... *-ista*........................... *-ito*............................
    -ería........................ *-mente*...................... *-izo*............................
    -illo......................... *-ura*........................... *-ecito*........................

- One of the differences between Spanish and English is the use of a more .... word order in Spanish.

- The word 'a' is often used before the direct object if the direct object is a

    ....

    Example: El perro ve al hombre
    Which means: ....

- Read through all the practice questions and their associated texts/passages in chapter 9.

CHAPTER 9 **PRACTICE QUESTIONS**

Now make a list of 20 words you are *not familiar* with. Without using a dictionary, use any of the strategies discussed in chapters 8 and 9 to work out what these unfamiliar words might mean.

	Spanish word	*Meaning*		*Spanish word*	*Meaning*
1.	....	....	2.	....	....
3.	....	....	4.	....	....
5.	....	....	6.	....	....
7.	....	....	8.	....	....
9.	....	....	10.	....	....
11.	....	....	12.	....	....
13.	....	....	14.	....	....
15.	....	....	16.	....	....
17.	....	....	18.	....	....
19.	....	....	20.	....	....

Only *after* trying yourself, check each of the Spanish words in a dictionary.

- Read through the **Practice Questions** in chapter 9, and their associated passages again. Write down 6 sentences in which the *subject comes after the verb*. Now write down the meaning of each of these sentences.

1. Spanish ....

   ....

   English ....

   ....

2. Spanish ....

   ....

   English ....

   ....

3. Spanish ....

   ....

   English ....

   ....

4. Spanish ....

   ....

   English ....

   ....

5. Spanish ....

   ....

   English ....

   ....

6. Spanish ....

   ....

   English ....

REVIEW SHEET

- Write down 10 sentences from the **Practice Questions** in chapter 9 in which the personal 'a' is being used; for each of these sentences write down the English meaning.

1. **Spanish**...

   English..

2. **Spanish**...

   English..

3. **Spanish**...

   English..

4. **Spanish**...

   English..

5. **Spanish**...

   English..

6. **Spanish**...

   English..

7. **Spanish**...

   English..

8. **Spanish**...

   English..

9. **Spanish**...

   English..

10. **Spanish**...

    English..

REVIEW SHEET

CHAPTER 10

WRITING: BASIC LEVEL

NATURE OF TASKS
ANSWERING QUESTIONS
WRITING LISTS
FORM-FILLING
DIARY ENTRIES
WRITING MESSAGES
WRITING POSTCARDS
WRITING LETTERS
VOCABULARY
COPING WITH PROBLEMS

GETTING STARTED

Although **writing** is a very important part of learning a language, it is *not* a compulsory paper in the GCSE. You can take just the *common core* (Basic Listening, Basic Speaking and Basic Reading) but the maximum grade you can then achieve is Grade E. You could take the common core *plus* one Higher Level component and achieve Grade D but, if you want to get a Grade C, you must take the **Basic Writing** paper. It does not matter how well you do on the other papers, if you do not at least attempt the Basic Writing test, you will not be eligible for the award of Grade C. But don't panic, read on! You will not lose marks by attempting Basic Writing, even if you don't do it well, so it is usually worth 'having a go'. (If you are aiming at Grades A and B, you must take Basic Writing AND Higher Writing.)

You may have noticed that we have placed the emphasis on 'attempting' Basic Writing, rather than on what you have to achieve in it. That is deliberate and reflects the requirements of the National Criteria. You could, in theory at least, score no marks on the paper and, provided you had both taken it and scored well on an additional Higher Level paper in another skill, you could be awarded Grade C. In practice, candidates likely to do well on any Higher Level paper should be capable of achieving something worthwhile in Basic Writing (as are many who find all the Higher Level papers very difficult).

As in Basic Speaking, you do not have to produce perfect Spanish in order to score full marks. The emphasis is very much on 'getting the message across', which carries far more marks than the quality of the Spanish used. The key questions are: 'Have you done all the tasks set?' and 'Would a Spanish-speaker with no knowledge of English actually be able to understand what you have written?'

ESSENTIAL PRINCIPLES

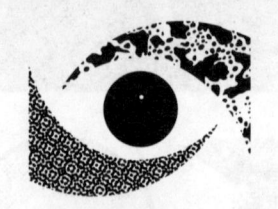

1 ▸ THE NATURE OF THE TASKS

In many cases, the tasks you have to do are the kind of things you have done to help you with learning the other skills. The tasks are designed to be fairly straightforward and predictable. Basic Writing is not intended to be any more difficult than any of the other Basic Level tests.

The writing tasks vary somewhat among the different Examining Groups. You will need to check carefully which topic areas you are expected to cover and which exercises you are required to do.

The tasks likely to be set by the different Examining Groups are shown below:

Tasks	MEG	NEAB	NISEAC	SEG	ULEAC	WJEC
Lists	Yes	No	Yes	No	Yes	Yes
Form-filling	Yes	No	No	No	Yes	No
Diary entries	Yes	No	Yes	No	No	Yes
Messages	Yes	Yes	Yes	Yes	Yes	Yes
Postcards	Yes	Yes	Yes	Yes	Yes	Yes
Letters	No	Yes	Yes	Yes	Yes	Yes
Completion of a model letter	No	No	No	No	Yes	No

Table 10.1 Tasks for Basic Writing of the various Examining Groups.

Not all of the possibilities will be set every year. Tasks set by ULEAC include some alternatives for candidates to choose.

In all exercises there will be clear instructions as to what you should include, and how much you are required to write. Usually the answer you have to provide will be outlined in English. However, you may be required to write a reply to a message, postcard, or letter written in Spanish, so it is important for you to get practice in reading and understanding Spanish handwriting. Your course book will no doubt contain examples and there are some in the sections on Reading as well as in the chapters on Writing.

❝ Pay attention to the instructions ❞

2 ▸ ANSWERING THE QUESTIONS

❝ Write as neatly as you can ❞

❝ Avoid writing in English ❞

❝ Plan your answer ❞

- You will need to communicate the information required in such a way that the person for whom the list/message/postcard/letter is intended can understand clearly what you mean.
  Clear handwriting is also an obvious advantage! If you do notice a mistake and wish to correct it, do so clearly and neatly. You will not get credit for anything an examiner cannot decipher!

- You do not have to write perfect Spanish in order to get your meaning across, but do try to be as accurate as possible. DO NOT WRITE ANYTHING IN ENGLISH. You will be given credit only for what is written in Spanish, so don't just write an English word when in difficulty.

- You must make sure that you include all the relevant information necessary for the exercise. If there are five points listed for you to mention in your note, message, postcard or letter, deal with all five. If you attend to only three, you can qualify for only three-fifths of the marks available.

- Make sure you keep within the word limits set for the question.

- Think carefully about what you are going to write, before you write your answer.

  This is especially important if you have to write your answer in a limited space, e.g. on a blank postcard or note-pad. There should be 'rough paper' for you to draft your answer.

> **Build on what you know**

- Always build on Spanish that you know. It is a good idea to learn and remember vocabulary and grammar in set phrases and then to use the phrases as 'building blocks'. You almost certainly already do this to some extent. You know *quiero* means 'I should like' and you know the Spanish for many items and for several expressions of quantity, so you can use *quiero* to ask for a whole range of things, including, for example, *Quiero un kilo de tomates*.

  Although it is sometimes tempting, don't think of what you want to say in English and then try to translate it into Spanish.

  Make notes in Spanish, using vocabulary and expressions with which you are familiar.

  IF YOU DON'T KNOW IT, DON'T USE IT.

- Try to use interesting material wherever you can, but make sure it is relevant.
- Make sure you check your work thoroughly.

We shall now look at the different types of writing tasks you are likely to have to do.

3 > WRITING LISTS

> **Check back to Chapter 3**

Writing a **list** is really not much more than showing that you have learnt certain items of vocabulary. Check the topic areas to be tested and learn the words! You can help yourself to learn the vocabulary by actually testing yourself regularly. You can also devise your own test lists to fit in with the kind of exercise you may have to complete in this section of the examination. Advice on learning vocabulary is given in Chapter 3.

The sort of list you will be required to write is likely to centre on the topic areas of shopping, clothing and personal belongings and free time activities, though these may not be the only topics tested. Possible lists could be :

> **A typical list**

- **shopping for food and drink**, e.g. for a party or picnic
- **shopping for presents**, e.g. to take home from Spain
- **describing the contents of a lost bag or case**
- **activities undertaken, or to be undertaken**, with a Spanish-speaking friend

Apart from knowing the individual words, you may be required to give further information, e.g. stating an appropriate quantity or amount (for food and drink), using adjectives of size and colour or stating ages, e.g. to describe clothing. You could also be asked to name the shop where you would buy each item.

Remember to make sure that what you include in your list makes sense for the task. For instance, if you are writing a shopping list for a picnic, it is unlikely that you would expect to buy a ready-made paella! Nor is it likely that you would wish to take ten different things to drink and nothing to eat!

> **Avoid repeating items in your list**

Make sure you do not repeat yourself. Each item you list will gain a mark only once. If you have to list five items of food and drink and the quantities of each, you could ask for

un paquete de.... *una botella de....*
un kilo de.... *un litro de....*
una lata de....

4 > FORM-FILLING

> **Useful items in form filling**

Form-filling often involves you in understanding the Spanish instructions or questions, so make sure you are clear about the difference between *Nombre* (First name) and *Apellido* (Surname). You also need to understand *Edad* (age), *Fecha* (date), *Domicilio* (home address), *Firma* (signature). Dates you may be asked for include: *Fecha de nacimiento* (date of birth), *Fecha de llegada* (date of arrival), *Fecha de salida* (date of departure). You could also be asked to list members of your family, any pets, your interests, subjects studied, etc.

5 > DIARY ENTRIES

Diary entries tend to be like lists, with the emphasis on activities and on the places where those activities take place. If the activities listed are plans for the *future* (e.g. what you will do on the different days when your penfriend will be staying with you), an *infinitive* will normally communicate very well, e.g.

JUEVES: Ir al centro. Comer en un restaurante.

If the diary entries are a record of what you *have done*, you will need to use the *Preterite tense*, e.g.

    VIERNES: Fuimos a Londres. Visitamos la Torre.

You might get away with a *noun*, e.g.

    VIERNES: Excursión a Londres. Visita a la Torre.

The one danger with that is that there could be situations in which it was not clear whether the entry referred to something done or planned.

6 > WRITING MESSAGES

The **messages** you have to write may not involve writing complete sentences – simple notes may be sufficient. Be careful, as always, to check all the instructions very carefully and cover all the tasks.

Again, refer to the topic areas tested at this Level by your Examining Group.

Some obvious possible messages could include:

- **leaving instructions for a Spanish-speaking visitor** explaining to him/her how to get to a particular place
- **noting down a telephone message**, e.g. Pablo rang up, he wants to go to the cinema tonight; the film is very good; please will you ring him; he is at home until 6 o'clock.
- **explaining why you have gone out and where, when you will be back, etc.**
- **making arrangements for some kind of activity**, e.g. planning a trip to town, to a concert, football match.

❝ Some common messages ❞

In order to be able to leave the right kind of message, you will need to be able to give details such as:

- **directions and places**, e.g. first left, straight on, at the café
- **methods of transport**, e.g. on foot, by bus/train/taxi
- **times and dates**, e.g. half past four, in the evening, on Friday
- **duration**, e.g. for five minutes, for half an hour
- **activities of interest**, e.g. cinema, concert, theatre, swimming
- **simple instructions/suggestions/invitations**, e.g. Can you come to the party?

❝ Details you might need for your message ❞

The above is not intended to be a complete list, but rather to show some examples of the kind of message to expect.

❝ Check verb tenses ❞

One area that can be a problem is **verb tenses**. You MUST make clear whether María has gone to the disco (*Ha ido a la dicoteca* OR *Está en la discoteca*) or is going to go (*Va a ir a la discoteca* or simply *Va a la discoteca*).

7 > WRITING POSTCARDS

As before, check all the instructions fully. You may have to write your answer on a blank **postcard** printed in the question paper. This means you have to plan what you are going to write very carefully, and stick closely to the word limits.

❝ Planning is even more important here ❞

It is normal to name the place (not the full address) you are writing from and put the date (in Spanish!) at the top. A good opening is *Hola!* or possibly *¿Qué tal?* Obviously you also sign the card at the end. You may choose to write *Un abrazo de* before your signature. What comes in between the opening and the end will depend on what you are told to do in the question paper but there are some fairly obvious things that you could be required to say:

❝ Useful hints for writing postcards ❞

- where you are
- what sort of accommodation you are in (hotel, campsite, youth hostel etc.)
- when you arrived
- who you are with
- how long you are staying there
- what the weather is like
- what you do (e.g. every day)
- what you have done since your arrival
- what you plan/want to do (tomorrow, next week)
- what the food is like
- what the hotel, campsite etc. is like
- people you have met there
- whether/why you are enjoying yourself

The topic areas PERSONAL IDENTIFICATION, HOLIDAYS, WEATHER and FREE TIME AND ENTERTAINMENT are obvious areas for revision for this section.

8 WRITING LETTERS

Identify the type of letter

At Basic Level **letters** are normally expected to be between 60 and 70 words.

It is important to be sure from the outset whether your letter is
- (a) **informal** – to a friend of about your own age
- (b) **semi-formal** – to an adult acquaintance
- (c) **formal** – to someone in an official position whom you do not know well

This will determine how you begin and end the letter. In all cases, though, you will begin by putting the name of the place you are writing from (not the full address) at the top right hand corner, followed by the date. All letters end, of course, with a signature.

INFORMAL LETTERS

These **begin**:

Querido.....: (*with a boy's name in place of the dots*) or
Querida.....: (*with a girl's name in place of the dots*)

You need to have two or three Spanish boys' names and two or three girls' names you can be sure of spelling correctly.

A typical **ending** is:
Un abrazo de (*followed by the signature, on the next line*).

Content of informal letters

The content of the letter will be very similar to the sort of thing listed for postcards, but you will have to write rather more. You could well be asked to give information about yourself, your family or your house, about a recent incident (such as a party, a meal out, an accident), about your school or college. You might have to issue, accept or decline an invitation or make arrangements to meet the other person. You might have to thank your friend for a present or you might have to thank him/her and his/her parents for a good holiday at their house and say something about your return journey.

Remember, in an informal letter you address the person you are writing to as *tú*.

SEMI-FORMAL LETTERS

A good **beginning** for these is:
Estimado.....: (*with a man's name in place of the dots*)
Estimada.....: (*with a woman's name in place of the dots*)

The names need to have a title (*señor/señora* + surname OR *don/doña* + first name), e.g.
Estimado don José:

It is also a good idea to have two or three typical Spanish surnames you can guarantee to spell correctly (e.g. *Díaz, Rodríguez* or *Gómez*)

A typical **ending** for this sort of letter is:
Un afectuoso saludo de (*followed by the signature, on the next line*).

The content is likely to be very much like that listed for informal letters but remember that you address the person you are writing to as *usted* (or *Vd.*)

FORMAL LETTERS

These normally **begin**:
Muy señor mío: (= *Dear Sir*)
Muy señores míos: (= *Dear Sirs*)
Distinguida señora: (= *Dear Madam*)

Typical **endings** would be:
Le saluda atentamente (*followed on the next line by the signature*) to a man
Les saluda atentamente (*followed on the next line by the signature*) to more than one person
Reciba un respetuoso saludo de (*followed on the next line by the signature*) to a woman

Content of formal letters

The content of such a letter is likely to be a request for information about holiday facilities, booking accommodation, making arrangements for a visit as part of town twinning, reporting or enquiring about lost property or possibly complaining about

CHAPTER 10 WRITING: BASIC LEVEL

things that were unsatisfactory at the hotel you stayed in.

Remember that you address the person you are writing to as *usted* (or *Vd.*).

COMPLETION OF A MODEL LETTER

Completion of a **model letter** is usually a fairly straightforward task in which you have to fill in the gaps is a standard letter so that it communicates the particular information that is required. It will be a formal letter and the content is likely to be of the type listed above for formal letters.

9 > VOCABULARY

You cannot suddenly expect to sit down and learn 1500 – 2200 words. Be systematic and learn vocabulary regularly and in short bursts. "A little but often" is a sensible approach. Fuller advice on learning **vocabulary** is given in Chapter 3.

Check Chapter 3

10 > COPING WITH PROBLEMS

If the tasks set require words or expressions you cannot remember, think how you can get round them:

- Do you know the opposite expression?

    If you cannot remember *lejos*, you can say *No está cerca*.

- Can you explain what you mean without the key word?

    If you cannot remember *nadar* or *bañarse*, you can still give the message that someone has gone swimming by writing: *Está en la piscina* or *Está en el mar*.

    If you have to say that someone is going to telephone the day after tomorrow and you cannot remember *pasado mañana*, why not head your note *Lunes* and write: *Va a telefonear el miércoles?* (It's cheating, really! But it conveys the message very effectively.)

    If you cannot remember how to say 'two hours ago', head your note with a time, *las 4 y media*, and refer to the event happening *a las dos y media*.

- Can you explain the function of the item?

    If you have forgotten the word for gloves (*guantes*), you could try *lo que me pongo en las manos cuando hace frío*.

Some useful hints if you cannot remember words or expressions

- Can you you explain by use of the word for a similar item?

    If you cannot remember the word for an overcoat (*abrigo*), you could write: *una chaqueta muy larga*. That might work but you would guarantee successful communication if you added *...que se usa para salir en invierno*.

It is a good idea to practise these strategies.

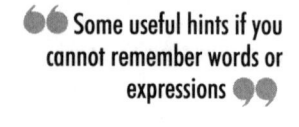

STUDENTS' ANSWERS WITH EXAMINER'S COMMENTS

Q1 LIST QUESTION

(a) In a recent letter, your pen-friend has asked you which subjects you are studying at school. Write down **in Spanish**, in the spaces provided, five or six subjects.

(3)

1. español — *Fine*
2. historia — *Fine*
3. mathematicas — *The 'h' should not be there and accent missed but the answer would be clear to any Spaniard*
4. ingles — *Missed accent but the answer is clear*
5. science — *No. This is English and will not score*
6. ....

Overall: It is a pity you gave only five answers. Another correct answer would have made up for the last one, which was not accepted. 2 marks out of 3

CHAPTER 10 **STUDENTS' ANSWERS WITH EXAMINER'S COMMENTS**

(b) You are camping in Spain and there is no restaurant at the campsite. Make a list **in Spanish** of what you might buy to eat and drink at the local *Supermercado*. Include five or six items. (3)

❝ Good ❞ → 1. el queso
❝ Good ❞ → 2. la cerveza
3. la hamburgesa

❝ There should be a 'u' after the 'g' but the meaning is absolutely clear ❞

❝ No. I think you meant *jamón* but what you have written is meaningless ❞ → 4. el ramon

❝ The Spanish is not very accurate – The word *de* should not be there, nor should the final 'e' – but the answer would still be very clear to a Spaniard. (You should use *el* before a stressed 'a', even for feminine words, but in fact there was no requirement to put *el* or *la* with any of these answers ❞ → 5. la agua de minerale
6. ....

(WJEC)

❝ Overall: Again it is a pity you gave only five answers (You were asked to give five or six). Another correct answer would have made up for the fourth one ❞

Q2 FORM-FILLING QUESTION

You want a Spanish penfriend, and your teacher gives you a form issued by a Spanish magazine for teenagers. You simply have to fill in the form below, so that the magazine can publish your details.

Answer each point on the form below wherever possible **with words in Spanish.**
(10)
(ULEAC)

```
Nombre  Williams              Apellido  Peter
Edad  16  años  2  meses.  Fecha de nacimiento  Leicester  (1)
Familia  4
                                                            (1)
¿Qué animales tienes en casa?  perro
                                                            (1)
¿Cómo eres tú?  como hamburgesas y patatas
                                                            (2)
Estudios y trabajo:
La asignatura
que prefieres  geographia                                   (1)
La asignatura
que no te gusta:  technolojia                               (1)
¿Qué haces para
ayudar en casa?  Ayuadar mi madre
                 Cortar la herba                            (2)
Intereses y pasatiempos
Me gusta más:  La Discoteca                                 (1)
Me gusta bastante:  El fútbol                               (1)
Firma  Peter Williams       Fecha  Leicester.
```

❝ You certainly don't get the first mark! *Nombre* means 'first name and *apellido* means 'surname'. Your age is all right but *Fecha de nacimiento* means date of birth'. Finally you should have given details of your family (e.g. *un hermano*) to score.
The animal is fine (1 mark)
You have misunderstood the next question. You were right to give 2 facts for 2 marks but the question is nothing to do with eating and it means "What are you like?' (0 marks) ❞

CHAPTER 10 **WRITING: BASIC LEVEL**

> *Geographia* should be spelt *geografía* but it communicates well. (1 mark)
> *Technologia* should be spelt *tecnología* but it communicates well. (1 mark)
> *Ayudar mi madre* does not say what you do to help (0 marks). (There should be the word '*a*' before '*madre*' if the Spanish were correct.)
> *Cortar la herba*: the last word should be *hierba* but the answer is clear (1 mark)
> *La discoteca*. Fine. (1 mark)
> *El fútbal* should be *fútbol* but the answer is clear (1 mark)
> You have signed in the correct place but *fecha* means 'date' – fortunately no marks depended on the last line!

Q3 DIARY QUESTION
You intend to enclose in a letter to your penfriend a list of the things you would like to do on each day during your visit to his/her home. Start to prepare this list by writing out some of these activities in the spaces provided below. You should list one activity for each day.

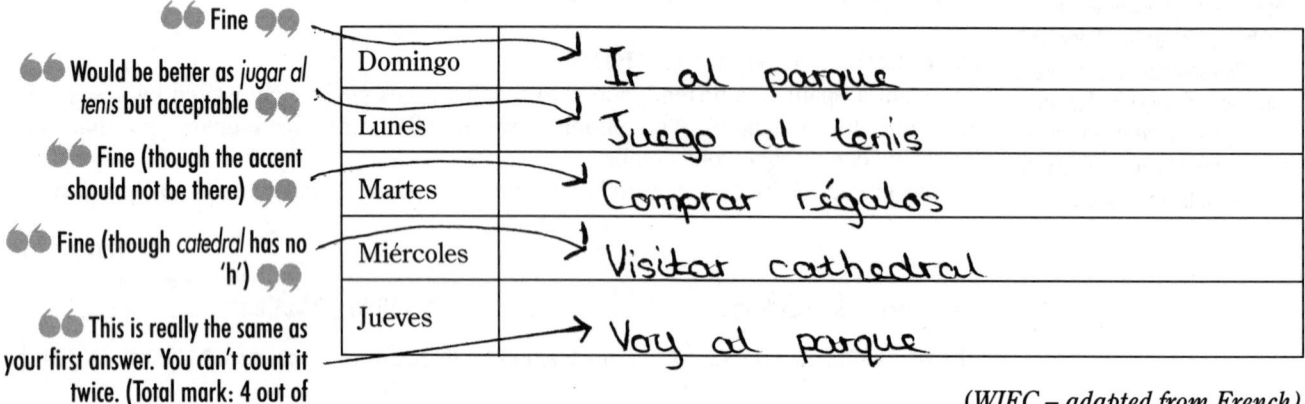

Domingo	Ir al parque
Lunes	Juego al tenis
Martes	Comprar régalos
Miércoles	Visitar cathedral
Jueves	Voy al parque

> Fine
>
> Would be better as *jugar al tenis* but acceptable
>
> Fine (though the accent should not be there)
>
> Fine (though *catedral* has no 'h')
>
> This is really the same as your first answer. You can't count it twice. (Total mark: 4 out of 5)

(WJEC – adapted from French)

Q4 MESSAGE QUESTION
While your Spanish penfriend is staying in your home, she decides one day to go shopping when you are at school. She offers to get you some things that you need. To make it easier for her, you write her a note in Spanish.
Write in Spanish about 30 words.
(a) Say that it does not cost much to go by bus.
(b) Say that you would like a film for your camera.
(c) Say that you need a blue biro.
(d) Say that the supermarket is not far from your school.
(e) Ask if she can meet you after school.

(20)

> Es barato la autobús.
> Por favor una pellicula para la camera
> Necessito un azul bolígrafo
> El supermercado cerca mi cellegio
> ¿Puedes ir al collegio a las quatro?

> Fine in spite of wrong gender for *autobús*
>
> This works all right, in spite of the mis-spelling of *película*. Camera is not acceptable, though – It is simply the English word
>
> This works well, in spite of the mis-spelling of *necesito*, the missed accent on *bolígrafo* and *azul* being in the wrong place. (It should come after *bolígrafo*)
>
> This answer just about gets the message across, in spite of the omission of *está* and *de* and the mis-spelling of *colegio*
>
> This is quite a neat way of avoiding the verb 'to meet'. It seems to work well, in spite of the mis-spelling of *colegio* and *cuatro*

(NICCEA)

CHAPTER 10 STUDENTS' ANSWERS WITH EXAMINER'S COMMENTS

❝ Overall: This candidate has communicated well, in spite of some obvious limitations of language. The mark is likely to be 14 out of 15 for Commication and 2 out of 5 for Quality of Language. (Total: 16 out of 20) ❞

Q5 POSTCARD QUESTION
You have just moved house and you receive a post-card from your Spanish pen-friend who is on holiday.

On the blank post-card below, write a reply in **Spanish** in about 30 words. Names and addresses are not required.

Mention the following points.
1. Greet your friend and ask how he/she is.
2. Say that you like the house because it is big.
3. Say you have lots of new friends.
4. Say that you are near a swimming-pool and the countryside.
5. Say that your teachers are very nice.

❝ This answer deals adequately with all the points and will score high marks for communication. The errors of Spanish do not in any way affect the meaning. Specific points: ❞

❝ 1. It should, of course, be *me gusta* ❞

❝ 2. The candidate has not said that he/she likes the house because it is big but that is certainly the implication of the way this is written ❞

❝ 3. It should be *nuevos*. ❞

❝ 4. The word *de* should be here ❞

❝ 5. *Campo* is masculine ❞

❝ 6. It should be *mis* ❞

❝ 7. It should be *son*. *Buenos* is just acceptable. (It should really be *simpáticos* or *amables* ❞

POSTCARD

¡Hola! ¿Qué tal? Me gusto [1] mucho la casa — ¡Es grande! [2] Tengo muchos neuvos [3] amigos. Estoy cerca [4] la piscina y la campo [5]. Mi [6] profesores es [7] muy buenos.
John.

(10)
(MEG)

❝ The mark for this piece of work should be either 9 or 10 out of 10 (depending on whether this particular question carries any marks for Quality of Language). ❞

CHAPTER 10 WRITING: BASIC LEVEL

Q6 REPLY TO POSTCARD

Before leaving for your holiday at a well-known holiday resort, you receive the following post card from your Spanish penfriend.

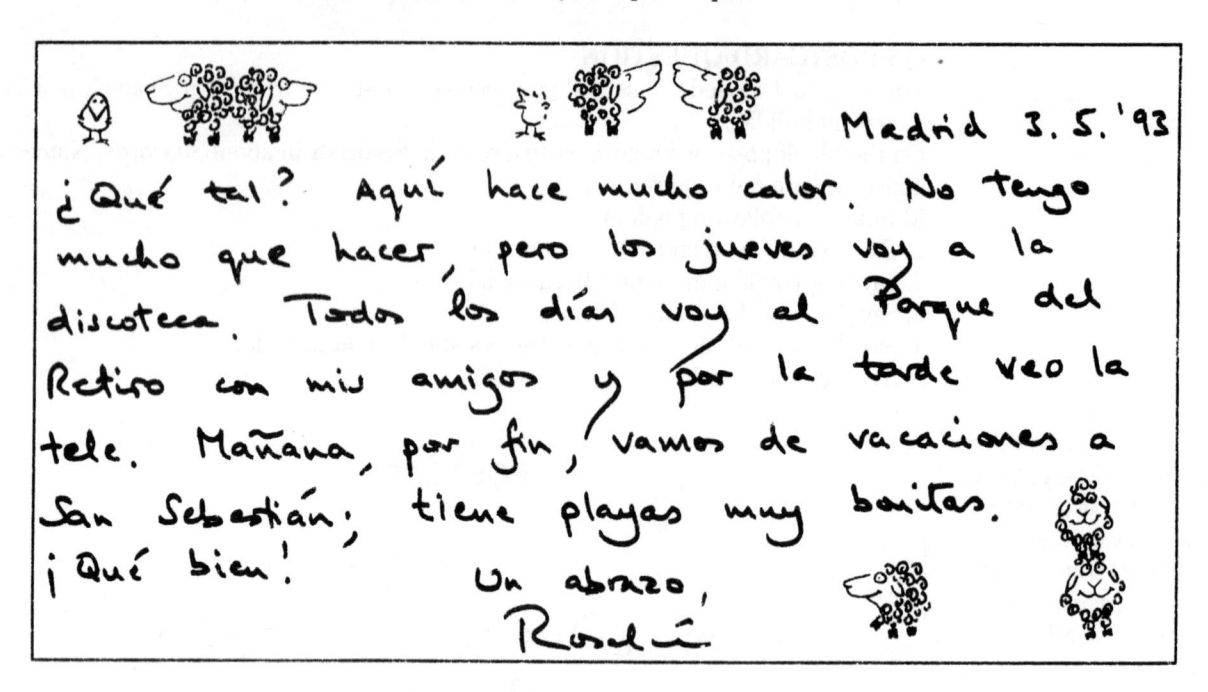

> Madrid 3.5.'93
>
> ¿Qué tal? Aquí hace mucho calor. No tengo mucho que hacer, pero los jueves voy a la discoteca. Todos los días voy al Parque del Retiro con mis amigos y por la tarde veo la tele. Mañana, por fin, vamos de vacaciones a San Sebastián; tiene playas muy bonitas. ¡Qué bien!
>
> Un abrazo,
> Rosalí

Write a postcard of 25 to 30 words **in Spanish** to your penfriend saying:
(1) you are staying on a large campsite
(2) there is a lot to do
(3) it is raining but it is warm
(4) you go to the swimming pool every day
(5) you want to go to the cinema tomorrow.

(10)

> ¿Qué tal? Estoy en un grande [1] camping. Tengo mucho que hacer. Voy a la discoteca y veo la tele. Aquí hace calor pero [2] lloviendo. Todos los días voy al [3] piscina. Mañana voy al cine.
>
> ¡Qué bien!
> Un abrazo,
> Sharon

❝ This candidate communicates the message very effectively. In the process she has also made very good use of the expressions contained in her penfriend's card – but only the ones that suit her purpose. Specific points: ❞

❝ 1. It should be *un camping grande* ❞

❝ 2. Really the word *está* should occur here but the sentence is clear. ❞

❝ 3. It should be *a la piscina* ❞

(ULEAC)

❝ None of these points restricts understanding. She will get full marks for Communication. If there is a mark for Quality of Language, she will get 1 out of 2, giving a total of 9 out of 10 ❞

CHAPTER 10 STUDENTS' ANSWERS WITH EXAMINER'S COMMENTS

Q7 LETTER QUESTION

You have been writing to a Spanish penfriend for a short time. He has now written asking for more information about you and your family.

Write him a short letter, in Spanish, of *about 60 words*.

Mention the following points:

(a) Say that you will be working during the summer holidays in a shop.

(b) Describe the shop and where it is.

(c) Say what you are going to do with the money you earn.

(d) Say what your father's or mother's job is.

(e) Say where you are going on holiday and for how long.

(f) Ask what he intends to do this summer.

REMEMBER TO BEGIN AND END YOUR LETTER CORRECTLY. (40)

(*NICCEA*)

> 1. In spite of the bold printed reminder, this letter has no correct beginning. This is simply throwing away the easiest marks to get!

> 2. It should be *vacaciones* but it is clear

> 3. It should be *bonita* but again the meaning is clear

> 4. It should be *comprar* but anyone would understand

> 5. You should only use *a* for visiting a person, not a place, but it is clear

> 6. You shouldn't use *un* or *una* when saying what someone's job is and there should be an accent on *policía* but neither point affects the reader's understanding

> 7. The same point as for 6. Double 's' does not occur in Spanish words

> 8. Don't do this! 'Scotland' communicates nothing in Spanish. If you don't know the word, say you are going somewhere else – that you can say in Spanish!

---

[1] Trabajo en las vaccaciones [2] de verano en una tienda. Es grande y bonito [3] cerca mi casa. Gano dinero – quiero compar [4] muchos discos y visitar a [5] Londres. Mi padre es un policia [6]. Mi madre es una professora [7]. Voy en las vaccaciones [2] a Scotland [8] – para dos semanas. ¿Dónde vas este verano? ¿Qué haces?

Un abrazo de
Richard

> Overall: The communication is good but marks are lost for one serious omission and one word that does not communicate. The quality of language is reasonable for Basic Level

CHAPTER 10 WRITING: BASIC LEVEL

Q8 REPLY TO LETTER

Write a letter **in Spanish** in reply to the letter below from your penfriend. You should write about 70 words and refer to **four points** made in the letter. Three points must come from the first paragraph. The last point must come from the **second** paragraph and should be answered at greater length because there are extra marks allocated for this part of your answer.

NB Be sure to begin and end your letter properly and to sign it. (20)

Salamanca
30 de abril

¡Hola!

Gracias por tu carta, que recibí esta mañana. Te contesto en seguida para decirte que pronto cambiamos de casa. La semana que viene iremos a un piso nuevo cerca del parque. Es muy bonito. Y, ¿cómo es tu casa? ¿Cuántos dormitorios tiene? ¿Cómo es el jardín de tu casa? ¿Dónde está tu casa exactamente?

Mañana iré a un partido de fútbol; juega el Real Madrid. ¿Qué deportes prefieres tú? Explícamelo todo. Pronto tendremos los exámenes — ¡qué horror! En tu próxima carta dime algo de tus exámenes. ¿Cuáles son los más difíciles y los más fáciles? Dímelo todo.

Un abrazo,

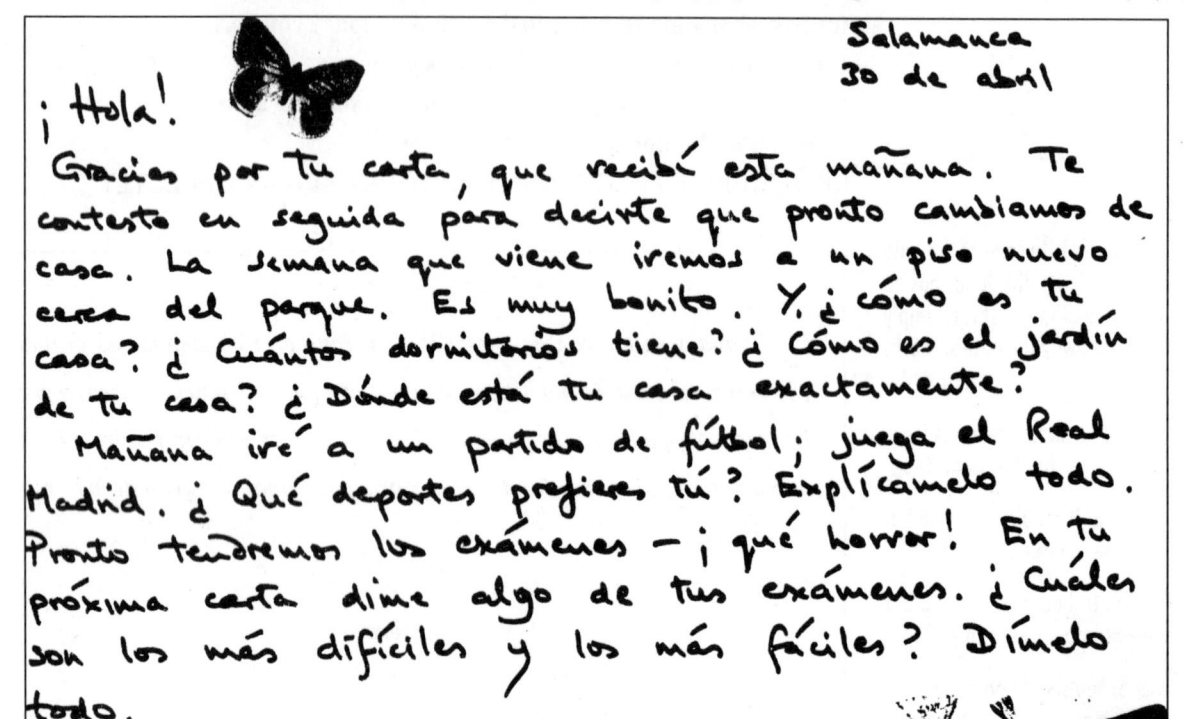

Ju—

(ULEAC)

Specific language points:
1. cuatro
2. bonita
3. es muy bueno
4. A mí me gusta mucho el fútbol

Leeds
5 de Junio

¡Hola!

Gracias por tu carta que recibí esta mañana. ¿Qué tal tu piso nuevo? Mi casa tiene cuatros [1] dormitorios. Es muy bonito [2]. El jardín es grande y bonito. Está en las afueras – cerca del parque.

¿Qué tal el partido de fútbol? El Real Madrid es bueno ¿no? El Leeds United también [3] muy bueno. A mi me gusto el fútbol mucho [4] Juego la semana que viene para el colegio.

Un abrazo,
Philip

❝ This answer is of almost exactly the length specified. It deals adequately with the number of points required and deserves full marks for communication. The language used is quite accurate, though perhaps a little limited in scope (e.g. repetition of *bonito* in successive sentences) and there is plenty of use of expressions drawn directly from the penfriend's postcard – but those expressions are well used. ❞

CHAPTER 10 STUDENTS' ANSWERS WITH EXAMINER'S COMMENTS

Q9 COMPLETION OF MODEL LETTER

Your parents want to plan a holiday in Benidorm, and ask you to write a letter to the local Tourist Office. Your teacher has given you a skeleton letter to help you. Following the guidelines given in the words or questions below the spaces, complete this letter **with words in Spanish** according to what your parents wish to know.

14.5.93

Muy señor(a) mío/a:

Le escribo de parte de mis padres, que quieren pasar sus **vaccaciones** ...
                                               (1) *holidays*

en España.

Viajaremos a Alicante **cómo ir en coche** .... y pasaremos
                        (2) *how will you travel?*

el mes de **augosto** .... en Benidorm.
           (3) *which month?*

Queremos saber algo sobre **las playas** .... y
                              (4) *the beaches*

qué otras atracciones turistas . de la ciudad. También nos
(5) *which other tourist attractions?*

gustaría hacer **excursiones** .... a otros pueblos.
                (6) *excursions*

¿Puede usted mandarnos **folletos** ....
                             (7) *brochures*

sobre Benidorm y los pueblos de la **playa** ....?
                                   (8) *coast*

Si es posible **mandarme** .... **un lista** ....
              (9) *I should like/I want*   (10) *a list*

de los hoteles de Benidorm.

Le ruego me conteste cuanto antes.

Le saluda atentamente,

.... (firma)

Examiner's comments:

- ❝ Wrong spelling but gets the message across ❞
- ❝ *En coche* on its own would be all right but the extra words confuse the issue. Don't translate the question! ❞
- ❝ Wrong spelling but clear ❞
- ❝ Fine ❞
- ❝ This is the same problem as Q2 ❞
- ❝ Fine ❞
- ❝ Good ❞
- ❝ Not quite what was intended (*costa*) but it works ❞
- ❝ Probably not quite what was intended (*quiero*) but it works ❞
- ❝ Wrong gender for *lista* but no problem of understanding. Overall mark: 8 out of 10 ❞

(10)
(ULEAC)

CHAPTER 10 **WRITING: BASIC LEVEL**

PRACTICE QUESTIONS

Here are a number of further questions for you to practise. You will find answers at the end of the section.

Q1 LIST
You are on holiday with Spanish friends in Spain and you are planning to go on a shopping expedition. Write a list in Spanish of five shops with one article you intend to buy in each shop. There is no supermarket in the town!

Shop	Article to be purchased

(10)
(MEG)

Q2 FORM FILLING

You have applied for an exchange in Spain. You receive a form to fill in because the teachers organising the exchange want certain information about you in order to match you with a suitable Spanish pupil. Part of the form is printed below.

Give the information about yourself which is required by filling in the appropriate spaces.

Your teacher tells you that you must write your answers in Spanish and that you must not answer any question by putting a dash in the space.

NACIONALIDAD/NATIONALITY

.... (1)

ANIMALES EN CASA/PETS

.... (1)

ASIGNATURA PREFERIDA EN EL COLEGIO/FAVOURITE SUBJECT

.... (1)

COLOR DE OJOS/COLOUR OF EYES

.... (1)

DEPORTE PREFERIDO/FAVOURITE SPORT

.... (1)

PASATIEMPO FAVORITO/FAVOURITE HOBBY OR ACTIVITY

.... (1)

OTROS PASATIEMPOS/OTHER HOBBIES

.... (1)

COMIDA QUE NO TE GUSTA/FOOD YOU DO NOT LIKE

.... (1)

COMIDA QUE TE GUSTA/FOOD YOU LIKE

.... (1)

BEBIDA QUE TE GUSTA/DRINK YOU LIKE

.... (1)

(MEG)

Q3 MESSAGE

You are spending Christmas in Barcelona. You go to the office where your Spanish friend works to invite him/her to lunch, but you are told that (s)he is busy. Write him/her a note of 35 to 40 words saying:

- You are there to invite him/her to lunch
- The secretary has told you that your friend is busy
- When you are returning
- What you intend to do in the meantime
- Where you would like to take him/her to lunch

(15)
(Bahamas GCSE)

Q4 MESSAGE

While your Spanish exchange partner is out, you are invited to a disco. You leave a message for him/her of about 25 words in **Spanish** telling him/her of the arrangements.

Include the following points in your message.

- say you are with a friend at the disco
- say the disco is opposite the cinema
- ask if he/she wants to come
- say the music is very good
- say you are coming home by bus

(20)
(MEG)

Q5 POSTCARD
While on holiday in Spain you decide to write to your Spanish teacher. You send a postcard which you write **in Spanish**.
On the postcard tell your teacher that:
- you are spending a week in León;
- the hotel has a swimming pool;
- it is sunny;
- you like the Spanish food;
- you are going to visit Madrid tomorrow;
- you are speaking lots of Spanish.

Write neatly and put down all the information you are asked to give. The number of words is not important.

(NEAB)

64 - LEON. Bellezas de la Ciudad.
Beauties of the City.
Beautés de la Ville.

....

....

....

....

....

....

....

....

....

....

....

....

....

....

(NEAB)

Q6 POSTCARD
You are in Miami for the weekend. Write a postcard of 35 to 40 words, to your Colombian pen-friend including these points:
- Why you are there
- Whether you are alone or accompanied by other people
- Where you are staying
- 2 reasons why you are enjoying yourself

(10)
(Bahamas GCSE)

Q7 LETTER
You are planning a summer holiday in Cantabria in Northern Spain. Write a letter to the Tourist Office in Santander. You should write and sign the letter, not forgetting the date and a correct beginning and ending. You should write between 70 and 80 words, but the length of the letter is less important than including all the following points:
- Say who you are and how old you are.
- Say that you are thinking of travelling to Cantabria.
- Tell them how you are travelling.
- Ask them when the weather is good in the region.
- Say you want to visit the city of Santander.
- Ask what there is to see and do there.
- Ask where you can go after Santander.
- Ask them for a list of hotels.
- Thank them for their help.

(20)
(SEG)

Q8 LETTER
Write a short letter **in Spanish** to your Spanish pen-friend. Use betwen 50 and 70 words to tell him/her about your summer holiday. Include **at least six of these points**.
(i) Tell him/her your are on holiday in Tenby in West Wales.
(ii) Explain that you are staying at your grandparents' house.
(iii) Say what the weather is like.
(iv) Tell him/her what you do in the mornings, e.g. go swimming or go shopping.
(v) Say how you spend the rest of the day, e.g. playing tennis etc.
(vi) Say how long you are going to stay in Tenby.
(vii) Ask you pen-friend to write soon.
(viii) Begin and end the letter appropriately. *(12)*
(WJEC)

Q9 COMPLETION OF MODEL LETTER
The following letter contains several numbered spaces. Using the list *below* the letter write out in Spanish the words which would apply to your own circumstances.

Londres (1).......................

Muy señor mío:
　　Quisiera pasar (2)............................ con (3)..
.... en el Camping Sierra Nevada.
　　¿Puede usted reservar sitio para (4)..
para (5).., a partir del (6).............................
............................? Quiero saber también si hay (7)...................................
.... y (8)..
　　Si es posible, mándeme folletos con (9)..
además de (10)..
　　Le ruego me conteste cuanto antes.
　　Le saluda atentamente.
　　　　　　　　　　.. (firma)

Answers:
(1) today's date
(2) how long?
(3) who is accompanying you?
(4) how many tents?
(5) how many nights?
(6) date you will arrive?
(7) hot showers
(8) swimming pool
(9) details about Granada
(10) price list for the campsite

(ULEAC)

SPECIMEN ANSWERS TO PRACTICE QUESTIONS

The answers that follow are examples of how the Practice Questions could be answered. They are not 'the correct answer' – there are countless correct ways of answering writing questions – but they do communicate all the necessary information and they are written in grammatically accurate Spanish. The language has been deliberately kept quite straightforward.

A1　Zapatería　　　　　　　zapatos
　　　panadería　　　　　　　pan
　　　tienda de ultramarinos　　queso
　　　confitería　　　　　　　caramelos
　　　papelería　　　　　　　sobres

A2 Británica
un perro y un gato
el español
azules
el tenis

oír música
la natación; el ciclismo
el cerdo
el pescado
la naranjada

A3 Querido Ramón:
Quiero invitarte a comer hoy. Dice la secretaria que estás ocupado con un cliente. Vuelvo a la una y media. Ahora voy de compras a la plaza. Quiero llevarte al Restaurante Mediterráneo.
          Simon.

A4 Pilar:
Estoy con mi amiga Luisa en la discoteca. La discoteca está enfrente del cine. ¿Quieres ir? La música es muy buena. Vuelvo en autobús.
          Elizabeth.

A5   León, 4 de agosto
  ¡Hola! ¿Qué tal?
Estoy pasando una semana aquí. Hay piscina en el hotel. Hace sol. Me gusta la comida española – sobre todo la paella. Voy a visitar Madrid mañana. ¡Hablo mucho en español!
          David.

A6   Miami, 13 de agosto
Estoy aquí en Miami visitando los sitios de interés. Está aquí también mi hermana. Estamos en un hotel muy bueno. Estoy muy contenta porque hay una piscina estupenda en el hotel y hace muy buen tiempo.
    Mary.

A7   Nottingham
                                                     el 7 de junio
  Muy señores míos:
Soy estudiante y tengo dieciséis años. Tengo la idea de ir a Cantabria este año con un amigo. Vamos a viajar en avión y en autocar. ¿Cuándo hace buen tiempo en Cantabria? Queremos visitar la ciudad de Santander. ¿Qué hay de interés en Santander? Y ¿qué se puede hacer allí? ¿Qué otros sitios podemos visitar después?
  Por favor ¿quieren mandar una lista de hoteles?
  Gracias por su ayuda.
   Les saluda atentamente
     Peter Williams.

A8   Tenby
                                                      el 8 de agosto
  Querida Teresa:
Estoy de vacaciones en Tenby, en el oeste de País de Gales. Estoy en casa de mis abuelos. Hace muy buen tiempo. Hace calor. Todos los días por la mañana voy a la playa. Por la tarde juego al tenis y después voy a una discoteca. Estoy en Tenby hasta el sábado.
Escribe pronto.
  Un abrazo de
  Suzanne.

A9 1. 5 de junio
     2. una semana
     3. mis padres
     4. dos tiendas
     5. siete noches
     6. cinco de agosto

7. duchas calientes
8. piscina
9. información sobre Granada
10. una lista de precios del camping

A STEP FURTHER

VOCABULARY PRACTICE

Think of a topic area, give yourself a time limit and then see how many words from that topic you can write down in the time allowed.

Think of a Spanish word and then see what new word comes into your head next, e.g. *bar, cerveza, botella, vino, camarero, cuenta, tapas, calamares...* This can be interesting to do with a friend.

Practise the strategies for coping with problems. Look back to Chapter 3 (Vocabulary).

PRACTICE IN WRITING

If you have contacts in or from Spain or another Spanish-speaking country, use them. Exchange letters, postcards, ask for help, make notes of vocabulary and expressions you think may help you.

Go over as many specimen questions as you can. There will be many exercises in your course books similar to those which occur in the GCSE examination.

Go over and revise exercises you have written in the past and try to do them again, only this time see if you can improve on your previous performance.

Make a note of any particular weaknesses that appear regularly in your writing and try to do something about them. Ask your teacher for help if you don't understand, or can't see why you often make the same mistake.

You will find a Review Sheet for this chapter at the end of Chapter 11.

GETTING STARTED

The **Higher Writing** test is important because you cannot be awarded Grade B or A unless you have taken it (both Part 1 and Part 2 for MEG). The tasks set normally require you to write a letter and may require either a second letter or a report or account of an incident. You will be expected to write between 200 and 250 words in all. The Examining Groups are interested in

- whether you 'get the message across'
- the accuracy of your Spanish
- the overall quality and variety of expression

Higher Writing is not intended to be easy but, if you know what is required, there is much you can do to prepare for the examination and to ensure that you gain positive marks.

CHAPTER 11

WRITING: HIGHER LEVEL

REQUIREMENTS

NATURE OF THE TASKS

MARKING SCHEMES AND ASSESSMENT CRITERIA

PREPARING FOR THE EXAMINATION

IN THE EXAMINATION

'INSTANT LETTER KIT'

COPING WITH PROBLEMS

CHAPTER 11 **WRITING: HIGHER LEVEL**

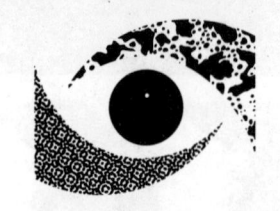

ESSENTIAL PRINCIPLES

1 REQUIREMENTS

Why Higher writing is important

Just as you have to 'attempt' *Basic Writing* to be eligible for Grade C, so you have to 'attempt' **Higher Writing** to be eligible for Grade B or A. If this is your weakest skill, all is not lost! Provided you have taken the examination, you can compensate for a very poor performance in it by doing very well in all the other papers (including Basic Writing) and still be awarded Grade A. On the other hand, if you are taking it, you might as well prepare thoroughly and do it as well as you can.

The number of tasks you have to do for each Examining Group, the approximate number of words *per task* and the time allocation for the paper are shown below:

What the Examining Groups require in Higher Writing

Group	Tasks	Words	Time
MEG Part 1	1	100	30 min.+
Part 2	1	150	35 min.+
NEAB	2	100*	50 min.
NISEAC	1	200	50 min.
SEG	2	100	60 min.
ULEAC	2	100	60 min.+
WJEC	2	100–120	70 min.

* The number of words shown for NEAB is an estimate of the approximate number needed to perform the tasks successfully. NEAB states clearly on its question papers ' ' 'The number of words is not important'.

+ For MEG and ULEAC the Higher Writing papers are taken in the same examination session as Basic Writing. For ULEAC you therefore have 105 minutes to complete both papers. For MEG you have 55 minutes for Basic + Higher Part 1 or 90 minutes for Basic + Higher Parts 1 and 2. The Basic and MEG Higher 1 answers are collected after the time allocated to them but you are free to move on to the next paper at any time. It is reasonable to assume that Higher Level candidates should complete the Basic papers well within the time allocated (and MEG certainly does assume this – you should really give yourself at least 45 minutes for a MEG Higher Part 2 paper).

2 THE NATURE OF THE TASKS

Letters are important here

You will almost certainly be required to **write a letter**, so make sure you know how to begin and end a letter correctly (see Chapter 10). There will probably be some marks allocated for the beginning and ending of your letter, so make sure you do get those marks; they are among the easiest marks to acquire, provided you have prepared yourself properly.

An account or report may be involved

If you have a second task to do, it is very likely to be an **account of an event or incident**. It could take the form of a *report* for the police, for a travel agency or hotel manager or for your penfriend's school magazine. On the other hand it could be *another letter* or, quite often, *part of a letter*. Read the instructions carefully and make sure you do what is asked. If it is a whole letter, you must begin and end it correctly. If it is not a whole letter, don't waste time and words making it look like one.

It is worth noting that the skills and language needed to write an account of an incident are very likely to be required in writing a letter, so we shall not consider them separately.

The presentation of the questions will be in the form of instructions in English, or a letter in Spanish to which you have to reply or it could be a series of pictures showing an event that you must imagine you witnessed or were involved in and that you have to recount in Spanish.

3 — MARKING SCHEMES/ CRITERIA FOR ASSESSMENT

❝ What examiners are looking for ❞

At Higher Level the Examining Groups seek to reward answers by marking positively across three main areas. In some cases the emphasis is slightly different, and the three areas listed below are sometimes merged to form just two areas. Find out exactly what your Examining Group is doing. You may also be able to obtain a copy of their marking scheme. The three main areas are:

1. Communication
2. Accuracy
3. Quality of expression

It is worth considering these aspects in more detail.

❝ Cover all the tasks ❞

1. Communication
This refers to the extent to which the relevant information is conveyed to the reader. Do you cover all the tasks and make yourself understood? Remember, if there are five tasks specified and you include only three of them in your letter, you can be awarded only three-fifths of the marks for communication (and, because communication is the main purpose of writing, there may also be a rule that says you cannot be awarded more than that proportion of the marks for accuracy and quality of expression).

❝ Be accurate ❞

2. Accuracy
This refers to the extent to which grammatical accuracy helps to convey the relevant information. Do you just manage to get the message across, or are you able to communicate the message clearly in largely correct Spanish?

❝ Be varied yet coherent ❞

3. Quality of expression
This is the extent to which the language you use helps to make your writing interesting and appropriate to the task. Do you use a variety of vocabulary, idioms, tenses, grammatical structures? Does your writing show coherence as a whole?

4 — PREPARING FOR THE EXAMINATION

- Check the topic areas to be tested in Higher Writing.
- Learn the vocabulary and structures required.
- Study as many specimen papers and past examination papers as possible.
- Devise a checklist which suits you, in order to check your work for accuracy and mistakes before and during the examination.
- Write as many practice letters and accounts as you can before the examination. Work to the times allowed in the examination and use your checklist.

DEVISING A CHECKLIST

It is important that the *checklist* you adopt is simple but thorough and that it also suits you. It should take particular account of the mistakes you make most frequently.
Outlined below is an example checklist for you to consider.

1. Have you answered the question including all the relevant information?

❝ Hints in preparing for the exam ❞

2. Have you kept within the word limits?
3. Have you checked your work for accuracy?

Verbs
- Do your verbs agree with their subjects?

    Mi hermana fue.... Mis padres fueron....

❝ Some useful checklists ❞

- Have you chosen the right tense? In particular

    Preterite for events; Imperfect for states of affairs/ habitual action/descriptions

- Have you chosen the right form of the verb?
    Entré (I went in)   *Entró* (He/she went in)

Gender
- Do the articles agree with the nouns in number and gender?

Las casas   Un café

- Do pronouns agree with the nouns they replace?
    El hombre tenía una bolsa. La dejó en el banco.

Adjectives
- Do your adjectives agree with the nouns they describe?
    Una catedral antigua   Unos folletos interesantes

Spellings
- Have you obeyed the key spelling rules?
    Particularly for -c- -z- -qu- -j- -g-
    Hice but *Hizo*
    Toqué but *Tocó*
    Jugué but *Jugó*
    Escogí but *Escoja usted*

- Have you obeyed the accent rules?
    Particularly for verbs of the *pretérito grave* group
    Dije Dijo; Puse Puso; Vine Vino; Estuve Estuvo etc.

5 > IN THE EXAMINATION

It is helpful to have a plan of action – the things to do once you have been told that you may start the examination. Your teacher will no doubt have discussed the importance of this but here again are some useful reminders and suggestions that are worth considering.

❝ Hints for the examination itself ❞

1. Make a quick note of any memory aids or checklists you may wish to refer to, including key expressions you particularly hope to be able to use or expressions in which you have often made mistakes.
2. Read the instructions on the question paper carefully, and make a sensible choice (where appropriate) from the questions available.
3. Plan what you are going to write before you launch into the writing itself. Make a note of key vocabulary and expressions to be included.
4. Allow enough time for each question.
5. Allow enough time to re-read and check your work.
6. Write clearly and legibly. A well-presented script creates a favourable impression on examiners and is easier for them to mark. Anything they cannot read will obviously gain no marks!

❝ Answer the queston set ❞

7. Make sure that what you write is relevant to the question. Reproducing material learnt by heart, however correct, will gain you no marks if it is not relevant to the question. If you have to write an account of an incident you saw in the street, the examiner does not wish to have to read an account of the meal you had in a restaurant just before the incident. He or she is likely to put a red line straight through the irrelevant material and all you will then have achieved is to reduce the number of words in which you can show how good you are at writing Spanish.

❝ Use the Spanish you know ❞

8. Use only Spanish that you know. Don't plan your writing in English and then try to translate it into Spanish. That is a recipe for disaster! Draw on the vocabulary, idioms, phrases and constructions that you are familiar with. On the other hand, it is important to 'show off' what you do know. The examiner can only award marks for what you have written, so make sure you reveal as full a range of your knowledge as you possibly can in terms of variety of vocabulary, idiom, construction, etc.

❝ Don't forget to check your answers ❞

9. Check that you have answered all aspects of the question.
10. Check that you have kept within the word limits.
11. Finally, CHECK YOUR WORK CAREFULLY FOR ACCURACY – Use your checklist.

6 > THE 'INSTANT LETTER KIT'

Writing with variety and accuracy can be made much easier if you have your own set of useful phrases that you know are correct and that you can use in a wide range of different situations. You do not have to find or invent a whole lot of new structures for each writing task you do. You can develop your own '**Instant Letter Kit**'.

It is a good idea to see how many of the useful phrases you used in your last piece of

> **Develop your own set of useful phrases**

written work can be re-used in the next – but do make sure that what you write is relevant to the task in hand.

Some people find it helpful to write the essential facts required by the task in as few words as possible and then to add useful phrases to improve the style of their writing, while bringing the total number of words up to the limit set.

As an example, let us consider part of a letter in which you have to mention a recent event. You decide to mention the meal you had in a restaurant to celebrate your friend's birthday, so you write:

Fui a un restaurante. Era el cumpleaños de mi amigo.

You now try to slot as many additional pieces of good (and relevant) Spanish as you can into those two sentences:

La semana pasada, precisamente el jueves por la tarde, fui con mi amigo David a un restaurante muy bueno y bastante famoso. Era el cumpleaños de mi amigo, que tiene dieciséis años, es muy simpático y vive a unos tres kilómetros de mi casa.

A quick check now reveals that your original ten words have become 42. More importantly, the extra 32 words are all expressions you know to be correct Spanish, the sentences have become more interesting and the quality of the writing has been improved. (And, although all the additional expressions can be pre-learnt, it is not possible for any examiner to decide you have introduced irrelevant material.) The sentences look more complex but in fact you have used a sort of 'building block' technique. In the first sentence the following expressions:

la semana pasada
por la tarde
con mi amigo David
muy bueno
bastante famoso

can each be included or omitted without in any way affecting the structure of the sentence itself. The one exception is *precisamente el jueves*, which clearly depends on *la semana pasada* for its meaning and which is essential if *por la tarde* is to have any real meaning. Each of the phrases includes more than one item that will improve your mark for quality of language. For example, *por la tarde* includes the correct agreement of *la* with *tarde* and good use of the preposition *por*. The phrase *bastante famoso* includes the correct (masculine singular) agreement of *famoso* with *restaurante* and good use of the adverb *bastante*.

You can build up your own set of useful phrases, beginning with the ones above and including the phrases added to the second sentence. Remember, you are dealing in phrases, not whole sentences.

Just to get you started, here are a few more suitable phrases:

> **Some useful phrases**

(des)afortunadamente	(un)fortunately
hace dos semanas	two weeks ago
tres horas más tarde	three hours later
como llovía	as it was raining
como hacía buen tiempo	as the weather was fine
con mucho cuidado	very carefully
sin dificultad	without difficulty
bastante despacio	quite slowly
no obstante	nevertheless
a pesar de la dificultad	in spite of the difficulty
cuando me di cuenta	when I realized

7 COPING WITH PROBLEMS

The strategies listed in Chapters 6 and 10 are likely to be useful here as well. One additional area that is worth considering is what to do if you are uncertain of the correct form of a verb. Let us suppose you wish to use the verb *poner*. You remember there is something unusual about it in the Preterite but cannot remember exactly what form it takes. You could always use the verb *decidir* before it. Instead of writing: *Puse la bolsa en el suelo* you write *Decidí poner la bolsa en el suelo*.

Other verbs that you could use in this way include:

empezar a	e.g. Empecé a andar	*I began to walk*
tratar de	e.g. Traté de explicar	*I tried to explain*
no querer	e.g. No quise decir...	*I refused to say...*

STUDENTS' ANSWERS WITH EXAMINER'S COMMENTS

You are recommended to work out how you would deal with each of these questions *before* you look at the students' answers and examiner's comments.

Q1 INFORMAL LETTER

Your Spanish pen-friend has just written to you and sent you this cutting to show what the family has given him/her as a birthday present.

Write a letter in reply, commenting on the present and explaining the sort of music you like and where you listen to it. Say where you went and what you did on your last birthday, giving details about what you received as presents. Tell him/her two things you hope to receive for your next birthday and why you are so keen to receive them.

CHAPTER 11 STUDENTS' ANSWERS WITH EXAMINER'S COMMENTS

Write about 100 words and **state at the end of your letter the number of words you have written.**

> 66 This is a piece of very accurate Spanish, with only three real errors and a missed accent (*esta* for *ese*; accent missed on *música*; *de* where it should not be; mis-spelling of *escucho*). The style is simple but there are several adjectives, all agreeing correctly with the nouns they describe, and there is good use of *bastante* and *estupendamente*. Overall it looks a good performance. But just a minute! The description of the bedroom is totally irrelevant to the question — so there can be no marks at all for those 29 words. The description of the restaurant and the wish to go there again can probably be accepted as just relevant but there is no mention of presents received, of two things hoped for next birthday or of reasons why those things are wanted. So, of the 10 things required in the instructions, five are missing and the candidate cannot really expect to score more than half marks. 99

Southampton,
el 3 de julio,

Querido José:

Gracias por tu amable carta. Esta [1] regalo es magnífico. Quiero tener uno igual. Me gusta mucho la musica [2] rock. Tengo muchos de [3] discos y los eschucho [4] en mi dormitorio. Mi dormitorio es grande y bonito. Tiene las paredes azules y las cortinas grises. Hay una cama, un armario, una mesa y una silla. También tengo allí muchos libros.

En mi cumpleaños fui con mis padres y mi hermano a un restaurante. El restaurante es bastante grande y muy bueno. Había mucha gente allí. Comimos estupendamente. Quiero volver allí el año que viene porque me gustó tanto.

Un abrazo de
Jeffrey.

(60)
(SEG)

Q2 FORMAL LETTER

Very near to the end of your holiday in Spain, you take a bus journey. You leave something on the bus. Once you have arrived back in England, you write to the bus company about your lost article.

Mention the following points in your letter. Marks are also awarded for additional relevant information.

1. Say what it is that you left on the bus and give a description of it.
2. Say who gave you this article, eg a relative and on what occasion, eg a birthday.
3. Give the date and time of the occurrence and information about the bus on which you left the article, eg where it was going, its number.
4. Say why you have not been able to go personally to collect the article.
5. Ask them to post it to you if they find it.

> *A comparatively simple and straightforward letter. All points have been dealt with effectively, so full marks for that. There is very little extra information – just the contents of the bag (possibly 2 or 3 marks) and perhaps there is an extra mark for giving slightly more than the minimum information about the bus. There is some effective use of 'Instant Letter Kit' style phrases (e.g. la semana pasada, al día siguiente) and the Spanish is generally very accurate. The grammatical corrections to be made are: [1] viajé; [2] dejé. Really the word for a long-distance bus is autocar. More seriously, the beginning and ending are inappropriate for a formal letter (See Chapter 10) and marks will be lost for that. Overall, quite a competent performance that scores good marks.*

Birmingham
el 3 de septiembre

Querido señor,

La semana pasada fui en el autobús de Madrid a Salamanca. Viajó [1] el lunes en el autobús de la tarde que sale de Madrid a las cuatro y media y dejó [2] una bolsa de cuero color marrón cuando bajé. Me gusta mucho la bolsa porque me la regaló mi hermana mayor por Navidad. Contiene tres libros, ropa y varias postales de Madrid. No fue posible ir a la oficina de objetos perdidos a pedir la bolsa porque tenía que volver a Inglaterra al día siguiente.

Si usted encuentra la bolsa, por favor mandarla por correo.

Un abrazo de
Lucy Wilson.

(20)
(MEG)

CHAPTER 11 **PRACTICE QUESTIONS**

Q3 ACCOUNT/REPORT

Imagine you are 1 of the 2 young people in the pictures. Write 100–120 words **in Spanish** to describe what happened in a letter to your pen-friend. Do not write the rest of the letter.

(*WJEC*)

> *Querido José:*
>
> *El lunes passado por la mañana saliba con mi hermana para ir a las tiendas. En el calle cerca el centro cuidad Mary tuvó un accidente porque un perro atacó ella. Se caió del bicicleta y rompió la pierna. El perro era muy grande y era marrón. El hombre con el perro muy asusto y ayudo. Yo llamo la ambulancía que vinó cinco minutos después y llevó Mary al hospital. Mis padres muy asusto. Compran flores y compro uvas. Visitamos Mary en la hospital por la tarde. Está en la hospital por una semana.*
>
> *Un abrazo de*
> *Adrian.*

❝ This answer is surprisingly easy to understand, in spite of the poor quality of the Spanish, and it will score quite a good mark for Communication. On the other hand, the language really is not good enough for Higher Level. Most of the verbs are wrong and some are in the Present Tense instead of the Preterite. This candidate does not know about the Personal 'a', is inconsistent in deciding the gender of *hospital* and has invented the expression *muy asusto* (and used it twice). There are one or two good accurate phrases (e.g. *por la mañana, por la tarde, para ir a las tiendas*) and the description of the dog is entirely accurate! The instructions were quite specific that this was only part of a letter, so the beginning and ending should not have been included. ❞

In the interests of accuracy, here is the same account corrected (though without any attempt to increase the range of expressions used):

> *El lunes pasado por la mañana salí en bicicleta con mi hermana para ir a las tiendas. En la calle, cerca del centro de la ciudad, Mary tuvo un accidente, porque un perro la atacó. Se cayó de la bicicleta y se rompió la pierna. El perro era marrón y muy grande. El hombre que estaba con el perro se asustó mucho y ayudó. Yo llamé para pedir una ambulancia, que llegó cinco minutos después y llevó a Mary al hospital. Mis padres se asustaron mucho. Compraron flores y yo compré uvas. Visitamos a Mary en el hospital por la tarde. Se queda en el hospital durante una semana.*

CHAPTER 11 PRACTICE QUESTIONS

PRACTICE QUESTIONS

You are recommended to ignore the word limits and work to the limits set by the Examining Group for the paper(s) *you* will take. There is an outline answer to the first question to give you an idea of what is expected.

INFORMAL LETTERS

Q1 You have received the following postcard from your Spanish pen-friend.

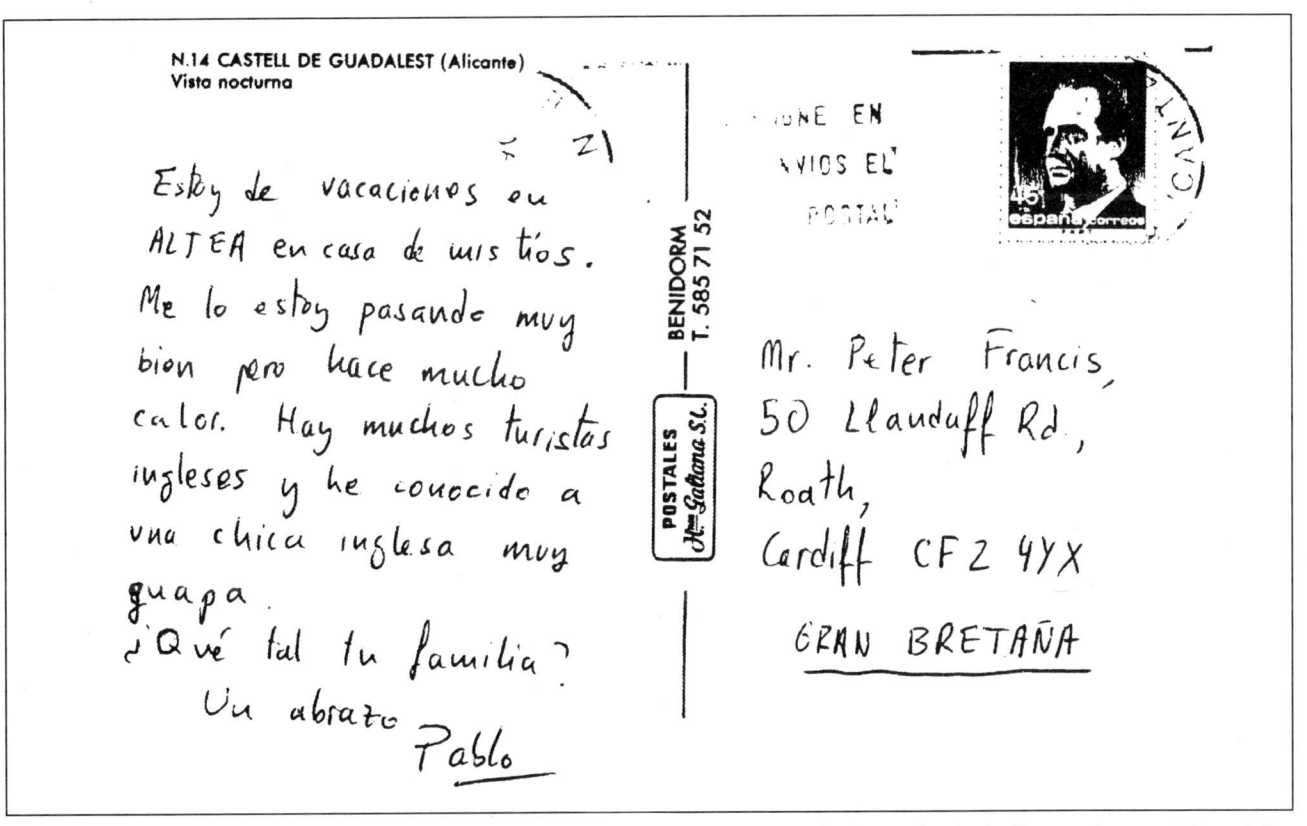

> N.14 CASTELL DE GUADALEST (Alicante)
> Vista nocturna
>
> Estoy de vacaciones en ALTEA en casa de mis tíos. Me lo estoy pasando muy bien pero hace mucho calor. Hay muchos turistas ingleses y he conocido a una chica inglesa muy guapa.
> ¿Qué tal tu familia?
> Un abrazo
> Pablo
>
> BENIDORM T. 585 71 52
> POSTALES J.ª Gaitana S.L.
>
> Mr. Peter Francis,
> 50 Llandaff Rd.,
> Roath,
> Cardiff CF2 4YX
> GRAN BRETAÑA

Write a letter **in Spanish** of 100–120 words in reply, including at least **eight** of the following points.

    (i)   Ask him how long he will be staying in Altea.
    (ii)   Ask him the name of the English girl he has met.
    (iii)   Ask how old she is and where she comes from.
    (iv)   Say that you and your parents are well,
    (v)   but that your brother is in hospital.
    (vi)   Explain that he has broken his leg and that
    (vii)   he will have to stay in hospital for a fortnight.
    (viii)   Send your regards to his parents.
    (ix)   Begin and end the letter appropriately.

(WJEC)

Q2 Your Spanish friend María is thinking of visiting the United States of America to attend an English language course in New York. She has sent you part of the brochure and has written to ask for your advice.

Write a letter to María **in Spanish** and try to persuade her to come and visit you in Britain instead.

Tell her:
- what you think of her plans to spend the holidays studying;
- that there are similar courses in this country;
- that she could come and stay with you and your family;
- what sorts of things you can do if she visits you;

- why else you think she should come here instead of the United States.

Ask her:
- what her parents think about her going to the United States;.
- how she feels about your ideas.

Write neatly and put down **all** the information you are asked to give. The number of words is not important.

(*NEAB*)

Q3 Write about 200 words in Spanish on the following.
You may use the visual material as a guide if you wish to do so.

Your penfriend thinks she might like to work as an au-pair when she's older. Your neighbours had an au-pair last year. Write a letter to your penfriend, including details about:

(i) who she was and where she came from
(ii) her appearance and character
(iii) the family with whom she stayed
(iv) some of the things she had to do while she was here.

(*NICCEA*)

CHAPTER 11 **PRACTICE QUESTIONS**

Q4 On holiday near Tarragona, you decide to write **in Spanish** to your Spanish friend to tell him/her about the excursion you went on yesterday to the *Rioleón Super Park*. You use the leaflet (below) from *Rioleón* to remind you of what you did. You have already prepared the following notes.
- Excursión a Rioleón, ¿cuándo y cómo, y con quién?
- Las atracciones: las que me gustaron más y por qué
- Los animales: los que me interesaron más y por qué
- Comidas y refrescos, y lo que hice al volver al hotel

(*40*)

[Please note that in the original GCSE paper the leaflet was printed in full colour.]

(ULEAC)

FORMAL LETTERS

Q5 Your family intends to take a trip to Mexico City. One of the hotels recommended to you is the Hotel María Isabel. Write a letter of about 100 words to the manager of the hotel. Include the following:

- Your arrival and departure dates
- The size of your family, type of accommodation you need and inquiries about the cost
- Ask about the following facilities: dining, entertainment, recreational
- Ask about the area in which the hotel is located, bearing in mind the needs and interests of your family members.

(20)

(Bahamas GCSE)

Q6 You are about to start your summer holidays and are looking for a job in Spain. A friend points out an advertisement in a Spanish newspaper (see below).

NECESITO, ESTUDIANTES INGLESES PARA TRABAJAR EN HOTELES DURANTE EL VERANO. ESCRIBIR CON DETALLES A Sr.Moreno. Calle Goya 4-3-A.Madrid.

Write a letter to Sr. Moreno in **Spanish** in about 100 words. Include the points below. Marks are also awarded for additional, relevant information.
1. Give personal details about yourself – eg your age.
2. Tell him how long you have been studying Spanish.
3. Tell him about other paid jobs you have done in the past.
4. Ask about the job he is offering – eg the pay.
5. Tell him when you must be back in England.

(20)
(MEG)

ACCOUNTS/REPORTS

Q7 While you were on holiday in Spain recently, staying with your exchange partner your hosts were burgled. Apparently the thieves got into the house through your bedroom window which you had left open when you went out. Now you have been asked to write your version of the incident for the Spanish police. Give a full account of all you know about the burglary saying why you were in Spain, what was stolen from you personally and also your alibi, in case the police suspect you of being involved.

(20)
(MEG)

Q8 While on holiday in Spain, you are involved in a minor accident while crossing the road outside your hotel. You were not seriously injured, but you have to provide the local police with a written report **in Spanish**. Make sure you cover the following areas.

- The circumstances leading up to the accident, e.g. where you were going, why you crossed the road.
- The car which hit you and what the driver was like.
- Your injuries and how they were treated.
- The effect the accident is likely to have on the rest of your holiday.

(40)
(ULEAC)

Q9 You have just returned from an exchange visit to the town of Puerto de la Cruz in the Canary Isles. Write an account of your visit for a language magazine saying when you went, what the family you stayed with was like, what you did, the places you visited and what you most enjoyed. You may find the plan below, taken from a local guide, useful.

(20)

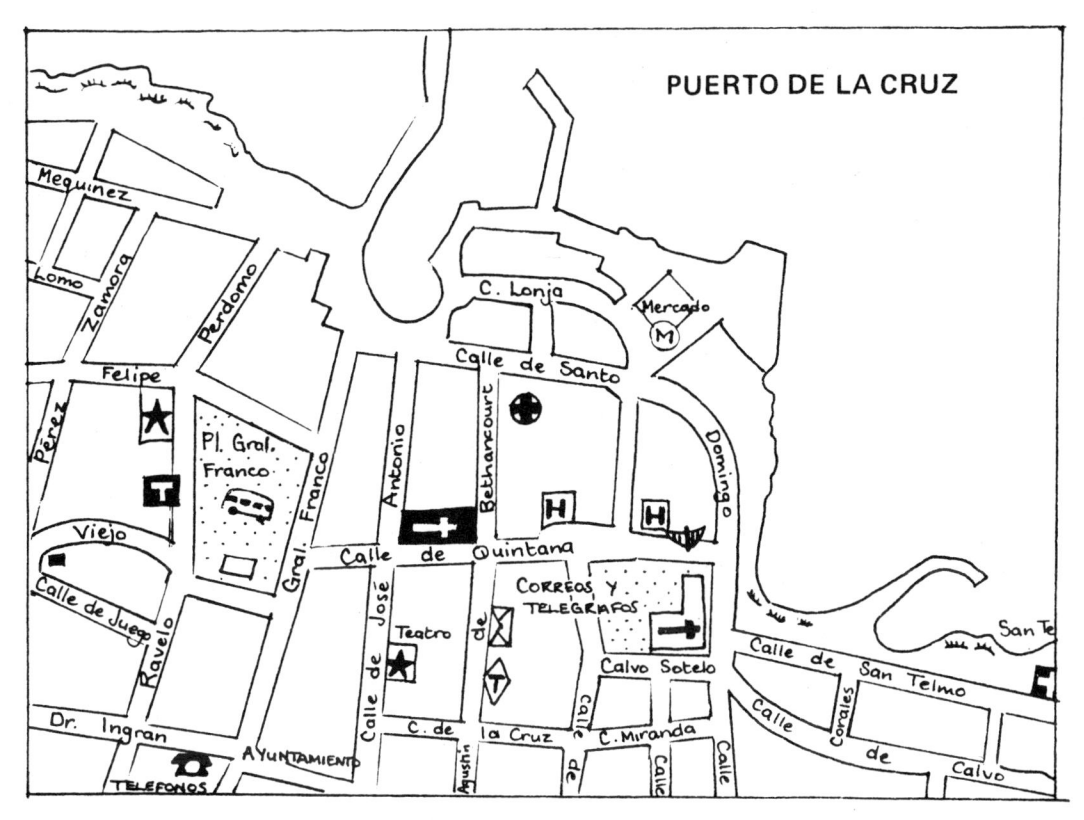

(MEG)

SPECIMEN ANSWER FOR THE FIRST PRACTICE QUESTION

Cardiff
el 3 de julio

Querido Pablo:

Recibí tu postal la semana pasada. Gracias. Altea parece bastante interesante. ¿Cuánto tiempo vas a estar en Altea? ¿Cómo se llama la chica inglesa? ¿Cuántos años tiene y de dónde es?

Mis padres y yo estamos bien pero desafortunadamente mi hermano está en el hospital. Se rompió la pierna hace cuatro días en un accidente bastante grave que ocurrió cuando iba de compras en su bicicleta nueva. Le atacó un perro enorme y muy feroz y se cayó de la bicicleta. Tiene que quedarse en el hospital durante quince días. No está muy contento.

Recuerdos a tus padres.

Un abrazo de
Peter.

A STEP FURTHER

First of all you can draw up your 'Instant Letter Kit'.

In order to improve the style of your written Spanish, it is a good idea from time to time to note down a dozen everyday nouns (words for things or people). Make sure you include some feminine ones and one or two plurals. Now write a suitable adjective (describing word) with each one, making sure it agrees (e.g. *una falda negra*). Finally, see how many could have an adverb (e.g. *bastante, demasiado. excesivamente*) added to them and still make sense. (Not all can.)

Another practice activity is to write six short and simple sentences involving past action (e.g. *Entré en la cocina*). Now write a suitable word or phrase to describe how the action was done (e.g. *Entré rápidamente en la cocina.*).

Remember, additional adjectives (provided they agree), adverbs and other additional phrases really do improve the style of your written Spanish – and gain you marks.

REVIEW SHEET

REVIEW SHEET: CHAPTERS 10 AND 11

BASIC LEVEL

- Write a list (in Spanish) of 12 items or words which might be involved in shopping for presents.

  1.................................... 2.................................... 3....................................
  4.................................... 5.................................... 6....................................
  7.................................... 8.................................... 9....................................
  10.................................. 11.................................. 12..................................

- Write a list (in Spanish) of 12 items or words which might be involved in describing the contents of a lost bag or case.

  1.................................... 2.................................... 3....................................
  4.................................... 5.................................... 6....................................
  7.................................... 8.................................... 9....................................
  10..................................

- Write a list (in Spanish) of 10 items or words which might be involved in going to the cinema or theatre with a Spanish friend.

  1.................................... 2.................................... 3....................................
  4.................................... 5.................................... 6....................................
  7.................................... 8.................................... 9....................................
  10..................................

- Write the *English* equivalent of each of these Spanish words.

  1. Nombre .... 2. Apellido ....
  3. Edad .... 4. Fecha..
  5. Domicilio.................................. 6. Firma...
  7. Fecha de nacimiento ....
  8. Fecha de llegada ....
  9. Fecha de salida ....

- Write down an appropriate **beginning** for each of the following:

  1. An informal letter...
  2. A semi-formal letter ....
  3. A formal letter ....

- Write down an appropriate **ending** for each of the following:

  1. An informal letter...
  2. A semi-formal letter ....
  3. A formal letter ....

HIGHER LEVEL

- Write down 40 useful phrases for your 'Instant Letter Kit'.

  1. .... 2. ....
  3. .... 4. ....
  5. .... 6. ....
  7. .... 8. ....
  9. .... 10. ....
  11. .... 12. ....
  13. .... 14. ....
  15. .... 16. ....
  17. .... 18. ....
  19. .... 20. ....
  21. .... 22. ....
  23. .... 24. ....

REVIEW SHEET

25.	26. ....
27.	28. ....
29.	30. ....
31.	32. ....
33.	34. ....
35.	36. ....
37.	38. ....
39.	40. ....

- Try to complete the following **rules** which will be useful in developing a *checklist*.

1. **Nouns:**
   - All nouns ending in *-aje* are ....
   - all nouns ending in *-ción* are ....
   - most nouns ending in *-o* are ....
     but two exceptions are 1. .... 2. ....
   - most nouns ending in *-a* are ....
     but two exceptions are 1. .... 2. ....

2. **Adjectives:**
   - Adjectives must agree in .... and .... with the noun or pronoun they describe.

3. **Adverbs:**
   - In most cases adverbs are formed by adding .... to the feminine singular of the adjective.

     Examples: rápido .... (rapidly)

     cuidadoso .... (carefully)

     probable .... (probably)

     Exceptions do however occur:

     Examples 1. .... 2. ....

     3. .... 4. ....

4. **Verbs:**
   - The **present tense** is used for ....

   - The **preterite tense** is used to ....

   - The **perfect tense** is used when ....

   - The **future tense** is used for ....

- Write out *hablar* in each of the tenses indicated

Present	Preterite	Perfect	Future
hablo	....	....	....
hablas	....	....	....
habla	....	....	....
hablamos	....	....	....
habláis	....	....	....
hablan	....	....	....

   - The **conditional tense** is used where in English we use ....

   - The **imperfect tense** is used for ....

   - The **pluperfect tense** is used for ....

REVIEW SHEET

- Write out *hablar* in each of the tenses indicated

Present	Conditional	Imperfect	Pluperfect
hablo	....	....	....
hablas	....	....	....
habla	....	....	....
hablamos	....	....	....
habláis	....	....	....
hablan	....	....	....

NB You can check these **rules** with the grammar chapter (12).

CHAPTER 12

GRAMMAR

NOUNS
ARTICLES
ADJECTIVES
ADVERBS
VERBS
PRONOUNS
THE PERSONAL 'A'
DATES, TIMES, NUMBERS AND QUESTIONS

GETTING STARTED

Many people become very worried about **grammar** and feel that it is too technical for them to understand. In fact it is simply an explanation of the way in which words are put together to convey meaning. We are using grammar whenever we say or write a sentence and we are also applying our knowledge of grammar to understand what we hear and read. In our own language we apply the 'rules' of grammar without thinking about them – and that should be exactly what we aim to do eventually in Spanish.

You can achieve a great deal by using the expressions you have learnt but a sound knowledge of the main points of grammar will enable you to develop a much wider range of language and also to ensure that you link different expressions correctly. At GCSE the accuracy of your Spanish is marked particularly in Higher Level Writing and Speaking but a good knowledge of grammar will improve the quality of your work in all skills and at both Levels.

The grammar section that follows contains fairly brief explanations of the main points of grammar that you will need for the GCSE examinations. You can use it for revision and also for reference.

Areas that are required for Higher Level only are marked with an asterisk *.

CHAPTER 12 **GRAMMAR**

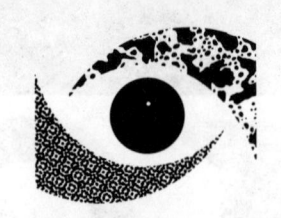

ESSENTIAL PRINCIPLES

1 > NOUNS

GENDER

All Spanish **nouns** are either masculine or feminine. You need to learn the **gender** with the word.

All nouns ending in *-aje* are masculine (e.g. el viaje).
All nouns ending in *-ción* are feminine (e.g. la natación).
All nouns ending in *-dad*, *-tad* and *-tud* are feminine (e.g. la verdad).
All nouns ending in *-umbre* are feminine (e.g. la cumbre)
Almost all nouns ending in *-o* are masculine. Important exceptions:
- la mano
- la radio.

Most nouns ending in *-a* are feminine but there are many exceptions, of which some of the most important are listed below:
- el clima
- el día
- el mapa
- el planeta
- el problema
- el sofá
- el tema
- el tranvía
- el telegrama (and all other nouns ending in -grama)

Nouns ending in *-ista* can be either masculine or feminine, depending on the sex of the person referred to (e.g. el/la tenista).

Notice also: el policía (*policeman*); la policía (*police force, policewoman*)
el guardia (*policeman*); la guardia (*policewoman, guard duty, protection*)

PLURAL

Here are some useful 'rules' for forming **plurals**.

Nouns ending in a **vowel** add -s
    el libro   los libros

Nouns ending in a **consonant** add -es
    la pared   las paredes
  except those ending in -s
    el lunes   los lunes
  but nouns ending in -s with an accented last syllable do add -es (and lose the accent)
    el inglés   los ingleses
    el autobús   los autobuses

Notice the variations in **written accent** (keeping the stress on the same syllable in singular and plural), e.g.
    el joven   los jóvenes
    la habitación   las habitaciones

Remember also to apply the spelling rules for words ending in -z
    e.g. el lápiz   los lápices

2 > ARTICLES

DEFINITE

	Masculine	Feminine
Singular	el coche (*the car*)	la casa (*the house*)
Plural	los coches (*the cars*)	las casas (*the houses*)

Notice also the neuter article 'lo', which is used with an adjective to convey the meaning 'the... thing' or 'the... part', e.g. 'Lo interesante es...' *The interesting thing is....;* 'Lo mejor es ...' *The best part is...*

INDEFINITE

	Masculine	Feminine
Singular	un coche (*a car*)	una casa (*a house*)
Plural	unos coches (*some cars*)	unas casas (*some houses*)

There is no word for 'some' in the singular (some coffee: *café*) and in practice the plural indefinite article (*unos/unas*) is usually omitted.

Quiero vino, por favor. *I'd like some wine, please.*
He comprado caramelos. *I've bought some sweets.*

ADDITIONAL USES OF THE DEFINITE ARTICLE

- When a noun is used in a **general sense** (so that the sentence could be taken to include every example of that noun that exists).

  e.g. Me gusta el queso. *I like cheese.*

  Notice that the sentence could be taken to mean that I like all cheese that exists. Compare that with

  Como queso. *I eat cheese* (where the statement clearly refers only to some of the cheese that exists).

- With parts of the **body** and **clothing** when used with a reflexive verb

  Me lavo las manos. *I wash my hands.*
  Se quitó la chaqueta. *He took off his jacket.*

- With **school subjects**: Las matemáticas; la historia.

- With **languages** (except after the verb 'hablar')

  El español es un idioma muy importante.
  but Hablo español.

- With **prices**: Cien pesetas el paquete. *100 pesetas a packet.*

- **Before titles** (other than *don/doña*) when speaking about someone

  El señor Gómez vive en Valencia (*but* Don Ramón vive en Granada).

OMISSION OF THE INDEFINITE ARTICLE

- When saying what someone's job is (*after* ser)
  Es peluquero. *He is a hairdresser.*
- With 'tener' and 'hay' in the negative
  No tengo coche. *I do not have a car.*
  No hay problema. *There isn't a problem.*
- After 'sin' (*without*)
  Llegó sin chaqueta. *He arrived without a jacket.*
- In exclamations
  ¡Qué sorpresa! *What a surprise!*
- * Before 'otro', 'tal', 'cierto'
  Otro tren *another train.* Tal libro *such a book.*
  Cierta ciudad *a certain city*

3 › ADJECTIVES

Remember to make **adjectives** 'agree' in number and gender with the noun or pronoun they describe.

Adjectives ending in *-o:*

	Masculine	*Feminine*
Singular	un coche blanco	una casa blanca
Plural	unos coches blancos	unas casas blancas

Adjectives ending in any other letter:

	Masculine	*Feminine*
Singular	un edificio grande	una camisa azul
Plural	unos edificios grandes	unas camisas azules

Adjectives of nationality or region:

	Masculine	*Feminine*
Singular	un libro español	una ciudad española
Plural	unos libros españoles	unas ciudades españolas

APOCOPATION

The following adjectives drop the final-*o* before a masculine singular noun

bueno:	buen	tercero:	tercer
malo:	mal	alguno:	algún
primero:	primer	ninguno:	ningún

e.g. un buen día (*but* un día bueno, una buena persona).

Note also that *grande* is shortened to *gran* when used before a singular noun of either gender, *e.g.*

un gran hombre, una gran idea (*but* unas grandes personas).

(Remember that in these cases *grande* means 'great'.)

COMPARATIVE

Más.... que.... *more.... than....*
Menos.... que.... *less.... than.... (not as.... as....)*
e.g. Las uvas son más caras que las manzanas.   *The grapes are dearer than the apples.*

El tren es menos rápido que el avión.   *The train is not as fast as the plane.*

Note the **irregular** comparatives:
- mejor *better*
- mayor *greater, older*
- peor *worse*
- menor *lesser, younger.*

* Tan.... como.... *as.... as....*
e.g. El libro es tan interesante como la película.   *The book is as interesting as the film.*

* SUPERLATIVE

Madrid es la ciudad más grande de España.   *Madrid is the largest city in Spain.*

POSSESSIVE ADJECTIVES

Singular		Plural		
Masculine	Feminine	Masculine	Feminine	
mi	mi	mis	mis	*my*
tu	tu	tus	tus	*your*
su	su	sus	sus	*his, her, its, your (Vd.)*
nuestro	nuestra	nuestros	nuestras	*our*
vuestro	vuestra	vuestros	vuestras	*your*
su	su	sus	sus	*their, your (Vd.)*

e.g. Mi libro, mis libros.

DEMONSTRATIVE ADJECTIVES

Singular		Plural		
Masculine	Feminine	Masculine	Feminine	
este	esta	estos	estas	*this, these*
ese	esa	esos	esas	*that, those +*
aquel	aquella	aquellos	aquellas	*that, those +*

+ *ese etc. is used for things or persons near the person being spoken to.*
+ *aquel etc. is used for things or persons near neither the speaker nor the person spoken to.*

POSITION OF ADJECTIVES

Possessive and Demonstrative adjectives come before the nouns they describe, *e.g.*

nuestro coche   este libro

Other adjectives usually follow the nouns they describe, e.g.
    un coche azul   un libro interesante

With the following adjectives the position affects the meaning:

	before the noun	after the noun
antiguo	*previous/former*	*ancient*
grande	*great*	*large/big*
pobre	*unfortunate*	*poor (with little money)*

e.g. una gran señora   *a great lady*
    una señora grande   *a large (or tall) lady.*

4 > ADVERBS

In most cases, **adverbs** are formed by adding *-mente* to the feminine singular form of the adjective, e.g.

rápido	rápidamente	*quickly*
cuidadoso	cuidadosamente	*carefully*
probable	probablemente	*probably*

Exceptions include:

bien	*well*	bastante	*fairly, quite*
mal	*badly*	muy	*very*
mucho	*a lot*	demasiado	*too, too much*
poco	*not very (much)*	aquí	*here*
despacio	*slowly*	ahí	*there, near person spoken to*
de prisa	*quickly*	allí	*there, near neither speaker nor person spoken to*
a menudo	*often*		
pronto	*soon*	ahora	*now*
de repente	*suddenly*	luego	*then, next.*

COMPARATIVE

Comparison of adverbs is very similar to comparison of adjectives:
Habla más de prisa que su hermano.   *He speaks faster than his brother.*
* Terminó tan pronto como su amigo.   *He finished as soon as his brother.*

* *Note also constructions such as:*
    Sabe más de lo que crees.   *He knows more than you think.*

* SUPERLATIVE

Note the construction:

Anduve lo más rápidamente posible.   *I walked the fastest I could.*

5 > VERBS

PRESENT TENSE

Use: The **Present Tense** is used for things that happen or are happening at the present time, e.g. 'I eat' or 'I am eating'.

Regular verbs

hablar	comer	vivir
hablo	como	vivo
hablas	comes	vives
habla	come	vive
hablamos	comemos	vivimos
habláis	coméis	vivís
hablan	comen	viven

Radical-changing verbs

encontrar(ue)	entender(ie)	pedir(i)
encuentro	entiendo	pido
encuentras	entiendes	pide
encuentra	entiende	pide
encontramos	entendemos	pedimos
encontráis	entendéis	pedís
encuentran	entienden	piden

Common irregular verbs

ser	estar	ir	tener	hacer	venir
soy	estoy	voy	tengo	hago	vengo
eres	estás	vas	tienes	haces	vienes
es	está	va	tiene	hace	viene
somos	estamos	vamos	tenemos	hacemos	venimos
sois	estáis	vais	tenéis	hacéis	venís
son	están	van	tienen	hacen	vienen

Verbs that are regular apart from the 1st person singular (yo *form*)
e.g. salir

salgo	*caer*: caigo, caes, etc.
sales	*traer*: traigo, traes, etc.
sale	*poner*: pongo, pones, etc.
salimos	*salir*: salgo, sales, etc.
salís	*ver*: veo, ves, etc.
salen	*dar*: doy, das, etc.
	saber: sé, sabes, etc.
	ofrecer: ofrezco, ofreces, etc.

(*All verbs ending in* -ecer, -ocer *and* -ucir *follow the pattern of* ofrecer.)

PRETERITE TENSE

Use: The **Preterite** is used to recount events or things that happened in the past, e.g. 'I spoke', 'She went', 'You arrived'.

Regular   **Regular – but note spellings**

hablar	comer	vivir	leer	oír	ver
hablé	comí	viví	leí	oí	vi
hablaste	comiste	viviste	leíste	oíste	viste
habló	comió	vivió	leyó	oyó	vio
hablamos	comimos	vivimos	leímos	oímos	vimos
hablasteis	comisteis	vivisteis	leísteis	oísteis	visteis
hablaron	comieron	vivieron	leyeron	oyeron	vieron

The following verbs are regular in the Preterite Tense, but note the effects of the spelling rules on the first person singular (yo form):

Empezar: empecé, empezaste, empezó, etc.   *Changes of this sort affect all*
cruzar: crucé, cruzaste, cruzó, etc.   *verbs ending in* -zar, -gar, -car.
jugar: jugué, jugaste, jugó, etc.
buscar: busqué, buscaste, buscó, etc.

Radical-changing -ir verbs:

sentir (ie)	dormir (ue)	seguir (i)	
sentí	dormí	seguí	*There are no radical*
sentiste	dormiste	seguiste	*changes in the Preterite*
sintió	durmió	siguió	*of* -ar *and* -er *radical-*
sentimos	dormimos	seguimos	*changing verbs.*
sentisteis	dormisteis	seguisteis	
sintieron	durmieron	siguieron	

'Pretérito grave' verbs:
These verbs have no accents in the Preterite.

estar	hacer	decir	
estuve	hice	dije	*andar*: anduve, anduviste, *etc.*
estuviste	hiciste	dijiste	*tener*: tuve, tuviste, tuvo, *etc.*
estuvo	hizo	dijo	*poder*: pude, pudiste, pudo, *etc.*
estuvimos	hicimos	dijimos	*poner*: puse, pusiste, puso, *etc.*
estuvisteis	hicisteis	dijisteis	*saber*: supe, supiste, supo, *etc.*
estuvieron	hicieron	dijeron +	*querer*: quise, quisiste, *etc.*
			venir: vine, viniste, vino, *etc.*

+ *Note that there is no* i *in this part of decir*. The same pattern is followed by:
traer: traje, trajiste, trajo, trajimos, trajisteis, trajeron
conducir: conduje, condujiste, condujo, condujimos, condujisteis, condujeron
and all verbs that end in -ducir.

Irregular verbs:

dar		ser		ir	
di	dimos	fui	fuimos	fui	fuimos
diste	disteis	fuiste	fuisteis	fuiste	fuisteis
dio	dieron	fue	fueron	fue	fueron

PERFECT TENSE

Use: The **Perfect Tense** is used when we would use the English Past Tense with 'have', e.g. 'I have eaten', 'Have you visited Spain?'.

Regular			**Irregular**
hablar	*comer*	*vivir*	*hacer*
he hablado	he comido	he vivido	he hecho
has hablado	has comido	has vivido	has hecho
ha hablado	ha comido	ha vivido	ha hecho
hemos hablado	hemos comido	hemos vivido	hemos hecho
habéis hablado	habéis comido	habéis vivido	habéis hecho
han hablado	han comido	han vivido	han hecho

The past participle of regular verbs is formed by removing the infinitive ending (-ar, -er, -ir*) and replacing it*
    for -ar *verbs with* -ado
    for -er *and* -ir *verbs with* -ido.

Note the accent required when -ido *is added to* a, e *or* o
    caer: caído.   leer: leído.   oír: oído.

Remember that you must not put any words between the two parts of the Perfect Tense. 'Have you eaten?' (addressing the person as 'usted') can be expressed in two ways:
    ¿Ha comido usted? *and* ¿Usted ha comido?

What you must **not** *do is put the word* 'usted' *in the middle (which is where we do put* 'you' *in English).*

* Irregular past participles:

abrir:	abierto	romper:	roto
cubrir:	cubierto	ver:	visto
decir:	dicho	volver:	vuelto
escribir:	escrito	morir:	muerto
poner:	puesto		

FUTURE TENSE

You are expected to recognize and understand this tense at Basic Level but you will be expected to use it only at Higher Level.

Use: The **Future Tense** is used for future events, e.g. 'I shall go', 'They will arrive'.

The endings of the Future Tense are the same for all verbs. The stem is normally the infinitive.

Regular		**Irregular**
hablar	*dormirse*	decir: diré, *etc.*
hablaré	me dormiré	hacer: haré, *etc.*
hablarás	te dormirás	poder: podré, *etc.*
hablará	se dormirá	poner: pondré, *etc.*
hablaremos	nos dormiremos	querer: querré, *etc.*
hablaréis	os dormiréis	saber: sabré, *etc.*
hablarán	se dormirán	salir: saldré, *etc.*
		tener: tendré, *etc.*
		venir: vendré, *etc.*

'IR A' + INFINITIVE

At Basic Level you can be expected to express future action by using the verb ir a *followed by an infinitive*

e.g. Voy a visitar a mi abuela.   *I am going to visit my grandmother.*
Van a reparar el coche para mañana.   *They are going to repair the car for tomorrow.*

CONDITIONAL

At Basic Level you should understand and be able to use:
Me gustaría... e.g. Me gustaría visitar Sevilla   *I should like to visit Seville.*
¿Te gustaría...? *Would you like...?*
¿Le gustaría...? *Would you like...?* (*addressing the person as* usted)
Nos gustaría... *We should like...*

* *At Higher Level you should be able to understand and use the Conditional of other verbs.*

Use: The **Conditional** is used where in English we use 'would' or 'should', e.g. 'I should like....' 'He would do it, if....'

The endings are the same for all verbs. The stem is the same as for the Future Tense:

hablar	divertirse	hacer
hablaría	me divertiría	haría
hablarías	te divertirías	harías
hablaría	se divertiría	haría
hablaríamos	nos divertiríamos	haríamos
hablaríais	os divertiríais	haríais
hablarían	se divertirían	harían

* IMPERFECT

Use: The **Imperfect** is used for things that 'used to happen' or 'were happening', e.g. 'When I lived in the North (= used to live...)', 'When I was having lunch...'

Regular			Irregular		
hablar	*comer*	*vivir*	*ser*	*ir*	*ver*
hablaba	comía	vivía	era	iba	veía
hablabas	comías	vivías	eras	ibas	veías
hablaba	comía	vivía	era	iba	veía
hablábamos	comíamos	vivíamos	éramos	íbamos	veíamos
hablabais	comíais	vivíais	erais	ibais	veíais
hablaban	comían	vivían	eran	iban	veían

* PLUPERFECT

Use: The **Pluperfect** is used for what 'had happened', e.g. 'Because I had lost my passport....'

The Pluperfect is formed by the Imperfect of haber + *the past participle*:

hablar		hacer	
había hablado	habíamos hablado	había hecho	habíamos hecho
habías hablado	habíais hablado	habías hecho	habíais hecho
había hablado	habían hablado	había hecho	habían hecho

CONTINUOUS TENSES

Any tense in Spanish can be made **continuous** (e.g. 'He will be eating'). This is done by using the verb **estar** in the tense and form required, together with the present participle

e.g. Está hablando.   *S/he is speaking.*
Estará comiendo.   *S/he will be eating.*
Habían estado trabajando.   *They had been working.*

*The **Present Participle** is formed by removing the ending (-ar, -er, -ir) from the infinitive and replacing it*
    for -ar verbs with -ando
    for -er and -ir verbs with -iendo.
    e.g. Entrar: entrando.   Comer: comiendo.

The ending -iendo has to be added to a consonant. If there is no consonant to add it to, change the i *to* y
    e.g. Leer: leyendo.   Ir: yendo

Any object or reflexive pronouns are placed either before the verb 'estar' *or on the end of the present participle*
    e.g. Lo está leyendo *or* Está leyéndolo.
        Se están lavando *or* Están lavándose
Note the addition of the accent when a pronoun is added to the end of a present participle.

COMMANDS AND INSTRUCTIONS

Usted/ Ustedes commands
These are formed by removing the -o from the yo *form of the Present Tense and adding these endings:*
    for -ar verbs: -e *and* -en
    for -er and -ir verbs   -a *and* -an

    e.g. Tomar (tomo):   Tome (usted);   Tomen (ustedes)
         Venir (vengo):   Venga (usted);   Vengan (ustedes).

The most important exceptions are:
    Ir (voy):   Vaya (usted);   Vayan (ustedes)
    Dar (doy):   Dé (usted);   Den (ustedes).
*For **negative** commands, simply put* 'No' *first, e.g.* 'No vaya (usted)' *(Don't go.)*

Tú commands
These usually have the same form as the 'he/she' form of the Present Tense
    e.g.   Hablar: Habla (*Speak!*)
          Empezar: Empieza (*Begin!*)

The exceptions are:
    Decir: Di.   Salir: Sal.
    Hacer: Haz.   Ser: Sé.
    Ir: Ve.   Tener: Ten.
    Poner: Pon.   Venir: Ven.

Vosotros commands
These are formed by removing the -r from the end of the infinitive and replacing it with a -d
    e.g. Comer: Comed.   Salir: Salid.
          Ir: Id.

* Negative tú and vosotros commands
These all begin with the word No.

For negative tú *commands, take the* Vd. *command and add an -s*
e.g. Beber (Beba): No bebas.   Ir (Vaya): No vayas.

For negative vosotros *commands, again take the* Vd. *command and remove the final letter, replacing*
        -a *with* -áis
        -e *with* -éis
    e.g. Escribir (Escriba):   No escribáis
        Ir (Vaya):   No vayáis.

REFLEXIVE VERBS

These are exactly like other verbs except that they require a reflexive pronoun with them. As an example look at the verb lavarse *in different tenses and forms.*

Present	*Perfect*	*Present Continuous*
me lavo	me he lavado	me estoy lavando
te lavas	te has lavado	te estás lavando
se lava	se ha lavado	se está lavando
nos lavamos	nos hemos lavado	nos estamos lavando
os laváis	os habéis lavado	os estáis lavando
se lavan	se han lavado	se están lavando

Tú *command:* Lávate   *Negative:* No te laves
Vd. *command:* Lávese   *Negative:* No se lave (usted).

GUSTAR

Remember that when the thing that is liked is singular, we use 'gusta';
when the thing that is liked is plural, we use 'gustan';
when the thing liked is a verb, we use 'gusta' + *infinitive.*

e.g. Me gusta el café. *I like coffee.*
Me gustan las uvas. *I like grapes.*
Me gusta jugar al tenis. *I like playing tennis.*

SER AND ESTAR

It is important to use the correct verb for 'to be'. The decision depends on what follows the verb.

a) When the verb is followed immediately by a NOUN or PRONOUN – use SER
   e.g. Mi tío **es actor**.
   Madrid **es una ciudad** en España.
   ¿Qué **es esto**?

b) When the verb is followed by a PRESENT PARTICIPLE – use ESTAR
   e.g. Cuando llegué, **estaban comiendo**.

c) When the verb is followed by an EXPRESSION OF PLACE – use ESTAR
   e.g. El libro **está en la mesa**.
   Granada **está en el sur de España**.   *But don't forget:* Granada es una ciudad en el sur de España. (Rule a)

d) When the verb is followed by a PAST PARTICIPLE:

   i) SER tells of the ACTION being done
   e.g. La puerta **es abierta** por el policía.   *The door is opened by the policeman.*

   ii) ......ESTAR tells of the SITUATION RESULTING from the action
   e.g. La puerta **está abierta**.   *The door is open.*

e) When the verb is followed by an ADJECTIVE:

   i) SER tells of an ESSENTIAL or PERMANENT characteristic
   e.g. El camarero **era simpático**.   *The waiter was nice.*
   María **es joven**.   *Mary is young (an essential, though not permanent, fact about her).*

   ii) ESTAR tells of TEMPORARY states
   e.g. Mi hermano **está enfermo**.   *My brother is ill.*

Some adjectives change meaning according to whether they follow 'ser' or 'estar':

ser malo *to be bad*	estar malo *to be ill*
ser listo *to be clever*	estar listo *to be ready*
ser aburrido *to be boring*	estar aburrido *to be bored*
ser cansado *to be tiring*	estar cansado *to be tired*

Notice also:
   ser alegre *to be cheerful by nature*
   estar alegre *to be happy at the time*

NEGATIVES

(a) *For the simple negative, put 'no' before the verb*
   e.g. No tengo paraguas. *I have not got an umbrella.*

(b) *With other negatives there is usually a choice of order*
   e.g. Nunca voy a Madrid *or* No voy nunca a Madrid. *I never go to Madrid.*

   The same choice is possible with 'nadie', 'nada' and 'ni...ni...'
   e.g. Nadie me habló *or* No me habló nadie. *Nobody spoke to me.*
   Ni el bolígrafo ni el cuaderno estaba en la mesa.
   or No estaba en la mesa ni el bolígrafo ni el cuaderno.
   Neither the pen nor the exercise book was on the table.

6 › PRONOUNS

PERSONAL PRONOUNS

Subject	Reflexive	Indirect Object	Direct Object	Disjunctive
yo	me	me	me	mí
tú	te	te	te	ti
usted	se	le (se)+	le, la	usted
él	se	le (se)+	le, lo	él
ella	se	le (se)+	la	ella
nostros/as	nos	nos	nos	nosotros/as
vosotros/as	os	os	os	vosotros/as
ustedes	se	les (se)+	les, las	ustedes
ellos	se	les (se)+	les, los	ellos
ellas	se	les (se)+	las	ellas

*The **subject pronouns** are usually omitted in Spanish (except for* usted *and* ustedes*). They are used to avoid ambiguity and also for emphasis,*
   e.g. Tengo un hermano y una hermana. Él tiene trece años; ella tiene doce.

*The **Indirect Object form** se is used instead of* le/les *if it is followed immediately by* lo, la, los *or* las.

Disjunctive pronouns *are used after a preposition*
   e.g. Lo he hecho para ella. *I have done it for her.*
   Remember that conmigo = *with me;* contigo = *with you.*

POSITION OF OBJECT PRONOUNS

(a) *Normally before the verb*: Lo compré ayer. *I bought it yesterday.*

(b) *On the end of a positive command*: Tómelo. *Take it.*
   But not on a negative command: No lo tome.

(c) *Position optional:*
   i) *with a dependent infinitive*
      either Lo voy a comprar *or* Voy a comprarlo. *I'm going to buy it.*
   ii) *with a continuous tense*
      either Lo estoy preparando *or* Estoy preparándolo. *I'm preparing it.*

ORDER OF OBJECT PRONOUNS

Indirect before direct: Me lo dieron ayer. *They gave it to me yesterday.*
Reflexive before either: ¿Las manos? Sí, me las he lavado. *My hands? Yes, I have washed them.*

TÚ AND USTED

Remember that *tú* (plural *vosotros*) is used when speaking (or writing) to
  close friends
  members of the immediate family
  people of your own age (at least while you are in your teens)
  younger children
  pets

Usted (plural *ustedes*) is used with
  older people
  people to whom you need to show some respect (usually people whom you would address as 'Mr...', 'Mrs...' or 'Miss...').

When addressing someone as *usted*, the verb form you have to use is the 'he/she' form. The form you use with *ustedes* is the 'they' form. Similarly the word for 'your' is *su* (plural *sus*).
e.g. ¿Tiene usted su pasaporte? *Do you have your passport?*

The abbreviations *Vd.* and *Vds.* are often used in writing for *usted* and *ustedes*.

7 > THE PERSONAL 'A'

Remember that when the Direct Object of a verb is a person we have to put '*a*' before it
  e.g. ¿Conoces a María? *Do you know Mary?*
    ¿A quién viste? *Who(m) did you see?*
    No vi a nadie. *I saw nobody.*
A fuller explanation of this point is included in Chapter 9.

8 > DATES; TIMES; NUMBERS; QUESTION WORDS

These are all dealt with in Chapter 3, in the section headed 'Key Words and Expressions'.

INDEX

Accommodation 19–20, 42–43, 106
Accounts/reports 216, 228–229
Active use 15
Addresses 6
Adjectives 237–239
Adverbs 239
Age 29
Agreement of adjectives 237–238
Aims of GCSE 2
Apocopation 238
Articles 236–237
Assessment 3–4, 217

Basic Listening 55–75, 97–100
Basic Reading 135–164, 189
Basic Speaking 101–115, 131–133
Basic Writing 193–213, 231
BGCSE 5

Checklist 217–218
Commands 243
Comparative (adjectives) 238
Comparative (adverbs) 239
Conditional tense 242
Continuous tenses 242–243
Conversation 111, 113–115, 125–127
Countries 29, 42

Daily routine 33, 126–127
Dates 25–26
Demonstrative adjectives 238
Describing people 29–31
Diary entries 195–196, 200

Emotions 25
Examination components 3–4
Examining Groups 6

Family 30
Finding the way 18–19, 41–42, 105, 108
Flexibility of word order 167
Food and drink 22, 49–52, 103–104, 108–109, 121, 124
Form-filling 195, 199, 207
Free-time and entertainment 17, 38–40, 114, 127
Future tense 241

Garden 33
Gender 236
Geographical surroundings 16, 34–35, 113, 127

Grades 4
Grammar 9, 235–246
'Gustar' 244

Health and welfare 21, 46–47
Higher Level skills 78, 166
Higher Listening 76–100
Higher Reading 165–191
Higher Speaking 116–134
Higher Writing 215–233
Holidays 19, 42–43, 114, 127
House and home 16, 31–33, 113, 126

IGCSE 5
Imperfect tense 242
'Instant Letter Kit' 218–219
Instructions, understanding of 138–139
'Ir a' + infinitive 242

Key words and expressions 25–28

Language problems 23
Language tasks 15–23
Letters 197–198, 203–205, 210–211, 220–222, 225–228
Life at home 16, 31–33, 113, 126
Listening 10, 55–100
Lists 195, 198–199, 206
Lost property 53, 107, 111

Messages 196, 200–201, 208
Model letters 198, 205

Narrator tasks 127–129
Nationalities 29, 42
Negatives 243, 245
Notices 138–139
Nouns 236
Numbers 27

Order of object pronouns 245

People 29–31
Perfect tense 241
Personal 'a' 167–168, 246
Personal identification 16, 28–31, 113, 126
Pluperfect tense 242
Plural 236
Position of adjectives 238–239
Position of object pronouns 245
Possessive adjectives 238

Postcards 196, 201–202, 209–210
Present tense 239–240
Preterite tense 240–241
Private transport 18, 41, 110
Pronouns 245–246
Public transport 18, 40–41, 109–110, 121–122, 124

Question words 28

Reading 10, 135–191
Receptive use 15
Reflexive verbs 244
'Registers' 77
Reports/accounts 216, 228–229
Revision 8–9
Role-plays 102, 103–111, 117–125
Rooms 31–33

School and college 17, 35, 114, 127
'Ser' and 'estar' 244
Services 22, 52–54, 119
Settings 14, 102
Shopping 21, 47–49, 105, 107, 108, 110
Signs 138–139
Social relationships 20, 44–46
Speaking 10, 101–134
Speed 27
Superlative (adjectives) 238
Superlative (adverbs) 239

Telephone 29
Time 25–27
Topics 14, 102–103, 112
Transcripts 68–72, 89–94
Transport 18, 40–41, 109–110, 121–122, 124
Travel 18, 40–42, 109–110, 121–122, 124
'Tú' and 'usted' 246

Understanding instructions 138–139
'Usted' 246

Verbs 239–245
Vocabulary 8, 9, 24, 138–141, 168, 213
Vocabulary lists 25–54

Weather 23, 54
Word order 167
Work and careers 17, 37–38, 127
Writing 5, 11, 193–233